Riot, Revelry and Rout

Riot, Revelry and Rout:

Sport in Lowland Scotland before 1860

JOHN BURNETT

TUCKWELL PRESS

First published in Great Britain in 2000 by
Tuckwell Press
The Mill House
Phantassie
East Linton
East Lothian EH40 3DG
Scotland

Copyright © John Burnett, 2000

ISBN 1 86232 003 9

The publishers acknowledge the support of the Scotland Inheritance Fund
in the publication of this volume

British Library Cataloguing in Publication Data
A catalogue record for this book is available
on request from the British Library

Typeset by Carnegie Publishing Ltd, Lancaster
Printed and bound by The Cromwell Press, Trowbridge, Wiltshire

Contents

Illustrations

Acknowledgements

The groundwork for this book was laid during a year as a Visiting Research Fellow in the School of Scottish Studies at the University of Edinburgh, and I am grateful to successive Directors, Professor Alexander Fenton and Dr Margaret Mackay, for their hospitality and support. Sandy Fenton provided thoughtful encouragement during the writing of the text, and many of the ideas in the book arose from discussions with George Dalgleish. Rob Close generously supplied inaccessible material of great interest from Ayrshire and Glasgow newspapers, and Sheriff David B. Smith's help went far beyond curling, the subject on which he is the authority. I owe a large debt of gratitude to each of these individuals.

I also thank Largs Historical Society, who gave me access to a typescript on the life of John Cairnie by Miss Mary B. Hall, and David Devereux of the Stewartry Museum, Kirkcudbright, who gave me a copy of notes by W. H. Clark on the Kirkcudbright Siller Gun.

Others who advised on points of detail or supplied references were Andrew Jackson and Robin Urquhart of Glasgow District Archives; Elspeth Alexander, Alastair Dodds and Naomi Tarrant, all of the National Museums of Scotland; David Brown, Tristram Clarke and Alison Rosie of the National Archives of Scotland; Sally Skilling of the Ulster Folk Life and Transport Museum; Iain Milne, Librarian of the Royal College of Physicians of Edinburgh; Bert Moorhouse of the University of Glasgow; and David McClure and David Trevarthen. David Hamilton allowed me to read the proofs of his book *Golf – Scotland's Game*.

The gathering of material would have been impossible without the help of many members of the staff of the National Library of Scotland.

Part of Chapter 7 has already appeared in another format in the *Proceedings of the Society of Antiquaries of Scotland* and I am grateful to the Society for their permission to reproduce it.

1. A detail from Charles Altamont Doyle, 'Winter Sports on Duddingston Loch'.
National Museums of Scotland.

CHAPTER ONE

Introduction

Some drove the jolly bowl about;
With dice and draughts some chased the day;
And some, with many a merry shout,
In riot, revelry, and rout,
Pursued the football-play.[1]

Thus Walter Scott described the recreations at a truce between the Scots and the English in *The Lay of the Last Minstrel* (1805). He places one sport, football, in the context of other kinds of recreation and implies the age-old idea of sport as a metaphor for war.

Sport relates in complex ways to the society in which it takes place. For example, shinty was played at Lady Fair at Innerpeffray, on the north bank of the River Earn near Crieff in Perthshire. Until it faded away in the middle of the nineteenth century, the fair was held on the 25th of March, Old Style: the use of the Julian calendar and a pre-Reformation name show that the fair was medieval in origin. It was held on a spot which had once been significant, by the old church, but by 1800 Innerpeffray was a hamlet, for Crieff had grown as a market town. The site was difficult to reach from the south. Access was by a ferry over the Earn: the boatman hauled the boat to and fro by a rope stretched across the river and on fair day his hands were blistered by the unaccustomed amount of work. The fair was held in the avenue from the church at the north end to the castle at the south, with the stalls set out at the north end. The shinty match between the parishes of Muthill and Crieff took place at the south end of the avenue. It was played until both sides were willing to stop, 'which was not often the case until a bloody battle had ensued, or some of the combatants got their legs wounded with a club'.[2] The participants relished the social violence, as in the Christmas football match at Monymusk in Aberdeenshire:

Of a' the ba'-men there was nane
But had twa bleedy shins.[3]

In other places there were clear links between sport and work. At Johnsmas Fair in Shetland, held at midsummer, overlooking Bressay Sound, the Shetland ponies which carried seaweed and peat were hired to Dutch fishermen who raced them.[4]

Sport is played for pleasure, for the release from the pressures of a disciplined life, to gain a reputation as a local hero, and for a dozen other reasons. Some sports were played on particular days in particular places, some were integrated into the administrative structure of a burgh, some were watched by tens if not hundreds of thousands of people, and some were tolerated in one century but condemned for their cruelty in others. Sport has many faces, many places in social life. The purpose of this book is to explore some of them in their Scottish context between the late Middle Ages and 1860.

Writers and Evidence

Most twentieth-century literature on the history of sport in Lowland Scotland has concentrated on developments from 1870 onwards, and much of the best academic analysis concerns football. Of works which deal with earlier sport, there is a small but good literature on curling, but that on golf is large and until recently, vastly unsatisfactory. Some notable studies on traditional sport were produced around the end of the Victorian era, partly as an outcome of the mild cultural – and milder political – nationalism of the period. Sir James Balfour Paul, Lord Lyon, author of the nine volumes of *The Scottish Peerage* (1904–14), and a great antiquary, wrote an admirable history of the Royal Company of Archers (1875), a book full of Scottish life and Scotsmen. He also edited ten volumes of the Accounts of the Lord High Treasurer (1900–16), setting out the Scots' monarchs personal expenditure between 1500 and 1566, and drawing attention to the evidence they furnished of sporting practice around 1500. A silversmith, A. J. S. Brooke, wrote valuable material in the 1890s in which he used his professional expertise: he concentrated on the trophies of archery and horse-racing.[5] The Reverend John

Kerr wrote authoritatively on curling.[6] *Sports and Pastimes of Scotland* (1891), by the Perth antiquary Robert Scott Fittis, is the obvious predecessor to the present work. A hundred years later far more information is available in print, and it is possible to go further than Fittis in framing explanations.

Three kinds of source have been used for this book: local histories, newspapers – particularly local ones – and poetry.

In its aim, local history is usually antiquarian: its concern is to record and explain a little, but not to analyse. It has an emotional content in that it is based on an enthusiasm for a place, often a love for it – but the irony is that most local historians fail to explain the peculiar nature of the place because they deal only with that place, and do not put it in context or compare it with other places. As far as sport is concerned, most local histories contain material of genuine value. Even books which appear to have been written on the premise that the sole inhabitants of the parish were the laird, his family, and the minister, usually reveal recreation in the Kirk Session's condemnation of Sabbath breaking. By assembling material from many local histories it becomes possible to see what is common, or unusual, or surprisingly early, and what gives the local flavour.

Two good examples are Midlothian parish histories by John Dickson, a retired Free Church minister who was born at Ford, near Pathhead. He showed the part played by sport in parish life and gave good descriptions of the carters' festivals, mixing detailed reporting with nostalgia and a little disapproval.[7] He said one of his books was 'a combination of wide research and pleasant conversations with the oldest residenters in the Parish'.[8] The only difficulty in using his work is that it is not clear what he had been told and what he himself remembered, and this applies to other authors of local histories too.

Newspapers are a rich source for many aspects of social life in nineteenth-century Scotland. In 1800 there were only 15 outside Glasgow and Edinburgh, and by the middle of the century there were dozens. In 1857 the duty on newspapers was removed and by 1880 there were nearly 150 local newspapers in Scotland. In this period one of the causes of the multiplication of titles was the desire to express different religious and political viewpoints. Predictably, the radical newspapers published more material on popular sports:

the *Ardrossan and Saltcoats Herald*, for example, which serialised the autobiography of a miner in 1890s, was also interested in popular leisure.

Newspaper reports of sport give the information which is of least interest to the historian – the result of the match. Comment appears rarely, and has to be sought diligently. Fortunately newspapers were edited by individuals who sometimes indulged their own enthusiasms. Thus good reports appeared in the *Dumfries Times* of the sports at Innerleithen in the 1830s, and in the *Ayr Advertiser* of the minor horse race at Newton-on-Ayr in the middle of the nineteenth century, simply because two men relished what they had seen. The drawback of the newspaper is that the more organised the sport, the more likely it was to be reported; the activities of lairds and urban dwellers are well covered, but not the leisure of the farm servant or the miner. Furthermore, it is also easier to find out what is happening in a medium-sized burgh such as Hamilton or Montrose than in Glasgow or Edinburgh: the city newspapers were taken up with politics, high society, coal and iron exports, and so had less space for sport.

Poetry is a rich source for traditional sport. For events before the twentieth century, it is the nearest thing to oral history. The poet has his licence to alter facts in the name of the Muse, but he also shows us the feelings of the players and spectators, and vivid details of the experience of being present at an event. Here are some of the people in Dumfries on the day of a shooting competition in 1777, leaning out of the windows to see the fun:

> O! happy they wha, up twa storey
> Saw the Procession in its glory!
> Alang the roads it left out o'er ye
>   Sic clouds o' stour
> Ye cou'na see ye'r thoomb before ye
>   For ha'f an hour! [9]

As this quotation shows, poetry also contains descriptions of sport in the language of the people, Scots. It also reminds the etiolated ethnologist in his ivory tower that sport was neither polite nor viewed from a distance, as on television. It was often raw, rumbustious,

2.   Badge of the Edinburgh Skating Club, 1790. *National Museums of Scotland.*

intemperate and immediate. It was played not with calculation and seriousness but with humour and full-throated enthusiasm like that of the Kilmarnock curler Tam Samson (1722–95) who, while still alive, was the subject of a funeral elegy by Burns:

He was the king of a' the core
To guard, or draw, or wick a bore
Or up the rink like Jehu roar
    In time o need;
But now he lies on Death's hog-score:
    Tam Samson's dead.[10]

The scope of this book

The present book gives a description of the sports which were enjoyed by Lowland Scots between the late Middle Ages and the middle of the nineteenth century. It does not pretend to make a careful distinction between traditional and modern sport: an exercise of this kind can make very good sense of the characteristics of folk football and rugby, for example,[11] but in other contexts it may imply more coherence in traditional sport than ever existed. It was very various indeed. For the purpose of this book traditional sport is that played before about 1860, before the domination of written rules, the steam intellect society, and the ideally athletic public schoolboy.

The sports and games which are described here are those which would have been recognised as leisure activities which involved physical exertion, with some exceptions. Field sports – hunting, shooting, deer stalking, fishing, falconry – have been left aside because they form a coherent group on their own, and do not relate particularly closely to the other sports which occupy the following pages. Also, field sports were the concern of a minority, and the chief concern here is with the majority.

The starting date in the fifteenth century is enforced by the limited evidence for the nature of the activities of medieval leisure in a poor country. Coherent evidence only becomes available after the Reformation, and its quantity is meagre until after 1660. By 1860 the modernisation of sport was well under way, and the scene was set for the sudden growth of spectator sport, particularly football. Sports which had taken place for centuries were dying out, and replacements such as cricket were being imported from England. Scotland and its people were changing rapidly.

The Lowlands were culturally distinct from the Highlands, and blended into another different culture in the north of England. So this book is concerned with activity in the Southern Uplands, the Midland Valley, the cities and north-east Scotland. Caithness, Orkney and Shetland have been left aside for reasons of space rather than because of any lack of interest in their traditions.

The approach which has been adopted is ethnological. Social and cultural history often aim to place something – a building, or a group of exiles – in their context, meaning principally in the social structures and events of their time. The ethnologist is aware of social practices which last for decades if not centuries, of traditions and the powerful emotions which surround them, and of the way they change over time. Ethnology often uses evidence which is seen as being of marginal importance by the historian such as objects, names of places and people and things. The ethnologist is always aware of language, names and physical objects, and of the specific nature of places and the importance to the individual of work, play, food and the structures of the day and of the year – and of a life. Ethnology is profoundly interdisciplinary, 'above all … prepared to make progress by all possible means'.[12]

REFERENCES

 1. Book V, vi, 19–23.
 2. Shearer (1881), 80–3.
 3. Crawford (1987), ii, 113.
 4. Fenton (1978), 240–1.
 5. Brooke (1890–91 and 1893–94).
 6. Kerr (1890).
 7. Dickson (1907 and 1911).
 8. Dickson (1911), 7.
 9. Mayne (1836), 35.
10. Burns (1993), 240.
11. Dunning & Sheard (1979).
12. Fenton (1992–93), 2.

CHAPTER TWO

Medieval Sport

The recreations of medieval Europe form a clear starting point for
Scotland's sporting traditions. As in other civilizations, the demands
of war brought developments in play. The tournament was a central
part of chivalric culture, and its presence in Scotland was the local
expression of a European phenomenon. In itself the tournament was
vivid and dramatic, and it may have been one of the sources for the
tradition of horse-racing which was to be particularly important in
Scotland, as we will see in a later chapter.

The tournament was the *ludus gallicus*: it originated in northern
France. Several other sports were created in the low-lying country
between Picardy in the south, the coast of Friesland in the north,
and the Ardennes in the east. Much of this area was in Burgundian
hands in the late Middle Ages, and if Venice was then the richest
city in the world, the Low Countries were undoubtedly wealthy.
They were also at the cross-roads of most of the major trade routes
of northern Europe, able to take ideas from all sides, develop them
and disseminate them.

The Tournament and the Horse Race

Tournaments were special events, marking the meeting of two
monarchs, a royal wedding, or something equally significant. If
possible, they were held on a notable day in the calendar: thus when,
in the *Niebelungenlied* (*c.* 1200), Siegfried came of age, his father
held a tournament at midsummer. When, in the same epic, the
Burgundians defeated the Saxons, they waited six weeks until
Whitsuntide to hold the celebratory sports and feasting. In the
twelfth century the tournament consisted of sword-fighting on foot,
and the typical forms were a combat between two sides and a general
melée. By the end of the thirteenth century this had been replaced
by jousting in an enclosed area.

The first tournament in Scotland was held in the reign (1165–1214) of William the Lion and the first jousting park laid out in 1329, the year of the death of Robert the Bruce.

The sites for tournaments in Edinburgh were at Craigingelt Well (near Greenside) and by the King's Stables, right under the Castle (now King's Stables Road), and in Stirling in 'the Valley' at the Castle. What is significant about these locations is that there was a natural place for spectators above the action – Greenside was one of the places where *Ane Satyre of the Three Estatis* was performed in the sixteenth century.

There were two principal forms of tournament. The tournament *à outrance* was conducted with the weapons of war – lance, sword, axe and dagger – and although the aim was to win honour, nevertheless injury and death were likely. Typically, knights represented their nations in a situation of war or something close to it, as on the borders of Scotland and England in the fourteenth century. The tournament *à outrance* reached its first peak between David I's return from France in 1341 and his defeat and capture at Neville's Cross five years later. The second peak of Scottish activity occurred towards the end of the century, most memorably when Sir David Lindsay defeated Lord John de Welles on London Bridge in 1390. This was thought to bring great honour to both combatants because they fought in front of the English king. When three Burgundian knights fought three Scots before James II at Stirling in 1448 there was ceremony, four or five thousand spectators, and – as in the *Niebelungenlied* and other stories of chivalric sport – the giving of presents of plate and money by the king to all the knights who took part.

The tournament *à plaisance* was less dangerous, though it was not unusual for it to result in death. Its significant phase in Scotland followed that of the tournament *à outrance* and occurred in the reigns of James IV (1488–1513) and James V (1513–42). It involved pageantry and courtly entertainment, and ladies were present. Tournaments were either held on festival days – James IV often jousted on Fastern's E'en – or to celebrate special events.[1] Thus the marriage of Perkin Warbeck in Edinburgh in 1496, and James IV's own wedding in 1503, were followed by jousting. James IV thus demonstrated to the English visitors that he was personally brave and had all the skills of war. When James V went to Paris in 1536 to meet his bride, the short-lived Magdalene, he was battered and bruised in the lists, and when he returned the following year to marry Mary of Guise the procedure was repeated.

James IV held tournaments in the courtyard at Holyroodhouse. The tournament was thus for spectators as much as for the participants. In the Middle Ages the practice of watching a sport was mostly confined to the tournament, though François I built the Château de Chenonceaux with a roof which could be walked on easily, so that ladies could watch the hunt. The decline of the tournament was matched by the rise of horse-racing: crowds of people of all kinds watched it. The tournament and the horse race are the sources for the modern practice of watching sport.

The final spectacle of the age of chivalry was held in 1520 when Henry VIII of England and François I of France met on the Field of the Cloth of Gold, a few miles inland from Calais, but even then it was seen as a conscious revival. Jousting continued for a few more decades, but its military function had vanished with the introduction of gunpowder.

The first notice of horse-racing in Scotland dates from the reign of James IV. A payment was made in 1504 to the jockey, 'the boy that ran the King's horse', at Leith. A few years later David Lindsay wrote:

> And sum, to schaw thare courtlie corsis
> Wald ryid to leith, and ryn thare horssis
> And wychtlie [vigorously] wallope ouer the sandis.[2]

In the last line, the poet gives a fair impression of sixteenth-century horse-racing. It was not a matter of sheer speed, like the modern sport. A race was usually run in three heats, so stamina was essential. Each heat at Leith was of several miles over wet sand, out and back: even the strongest animals did not gallop the whole course. Racing was still closely linked to the desire to select the best horses for hunting and war, and to the prestige to be gained from owning the beast that was fittest for these aristocratic activities.

One race stands out from all the other sixteenth-century Scots horse races: that at Haddington. It was first held in 1552. Its significance is that it was repeated annually. The burgh records said:

> 1552, May 10. The quhilk day John Forrois, burgess of Haddington, came cautioner that ane worthy and mychty lord, George lord Seyton, sall bring the silver bell that his horse wan upon the X day of May the yeir of God Im Vc fifty twa yeiris, to the said burgh of Haddington, upon the third day of November the samyn yeir of God, and present the same to the provost and bailies of the said burgh, with ane augmentation lyke as the said lord pleases to augment for his honour; and the same bell to be run for the same day, swa that the wynnar thereof may have the same again; and for the observing of thir premissis the said John Forrois has actit himself in the common buyk of Haddington, the said X day of May ...[3]

The Haddington race is the only pre-Reformation race which was established with the intention that it would be repeated. Like many later trophies each winner was expected to provide an 'augmentation', a silver medal, which commemorated his victory.

Unlike the tournament, the sports of the people led directly to traditions which can be followed down to the present day. Football was played all over Europe, usually on holidays. This was a game in which dozens if not hundreds of men would struggle in two teams over miles of countryside to take a ball to a nominated spot such as the church door or a stretch of river. It has been argued that its origin lies in the emulation by the people of the jousting of knights.[4]

Folk football is still played in a few places in Scotland, including some of the Scottish Border towns and in Kirkwall in Orkney. Reconstructed in English public schools in the middle of the nineteenth century it became the modern association football. The historical importance of folk football lies in that it was the most widespread team game and therefore is one of the bases for the growth in team sport in the nineteenth century.

The descent into disorder was part of popular leisure. The fifteenth-century poem 'Christ's Kirk on the Green' may begin with young women dressed in their best clothes, but when it comes to the sport one archer is so forceful that the bow flies to pieces and another sends an arrow over the byre:

> And cry'd fy, he hath slain a Priest
> a mile beyond the Mire.[5]

Archery was an art of war which, as 'Christ's Kirk' shows, was also an amusement. The English developed the use of the longbow and James I, educated at the English court, in 1424 framed the first Act requiring archery practice after mass on Sunday. There are still areas called the Butts or the Bow Butts in several burghs – St Andrews and Haddington, for example. The development of firearms removed the need for the archer as well as the mounted knight on the battlefield, and archery was transformed into a recreation for the burgher and the laird.

The Sports of the Low Countries

Scotland and the Low Countries were in close contact from the late Middle Ages until the eighteenth century. The east coast of Scotland was nearer to the Netherlands, in terms of sailing distance, than to London. Scots mercenaries served in the Low Countries, and the Dutch shared Calvinism and a legal system based on Roman law. A young Scot with legal ambitions might be sent to study in the Low Countries, as James Boswell did at Utrecht. From the seventeenth century, the medical school at Leiden attracted many Scots. The 'famous Synod of Dort' [Dordrecht] of 1618–19 has its place in the development of religious doctrine in Scotland.

There were trading links: coal was exported from Fife where the mines were drained by Dutch windmills, lead from Leadhills in Dumfriesshire made the glaze for Delftware factories in North Holland, and a variety of goods was imported, most of them the high-value products of advanced technologies which were yet to develop in Scotland, from church bells to polished marble for a floor at Hopetoun House. Scots wool and other goods were exported through the staple at Veere until 1794. It was from Veere that 'a young lion, a royal animal, well tamed' was sent to king James III in 1474. From Middelburg, close to Veere, came chalices of silver and copper to St Andrews and Aberdeen in 1497–98. These are representatives of the flow of luxury goods, the work of skilled craftsmen, and the products of a region in which there were many advanced crafts and industries which a small, poor and undeveloped country like Scotland could not support. There were Scots merchants in the Low Countries who smoothed the passage of wool and goods, and a few made the move in the other direction, and were given family names such as Fleming.[6]

The social practices of the Low Countries were also more advanced than those in Scotland. New sports and pastimes were created, and inevitably the flow of ideas about sport was from the Continent to Scotland. The diffusion of various sports at the end of the nineteenth century from England to all parts of the world as part of the English cultural hegemony has its counterpart in the emulation in the sixteenth and seventeenth centuries of the games of the people who lived in and around the world's trading centres – Antwerp first, then, after the closing of the River Scheldt in 1585, Amsterdam.

The relationship between the sports of the Low Countries and those in Scotland has been discussed most often, most passionately and most inaccurately through the case of golf. Several sports, however, came from the Netherlands to Scotland, including caich and curling. A general sporting term, the Scots word *bonspiel*, now confined to curling, was used in the sixteenth century for any game between groups of men from different places. It probably comes from the Dutch *verbond*, an alliance or covenant; and the Middle Dutch or Middle Low German *spel*, from the verb *spelen*, to play.[7]

Scottish archers purchased their equipment from the Low Countries, as when in 1612 duty was paid on 'schooting arrowes the groce ... 24 li[bri], bowes called hand bowes the dozen 24 li., bow staves the hundredth, 40 li., bowe stringis the dozen, 5s'.[8] The number of shooting guilds in Flanders created a market in which highly skilled craftsmen had the advantage: for centuries the arrows of Ghent were reckoned the best in Europe. The form of archery known as papingo shooting, involving the use of an elevated target in the form of a parrot, probably came to Scotland from the Continent, and not through England.[9] Skittles was sometimes called *Dutch pins* in Scotland.

Caich – the ancestor of squash, played with the hand rather than a racket – probably reached Scotland through the Netherlands rather than England. It appeared in Scotland at the end of the fifteenth century, and may have depended on the arrival of shrunk-skin balls from the Low Countries: caich is a simple game, but the technology of its ball is more complex. Tennis balls also were imported.

The origins of curling lie partly on the Continent. In Scotland early curlers used stones lifted from the beds of rivers: they were irregular in shape but had a satisfactory weight. The first Scots reference to curling dates from 1540–41: contemporary with this are representations of a similar game on the ice in the Netherlands. They occur in the paintings of Pieter Brueghel the elder (*c.* 1525–69) and others.[10] Stones could not be used in Holland because of the absence of outcrops of rock: thus the pieces are cylindrical, probably made of wood, and have handles. Among other materials, curling 'stones' of wood were used in seventeenth-century Scotland, and the apparent regularity of the Dutch pieces suggests that they too were wooden.

Before discussing golf we must divert for a moment and look at the character of traditional sports.

There are two principal sources of misunderstanding in any discussion of the origin of any sport which evolved rather than having been deliberately invented. The first is the idea that a sport (or indeed any other cultural phenomenon) has a single origin: in popular culture slow change, and combination of different entities is to be expected. The second is to imagine that modern categories existed: in terms of sport, it is essential to see that similar players with similar implements would vary the practice of a sport according to the number of players and sticks available, the weather, the dampness of the fields or the presence of ice, the state of the crops, the condition of the ball, the time free for the play, the number of young women watching, and so on. For example, golf, cricket and hockey have all tried to claim for their own a figure in stained glass in Gloucester cathedral. The 'Crécy window' provides evidence for the existence of stick-and-ball games, not for any specific game. 'Far and sure' may be the motto of the golfer, but the golf historian prefers 'Gang warily'.

The game of golf is the product of two sporting traditions – *kolf* from the Netherlands and shinty and other stick-and-ball games in Scotland.[11]

Kolf was played in the Netherlands from at least the middle of the fourteenth century.[12] But what was this *kolf*? Gillmeister concludes reasonably that *kolf* was the game played with a stick called a *kolf*.[13] Thus all the stick and ball games bore the same name. There is one unambiguous record of a game played across country towards a distant target, counting the number of strokes, at Loenen aan de Vecht at the startlingly early date of 1297 – but it appears to have been a unique event, and not part of a tradition.[14] The visual evidence for *kolf* in the sixteenth and seventeenth centuries is of two kinds: portraits of children and of paintings of winter games played on ice. The latter suggest that the game was played over short distances: the painters do not show the use of distant targets, but rather ones which are a few tens of metres away, and the ball is seen to be struck with gentle precision rather than with strength.

Turning to Scotland, hurling or shinty was already popular in the *Gàidhealtachd* in the first millennium AD. The word *shinty* was recorded in the nineteenth century in forms such as *shinnie* and *shinnop* over the whole of Lowland Scotland, and in northern England. Shinty must have been played all over Scotland in the fifteenth and sixteenth centuries.

The great Irish story, the *Tàin*, recounts how Cùchullain arrived at Emain Macha, near the present-day Armagh. First he played a hundred and fifty boys at hurling or shinty, then at another game in which first Cùchullain defended a single hole while the hundred and fifty each tried to strike a ball into it, then he attacked and holed the ball despite their massed defence. This game was still played in Scotland at the beginning of the nineteenth century when it had become *kirk the gussie*, so it must have been played in the fifteenth century. Leaving aside the heroic exaggeration of the *Tàin*, it would have been a game played by a handful of boys. Stick-and-ball games of various kinds were well established in Scotland in the Middle Ages.

It is almost certain that the Scots word *gouff* or *golf* in its first two or three centuries had more than one meaning. The first reference to *golf* in the Scots language occurs in an Act of Parliament of 1457,[15] where it is banned along with football in order to promote archery practice. This sounds like a more violent game than the modern golf, and there is a parallel in the prohibition against Englishmen playing hurling in Galway in 1527.[16] A surprising number of deaths from blows of a golf club are recorded: for example, at Brechin in 1508, Stirling in 1561, Kelso in 1632 and Falkirk in 1639,[17] and there must be a strong suspicion that they were suffered during a shinty-like game. Most of the sixteenth-century censures of golfing, whether in Acts of Parliament, or by presbyteries or kirk sessions, associate it with other violent sports such as football and shinty. Only at the very end of the century does a prohibition appear which links it with a less energetic game, when the Presbytery of Glasgow banned golf and alley bowls on Sundays.[18]

At the same time, *golf* also denoted a sophisticated game which was played by nobility and royalty at least as early as the first decade of the sixteenth century, when James IV bought equipment. This game was the chief source for modern golf. However, it took other forms. Hamilton has argued that there was widespread popular game which was a simplified form of the noble game, based on the use of simpler sticks and wooden balls. He reasonably suggests that this form of golf has been ignored because it left few traces in the historical record and did not result in the formation of clubs. Like the noble game, it seems to have been localised on the east-coast links.

When *kolf* came to Scotland, probably in the fifteenth century, it brought with it the *put* and the *bunker* from the Low Countries. As Gillmeister explains, the word *bunker* comes from:

> the Flemish *bancaert*, a synonym of *bastaert*, meaning 'illegit-imate child' ... The evolution of the term can thus be conjectured to have proceeded along the following lines: Flemish *bancaert slach*, 'bungled stroke into a sand pit', gave rise to *bancaert kolf*, 'implement with which bungled strokes are reme-died'. This was adopted into Scots as *bunkard club*, whence by back-formation, *bunker*, 'place where the bunkard club is used'.[19]

Golf balls were exported in some quantity from the Netherlands to Scotland in the last two decades of the fifteenth century, including the comparatively large quantity of six barrels of them in 1494.[20] Part of the argument which James Melville used in 1618, when he successfully asked James VI for a monopoly of golf ball making, was the amount of money which was being sent from Scotland to the Netherlands for balls.

Thus golf came from the Low Countries to Scotland, where there was already an established tradition of playing stick and ball games. The most convincing definition of the Scots' distinctive contribution to the development of golf, recently advanced by Hamilton, is that the Scots took the 'short game' – as we might retrospectively label it – of *kolf*, and lengthened the play so that a new range of possibilities emerged.[21] In particular, the terrain and the weather played far larger parts than before. This introduced an element of luck, for a fine shot might bounce unhappily and end beneath a whin bush. Yet whilst strength gave an advantage, skill was emphasised.

The Dutch *kolf* club in the form used between about 1425 and 1700 had a head of cast lead. It would have been fragile and liable to break if it was used on rough ground. An anonymous Dutch poem of 1657 includes the lines:

> When the sides have been drawn he braces himself and strikes
> his club
> Weighted with lead or his Scottish cleek of boxwood
> Three fingers wide, one thick
> With lead in it at the feather ball.[22]

The fact that the nineteenth-century cleek had a metal head is not relevant here: what is being described is the standard wooden golf club of the seventeenth and eighteenth centuries. The poem shows that by this date the Scots had achieved independent innovation by creating a light club suitable for use on the tussock-covered links: they were already making golf their own.

REFERENCES

1. Edington (1995), 102.
2. Lindsay (1931–36), i, 44.
3. Quoted by Fairfax-Blakeborough (1973), 289.
4. Gillmeister (1990a), 151.
5. Wood (1977–91), i, 3.
6. Smout (1992).
7. *DOST*, s.v. bonspiel.
8. Robertson & Wood (1928), 151.
9. Burnett & Urquhart (1998).
10. Smith (1981), 4–7.
11. The best discussions of early golf are Geddes (1992) and Hamilton (1999).
12. van Hengel (1982), 12.
13. Gillmeister (1996), 279.
14. van Hengel (1982), 17–18.
15. Reproduced by Geddes (1992), vi. Strictly speaking it is an Act of the Parliament of 1457, which continued into the following year. The Act concerning golf was passed in 1458. I am grateful to Dr Alan Borthwick for this point.
16. Gillmeister (1990b), 279; MacDonald (1932), 62. The word *hockey* was used to describe the game, raising the possibility that it was not the native game of *hurling* (see *OED*).
17. Hamilton (1999), chapter 2.
18. Johnston & Johnston (1993), 52.
19. Gillmeister (1990b), 280–1.
20. van Hengel (1982), 51.
21. Hamilton (1999).
22. Translation given by van Hengel (1982), 50.

CHAPTER THREE

Reformation, Royalty, Restoration

We now enter on a period of a little more than a century during which those in power alternately placed curbs on sport, or encouraged it. Religious reformers, wishing to control behaviour on the Sabbath, often tried to stop sport on Sunday. This was a reversal of the policy of the Stewarts, who had supported archery practice after mass. There was a reaction under James VI, whose reign of 58 years began in 1567 when he was an infant: he approved of sport and in his time many long-lasting competitions appeared for the first time. After his son Charles was marginalised in 1638, the extreme reformers in the kirk were able to place restraints on sport. When Charles II, crowned at Scone in 1651 on a brief visit to Scotland, returned in 1660 there was an anti-puritan flowering of sporting activity.

Reformation

The Reformation changed daily life in Scotland because it removed most religious festivals from the calendar, and because it introduced a moral vision of life and means for enforcing it – the kirk session and the presbytery. Thus many traditions came to an end or were significantly altered, for holy days had been for eating, dancing and sport as well as for worship. At the same time, Scotland's relations with the rest of Europe were redefined: contact with Catholic countries was more limited than before, an additional cause for suspicion of the English was introduced, and the protestant Netherlands became Scotland's closest relation on the Continent.

In *Ane Satyre of the Three Estatis* (1540) Sir David Lindsay imagined a priest boasting of his sporting ability:

> Thocht I preich not I can play at the caiche:
> I wait thair is nocht ane amang yow all
> Mair feirlie can play at the fut-ball.[1]

Fut-ball was the violent game played by dozens of men over miles of country and *caich* was a form of the *jeu de paume* played by striking a ball against a wall. They were both highly active sports which were played by the common people. Football was the antithesis of the restrained pleasures which the Calvinist ethos could accommodate. Thus it was particularly undesirable for a priest, a religious and social leader, to be a footballer.

Lindsay's lines stand for much of the criticism of the Roman Catholic Church in Scotland in the first half of the sixteenth century: the behaviour of the clergy was one of the clearest foci for dissatisfaction. Yet similar complaints had been made all over Europe for centuries – one thinks of Chaucer's 'manly man, to been an abbot able'.

The Reformers wished to control behaviour, particularly on Sundays, but at first much of their emphasis was on economic activities – *killing [kilning] and milling* – and on behaviour such as drinking and gaming which suggest disorder and the irrational. Nevertheless, sports were censured from time to time. A complaint was made in Dundee in 1558 'agains diverse persons of the burgh that, by all order, use playing at bowls and pennystanes, stenting of claith, stricking of stakes, stamping down of the gerse [grass] in the Meadow ..'.[2] on Sundays. At Elgin in 1599 at attempt was made to control Christmas festivities by prohibiting 'snaw balling, singing of carellis or uther prophane sangis, guysing, pyping, violing', though football was allowed provided it was played in the Chanonrie kirkyard. In later years it, too, was forbidden.[3]

The reign of James VI

Loquacious and intelligent, James VI (1566–1625) was learned but not always bookish. He rode well, revelled in hunting and on Newmarket Heath established the centre of horse-racing. Although he could not remove all of the puritan hostility to sport, his fondness for games and physical activity led to an increase in the quantity of sport both in England and Scotland.

James encouraged his eldest son to enjoy sports. Prince Henry Frederick, who died in 1612 at the age of 18, was fond of riding, golf and tennis, though he did not share his father's passion for hunting. In 1603 James bought him bows, arrows and a quiver, and 'twa golf clubbis twa staffis and four rakketis'.[4] The staffs were probably bowstaffs, though they may have been quarterstaffs, and the rackets were for tennis. Henry was a tennis addict: he played for hours wearing only his shirt – more like an artisan, said an observer.[5] James and his son may have found, or felt, a greater freedom to relish sport when they were in England. In Scotland, sport on Sundays was still the subject of aggressive criticism.

In 1617 James VI returned to his native country, which he had not seen since 1603. Thomas Erskine, Viscount Fenton, wrote to the Earl of Mar concerning James's impending journey to Scotland:

> One derektione I had almost forgottin from his Majestie, and that is that your Lordshipe should be all means possibill, ather be command or bye incitatione, to deall soe as the football and the rowbowles and sutche manlye exercisses may be practysed and exercised befor his Majesties cumming to Scotland, that theis pepill heir maye see the owld exerceisses of that cuntrye.[6]

When travelling back to London James found that in Lancashire the Puritans were preventing sport after the church service on Sunday. He supported the country people who had complained, not so much because of love of sport as because he wanted to lessen the political power of the Puritans. James had the Bishop of Chester write *A Declaration of Sports* in his name, attacking the ban:

> For when shall the Common sort of people have leave to ex-cercise if not vpon sondaies or holidaies, seeinge they must plie theire labors & winn theire livings in all workinge daies?[7]

In the reign of James VI horse-racing emerges as the sport of royalty, noblemen and lairds. One suspects that in the sixteenth century races were widespread if not frequent; as so often in the history of sport in this period the difficulty is the paucity of evidence. Record of races usually survives because something other than racing happened at them, as when Border rievers met at a race to plan a raid, or when a spectator was shot at Ayr in 1576.[8]

By the early seventeenth century the major races were associated with the burghs. The race at Peebles possibly began as early as 1573 and the one at Stirling was being run by 1598. There was a *bell race* at Glasgow in 1606.[9] From its hallmarks we know that the Lanark Bell was made in 1608–10, though the oldest medal attached by a winner dates from 1628. The race at Peebles was prohibited in 1608: 'the Lords of Secret Council … ordains that the same sall be nawise halden nor keepit this year' because the watchers used it as an opportunity for settling personal grievances. The Burgh of Paisley decided to buy a bell in the same year though they did not do so, nor start a Burgh race, until 1620. There is no record of the purchase of the silver bell at Dunfermline, but a race was certainly held on the Stirling road in 1610.[10] The race at Cupar started in 1610.[11]

It is impossible to be clear about James VI's role in promoting horse-racing in Scotland. He gave no prizes: he may either have encouraged others to award them, or have created a climate of opinion in which racing was well regarded.

The burghs were important for horse-racing, and horse-racing was important to the burghs. Both Lanark and Paisley had their arms engraved on their bells. At Dunfermline the Council required that the winner:

> produce Befoir ye provost and bailleis of ye said burt [burgh] In ye tolbuith yrof upon the fourt day of apryll In ye yeir of God sixteent ct [hundred] and eleven yeirs next to cum at ten houris bfor noon. The sylver Race bell double overgilt his majesties name and arms gravin yrupon …[12]

The council's wish to show their control over the prize, and the emphasis they placed on its value and its royal connection, indicates that the holding of a race gave status to the burgh. It certainly attracted the nobility and others who were sufficiently wealthy to own fast-running horses.

The Carlisle Bells of 1590 and 1597 are the oldest horse-racing trophies in Britain. They are small, round silver bells. They may have been preceded by the silver bell which Henry, 2nd Earl of Pembroke (c. 1534–1601) gave at an unknown date for a race at Salisbury: it was reworked into a cup about 1630.[13] The phrase *bell-course* was used in England for a horse race.

In Scotland, the expression to *bere the bell* meant to win or rank

above all others. John Rolland of Dalkeith, writing about 1550, said
Gavin Douglas 'Into his dayis abone all buir the bell' as a poet,[14]
and the preface to the 1568 edition of the *Workis* of David Lindsay
judged that:

> Thocht [though] Kennedie, and Dunbar bure the bell
> For the large race of Rethorick thay ran[15]

– still Lindsay was the best at criticising unreformed religion.

Why a bell as a trophy? Since the Middle Ages horses had been
decorated with bells and ribbons, and it was customary to adorn
horses with them on the first of May. It was common for other
animals to wear bells as adornment, 'Litile doggis and messanys' –
work dogs and lap dogs – 'with thar bellis'.[16] The bell at Paisley race
was to be 'hung at [the winner's] horse heid'.[17] In addition, in
heraldry, bells referred to acts of devotion and nobility.[18] The two
surviving seventeenth-century bells, those of Lanark and Paisley are
similar to one another, being (as it were) bell-shaped rather than
spherical: possibly the burgh connection was emphasised by the bell
being the same shape as the ones in the tolbooth or kirk.

The first shooting trophies date from the reign of James VI. They
were for burgh competitions: we will discuss them later. There were
also informal shoots. For example, John Somerville (1596–1677) was
sent to school at Dalserf in Lanarkshire when he was nine years old.
Young Somerville rode to Hamilton, and bought:

> ribbons of diverse coloures, a new hatt and gloves. But in noth-
> ing he bestowed his money more liberallie then upon
> gunpowder, a great quantitie whereof he buyes for his oune use,
> and to supplie the wantes of his comerades.

He returned to Dalserf, fixed the ribbons to his hat, and:

> with his little phizie [fusée] upon his shoulder, he marches to
> the church-yaird where the May-pole was sett up, and the
> solemnitie of that day was to be kept. There first at the football
> he equalled any that played; but for handeling of his piece in
> chargeing and dischargeing he was so ready, and shott so near
> the marke, that he farre surpassed all his fellow schollars ...[19]

The maypole, discouraged by reformers, was both a pagan fertility symbol and a mark of loyalty to James VI and his opposition to puritanism.

From the same period comes 'The Life and Death of the Piper of Kilbarchan', by Robert Sempill of Beltrees (*c.* 1600–*c.* 1660). Sempill describes Habbie Simpson as the universal presence at every social occasion, at harvest, at weddings, at Beltane and St Barchan's Day, 'At every Play, Race, Feast and Fair':

> At Horse Races many a day
> Before the Black, the Brown the Grey
> He gart his Pipe when he did play
> > baith Skirl and Skreed
> Now all such Pastimes quite away
> > sen Habbie's dead.[20]

Habbie Simpson was dead, and the Reformers were in power again.

Disorder

After Charles I lost control of Scotland in 1638, there was a period of twenty-two years when there were two Scottish civil wars, Scotland was drawn into the English civil war and then occupied by English forces. Bubonic plague ravaged the people in 1644–49. Various kinds of religious extremist held the centre of the stage. Polemic and protest were the order of the day: the unbiased commentator was not prominent.

In this period people were often censured for indulging in sports on Sundays. As half a century earlier, it was the breaking of the Sabbath, not the sport itself, which was seen as the fault. Sports and games may have been viewed with disapproval by extremists. They certainly managed to put a stop to some sports, for example *barla breaks* which, like dancing, they found intolerable because men and women touched one another. But public events such as horse races continued to be held.

In 1638 Henry Adamson (d. 1639) published *The Muses Threnodie or Mirthful Mournings on the Death of Mr Gall.* Sport appears at the beginning of this long poem, as the activity which must be given up by the mourners, and as the enthusiasm which Gall and Adamson had shared. The implication is that this was the central part of their social activity, and they were probably typical of young men of a little wealth in the medium-sized and larger burghs who had been brought up in the reign of James VI. Adamson was encouraged by William Drummond of Hawthornden to have his work printed: Drummond was the monarchist who famously expired on learning of the execution of Charles I. He was unsympathetic to reformed religion and its social strictures. Adamson's aggressive nostalgia must have appealed to him:

> How can I choose, but mourne? when I think on
> Our games Olympick-like in times agone.[21]

In the same decade the Lanark-born William Lithgow (*c.* 1582–1650) wrote in praise of physical exercises in *Scotlands Welcome to King Charles 1633*:

> For manly exercise, is shrewdly gone
> Foot-ball and Wrestling, throwing of the Stone:
> Jumping and breathing, practices of strength
> Which taught them to endure, hard things at length.[22]

This is not nostalgia, but a political statement. The strength of the nation depended on the strength of its men, and Lithgow saw it being eroded by the curtailment of sport on Sundays.

The presbytery of Lanark declared in 1650 that 26th December was a fast day 'to be keeped by the Kings Majestie, and whole congregation of this kirk' for James VI had brought in bishops, ceremonials, and tolerated 'sabbath breakings, at law publictlie avowed by him many things, by the Book of Sports'.[23] Thus there is evidence that the *Book of Sports* was known in Scotland. The date also is significant, for St Stephen's Day was (and in some places still is) important for sports and games, and the presbytery wished it instead to be a fast.

The Return of Monarchy and Sport

The Restoration brought a widespread revival of sport in England. In May 1660 Charles II landed at Dover, and on his birthday, 29th May, he entered London – on the same day as the burgh of

Haddington revived their horse race, for the prize of a silver cup bearing the town's arms, showing their loyalty to the monarch and their rejection of puritan values.[24] The players and showmen who had been dispersed during the Interregnum immediately congregated in London. Charles extended Bartholomew Fair from three to fourteen days and the level of licentiousness achieved a new extreme. Samuel Pepys loved it.[25] In the reign of Charles II sport was not merely acceptable, but fashionable.

The best single source for sport in Scotland in this period is an odd weekly periodical, the *Mercurius Caledonius*. It included politics, propaganda, news of trials and executions in London, notices of horse races in Scotland, and extravagant humour most of which was nonsensical. Its title varied. In the week that it was *Bourlesque News from the Antipodes*, it recorded 'That the Citizens of Dunkellia be permitted to make a Bowling Green of *Gillycranky*' – that is, of the rugged pass of Killiecrankie. Despite its variousness, the purpose of *Mercurius Caledonius* was political; its first sentence declared: 'our clouds are dissipate'.[26]

The issue for 1st February 1661 reported that the outbreak of a disease among horses had died out, so that 'Hauking, Hunting; and horse Coursing' could be safely carried out.[27] A few weeks later it announced:

> The famous horse race of *Couper* in *Fyfe*, which by the iniquity of the times, hath been so long buried to the great dissatisfaction of our Nobility and Gentry, is to be run, conform to the institution, upon the second Tuesday of *April*: There is a considerable number of Horses to carry on the work of the day …

Thus far we are in the realm of fact, though it is not clear why the Cupar race should have been 'famous' when other races did not enjoy this distinction. The paragraph continued:

> … among others, a *Waywood* of *Polonia* hath a Tartarian horse. This noble Gentleman was pleased to come to this Nation, to congratulate our happy Restauration; And it is to be desired, that such curious Gallants as come from Forreign Nationes, to see the Course, that they do not as others formerly

did, sleep in the time of the Solemnity. It is now clearly made
to appear by a frequent concourse of Gentry in these fields, that
the report of the Horse Infection was an absolute aspersion.[28]

We now find ourselves in the midst of politics and metaphor: was
the disappearance of the distemper actually a political comment?

A few weeks later the periodical gave itself entirely to comedy
describing *The Prince of Tartaria his Voyage to Cowper in Fife.* It
recounted on its final page how one of the races had been won by
a horse 28 years old whose speed had been concealed 'during the
time of the Usurper', and which had been so revitalised by the
Restoration that it had grown new teeth. The Duke of York, later
King James VII, was 28 in 1661. A diarist's account of the race makes
no mention of a distinguished Polish visitor.[29] The Prince made his
last appearance in *A Variety of News for all Pallets*, having a corn
sucked out of his toe by 'the Bailies daughter of Bervy',[30] planning
to make for Whigmeria.

In the first years after the Restoration there was horse-racing every
Saturday at Leith. The revived interest in sport among the gentry
was partly a reaction against Puritan discipline, and partly due to
the court making gambling fashionable. At Lanark the horse race
was revived and the advertisement for it, in an attempt to emphasise
its age and importance, exaggerated dramatically and said that it
had been started by King William the Lion six hundred years earlier.
About 1664 Dumfries Town Council bought a cup for a race for the
horses of noblemen and gentlemen. The Town Council of Stirling
offered a cup for a horse race in 1664, and in 1684 the Earl of Huntly
gave the Burgh of Banff the cup he had won there.[31]

Almost all of the horse races were held in royal burghs. So, too,
were most of the other annual sports which we have notice of before
the end of the seventeenth century: the shooting for the siller guns
at Dumfries and Kirkcudbright, and the archery competitions at
Musselburgh, Stirling, Peebles and Selkirk. Two instances of
competitions which were not in royal burghs were special cases: the
Kilwinning Papingo and the Red Hose Race at Carnwath, both
discussed below. Two horse races were not at royal burghs: at
Paisley, which was nevertheless a large town which had grown up

beside an abbey, and at Huntly in Aberdeenshire where the role of the Duke of Gordon as patron is quite clear.

Leith became the sporting capital of Scotland in the 1660s. There was golf on the links, a cockpit from 1683, the Company of Archers shooting, and of course horse-racing. There was also a bowling green, where the Renfrewshire laird William Cunningham of Craigends played in the 1670s, losing a little money and refreshing himself with ale and *grosarts* – gooseberries.[32]

Sir John Foulis of Ravelston had his country house three miles west of Edinburgh. There is no reason to suppose that his sporting enthusiasm was anything other than typical of a Scots laird of the period. At Ravelston he enjoyed country sports: hare coursing, fishing and hawking. At Leith he played golf. In 1672 he bought a golf club for his son Archie, and thirty-five years later a club and balls for two of his grandsons. Sir John was also a bowler.[33] His contemporary, General Tam Dalyell, the staunch royalist who did not shave his beard again after the execution of Charles I in 1649, died in 1685. In the inventory of his house in West Lothian, the Binns, there were swords and firearms – he pursued the Covenanters with vigour – '2 Quivers with arrows. 7 bows ... 3 iron [golf] clubs. 17 plae clubs ... A Curling stone of stone. A Curling stone of leid & iron. A Timber Curling stone ...'.[34]

Another minor laird, James Somerville (1632–90) said:

> The having of bowlling-greenes, buttes for archerie, tinnes-courts, and bulliart tables, in and about noblemen and gentlemen's houses, is better by farre ffor manly exercize, then to pass that tyme in drinking, smocking tobacco, ffingering of cards and tables [backgammon].[35]

This is a resolution of the antagonism which the religious reformers had perceived between sport and social discipline: Somerville says that some sports and games are healthy, and are distinct from others which involve dissipation. It draws on the idea, developed in ancient Greece and revived in Italy in the Renaissance, that sport was a suitable recreation for gentlemen. In the Middle Ages writers on education had encouraged young men of rank, destined for military service, to practice warlike sports and also those such as throwing games which would increase their strength. In the second half of the seventeenth century brute strength was seen as being less valuable to a gentleman: bowling, archery, tennis and billiards were all games of skill, and increasingly a value was set upon skill.

As we see in following chapters, there was a range of sports which people enjoyed as players or spectators. The gentry had access to a wider range, either because they could afford the equipment of the sport – the extreme case was to own a racehorse – or because they had the time, money, land and servants to be able to participate in field sports. Town dwellers were able to play a greater variety of sport than folk in the country.

REFERENCES

 1. Lindsay (1931–36), ii, 317.
 2. Maxwell (1891), 387.
 3. Cramond (1903–8), ii, 76.
 4. Anon. (1835), lxxvi–lxxvii.
 5. Anon. (1835), xxxvi.
 6. Paton (1930), 72.
 7. James VI (1982), 104.
 8. Fairfax-Blakeborough (1973), 1.
 9. Anon (1876), 473.
10. Seton (1896), ii, 645.
11. Brook (1890–1).
12. Quoted by Brook (1890–91), 181.
13. Aubrey (1847), 118.
14. *DOST*, s.v. bell.
15. Lindsay (1931–36), i, 404.
16. *DOST*, s.v. bell.
17. Brook (1890–91), 181.
18. Houwen (1994), i, 61.
19. Somerville (1815), ii, 145–6.
20. Wood (1977–91), ii, 52–4.
21. Adamson (1774), 20.
22. Quoted by Magoun (1931), 7. *Breathing* refers to the practice of holding one's breath in competition with others.
23. Anon (1839), 89–90.
24. Gray & Jamieson (1944), 125.
25. Addison (1953), 54, 99.
26. *MC*, 1. See also Buckroyd (1975).

27. MC, 21.
28. MC, 90–1.
29. Lamont (1830), 135–6.
30. Perhaps Inverbervie.
31. Brook (1890–1).
32. Cunningham (1887), 38, 112.
33. Foulis (1894), passim.
34. Dalyell & Beveridge (1923–4), 357.
35. Somerville (1815), ii, 141.

CHAPTER FOUR

Sports Played from Day to Day

Some of the most conspicuous sports were played on holidays. These included football and animal sports, to which we turn in Chapter 5, and later chapters will be devoted to horse-racing and to burgh sports, all of which took place on particular days of the year. There were, however, many sports which were less dependent on the calendar, indeed their pattern was probably affected more by the weather. These included bowling games, curling and golf. Some of these games were enjoyed by all the male population, at least in the sixteenth and seventeenth centuries, whilst others were limited in their appeal because of the cost of their implements. Burke has observed that traditional popular culture was not purely a matter for the common people, but also for landowners, professional men and their families; high culture, however, was restricted to the latter groups.[1] This pattern is repeated in Scottish sport. Bowling and throwing games were the province of all down to the middle of the eighteenth century. The *jeu de paume* was found in various forms depending on the ability of the players to afford rackets, ball and court, and golf was played by aristocrats as well as by apprentices.

It is striking that the two sports which changed and modernised in the first half of the nineteenth century, bowling and curling, were altered by the actions of men in the middle ranks of society. Lawyers wrote their rules and made them more 'rational'. By 1800 golf was already a complex game. In its most sophisticated form, played with feather-filled balls and costly clubs, it was part of the high culture of sport. The invention of a new, cheap and robust ball made of gutta percha, however, allowed the game to be taken up after a few years by the burgeoning middle classes.

Bowling and throwing games

The origin of bowling and throwing games is unknown, though the simplest arise from the basic human activity of throwing and are not dependent on a specific cultural context. By the Middle Ages any game in which an object is projected at a target is likely to have been strengthened by, if not directly derived from, archery. If folk football is the people's version of jousting then safe target-based competitions which could be played by people of all ages may have developed from archery. Evidence for bowling and throwing games is limited in quantity, but widely scattered. These games are found under many names implying that they were played in a variety of places which had their own local traditions. The likelihood is that bowling and throwing games, taken as a whole, were the most popular and widespread among the common people of Scotland, and indeed most parts of northern Europe, from the Middle Ages until the end of the eighteenth century.

BULLETING

Bulleting is the most common name in Scotland for the sport which is still played in Ireland under the names of *road bowling*, or *bowl-playing*. Both in Scotland and Ireland the ball is the *bullet*. The object is to reach a defined point – a tree or a public house, say – in the smallest number of throws. It is played on a road because this introduces the skill of landing the bullet on the road so that it bounces and rolls for the maximum distance. Unlike most throwing games, distance is as important as accuracy in bulleting.

In Scotland it has been called *lang bowlis*, *long bullets*, *langie-spangie*, and *knappar*, and in the nineteenth and twentieth centuries *hainching*. Bulleting first appears as *lang bowlis* in the Lord Treasurer's accounts in 1496. In *The Merour of Wyssdome* (c. 1490), John Irland, rector of Hawick, recommended that young nobles should practice archery, not football or *bowlis*,[2] implying a vigorous game, probably *long bowlis*. *Lang bullets* was still the name used in the prosecution of two shoemakers and a weaver for playing on the road between Kilmaurs and Fenwick in Ayrshire in 1858.[3] The *English Dialect Dictionary* records the name *langie spangie* – a *spang* being a long step – in Aberdeenshire in 1904.

In Lowland Scotland, bulleting was widespread by the mid-seventeenth century: it appears frequently in kirk session records, when men were censured for playing on the Sabbath. There is a story of the Marquis of Argyll who:

> was playing at the bullets with some gentlemen of the country; and one of them, when the Marquise stepped down to lift the bullet, fell pale, and said to them about him, 'Blesse me! What is that I see? My Lord with his head off, and all his shoulder full of blood![4]

This was a premonition: the marquis was beheaded in 1661. William Cunningham of Craigends (Renfrewshire) recorded in 1674 in his expenditure book that he 'Lost at bullets among our servants … 4s',[5] confirming that landowners played this game, as well as ordinary people. The last reference to a man of some substance bulleting occurs at Tranent in East Lothian in 1756. Bulleting went into decline at the beginning of the nineteenth century, and where it did survive it was a working-class sport.

James Hardy, the Berwickshire antiquary, gave three reasons for the demise of bulleting. First, it was played on public roads, which were becoming more heavily used. Bulleting was best played on a road with a hard surface, and, as the quantity of traffic increased, the dangers inherent in the sport became an increasing cause for concern. The Irvine District Road Trustees minuted on 5 July 1837:

> There was also laid before the meeting, an information lodged by James Willis one of the Surfacemen on the road from Kilmarnock to Stewarton against James Miller shoemaker in Kilmaurs for throwing the bullet on the public road near Kilmaurs and for being abusive when challenged. The Trustees instructed the Complaint to be put into the hands of the Fiscal with instructions to prosecute for the Penalties under the Road Act.[6]

David Murray, speaking of the Glasgow area about 1850, commented 'As the ball ran a long distance at a high speed and was apt to skite if it met an obstacle, it was dangerous to all who were upon the road and terrifying to horses'.[7] The physical danger of the game was also the reason for its being banned in Ireland.

Second, Hardy said that there had been 'a revolution in manners and customs': this is the same social change which brought disapproval of other dangerous or cruel sports, such as dog and cock fighting. Finally, he drew attention to the adoption of new farming techniques: previously farm labourers had had little work to do after the harvest had been brought in, and could find time for sport in autumn and winter.[8] Another reason can be added: the rise of quoiting, played on a plot of ground away from the road, and using quoits which could be made by the increasing number of blacksmiths and small foundries.

Bulleting left traces in street names. *Bullet Road*, Kilmarnock, is now Dundonald Road, and there was a *Bullet Road*, now *Ballot Road*, in Irvine. In Moffat there is *Ballplay Road*: though the name refers to a general sporting artefact, bulleting was the one game which was played on the road which did not have a more specific name such as *shinty*. South-west of Tarves in Aberdeenshire is a farm called *Boolroad*.[9] In Forres there was *Bulletloan*, which was renamed St Leonard's Road in 1890.[10] This obvious etymology has been challenged unconvincingly: 'Bulletloan. – The old form of *Bullag loan*, which is evidently from the Gaelic *bolg* or *builg*, and applied to soft places. The latter part is *lon*, a marsh or morass. The word is a tautology'.[11]

At the beginning of the nineteenth century the word *hainching* began to supplant *bulleting*. The word comes from the Scots *hainch*, the haunch, also used for an underhand throw in which the arm strikes the thigh at the moment the projectile is released – and thus for the game in which this is the accepted technique. The sport of hainching in the nineteenth century is identical to the earlier bulleting. Such evidence as exists suggests that it was played mainly in Fife, and probably was not particularly common there: references to it are far rarer than to quoiting, which took the place in the working man's leisure time which had earlier been occupied by bulleting.

Yetlins is the late nineteenth-century name for a form of bulleting played on a flat outcrop of rocks – the *Skerries* or *Skellies* on the shore at East Wemyss in Fife. Around 1840 whinstone bullets, water-worn stones from the beach, were being used, and they were superseded by *yetlins*. As a noun, *yetlin* usually referred to a cast-iron pot or more generally to anything made of cast iron. The balls for *yetlins* were cast in a local foundry, about 2¼ inches in diameter, weighing 1½ pounds. The length of the course across the rocks is variously given as ¼ or one mile, and the object was to score a *hail* by being the player to traverse the course in the fewest throws. When a player reached an agreed number of *hails*, the game was over. It took place on Hansel Monday, but did not survive the First World War.[12]

THROWING OR BOWLING AT A SINGLE FIXED TARGET
Pennystanes. A pennystane was a flat, round stone. In John Barbour's *Bruce*, written about 1375, a distance is referred to as a 'penny-stane cast'.[13] Edinburgh Town Council in 1592 drew attention to Sabbath-breaking by playing various sports, including *rowbowllis* and *penny stane*.[14] It occurs in Kirk Session records during the period of rigid control over behaviour on the Sabbath, as at Dundonald in Ayrshire,[15] and though it was less common than bulleting, it was certainly widespread. It was replaced by quoiting around 1800. The game was to throw the pennystanes at a target on the ground.

Quoiting. Quoiting, pronounced *kitin* in Scotland, is a sport in which heavy metal rings, usually weighing 8 to 12 lbs (3.6 to 5.5 kg), but sometimes as heavy as 23 lbs (10.5 kg), are thrown at a pin in the ground.[16] The distance of the throw has varied: 22 yards was a common length, though 18 is now the standard. In England the word has been used since the fifteenth century though the early references show nothing more than that it was a throwing game: they do not reveal whether a stone or some form of ring was used. Quoiting is the same game as pennystanes, but played with a wooden or iron quoit instead of a stone. It became very popular in Scotland from about 1820 onwards as a result of the availability of cheap but robust cast iron quoits.[17] Quoiting was in its essentials the same game as curling or bowls, but could be played on rough ground.

There is some evidence that it was originally played by the gentry. In the 1820s the Six-Feet Club, mostly Edinburgh lawyers, had a quoit as their badge and included quoiting among their sports, but soon it was exclusively a working man's sport. At a competition in Ayrshire in 1834 it was said that the losing finalists had for six hours been throwing quoits, 'a couple of which would almost be a load for a Glasgow porter'. The same report added: 'We should like to see our gentry taking an interest in this sport. The game has nothing of the brutality of the English prize-ring, while it possesses all that is necessary to prevent the people from sinking into that state of enervation and effeminacy which is the certain precursor of the decline and fall of all empires'.[18] In 1842 there was a competition at Craigie for a silver quoit given by Claud Alexander of Ballochmyle. Alexander paid for dinner for the quoiters and umpires: 'Mr Alexander entered the room during the evening', and spoke to the men – but did not dine.[19] In 1881–83, within a 12-mile radius of Stirling, almost all golfers, 74% of curlers and 69% of bowlers were in social classes A or B. But only 11% of quoiters were in these classes, and 72% in class C.[20]

Quoiting was for many years associated in the middle-class mind with gambling and heavy drinking. Many quoiting rinks were beside pubs. When entries were sought for a 'County Match' at Riccarton in Ayrshire in 1841, each parish to send up to three pairs, stakes were to be sent to John Morton of the Wheatsheaf Inn.[21] In a dispute after a match at Milton of Balgonie in Fife 'fists and quoits were thrown'. At nearby Leslie the sport was banned by the Town Council in 1858.

There were still several hundred clubs in Scotland after the Second World War, but the sport collapsed. It required the strength and stamina which were maintained by heavy manual work, and it was impossible for players to stay clean. The thrower of the quoit has a partner, the paperer, whose role is to mark the spot for which the thrower should aim, and then crouch over the spot with his hands about eighteen inches apart: when the quoit lands it spatters the paperer with clay. By 1994 there were only six clubs left, and their distribution indicates the sport's former ubiquity in the Lowlands: Prestwick (Ayrshire), Linwood Redan (Renfrewshire), Birkenside and Shotts (Lanarkshire), Stonehaven (Kincardineshire) and Canonbie (Dumfriesshire).

Allay bowls. The use of the name *lang bowlis* in Scotland implies the existence of a parallel game played over shorter distances. This first appears as *rowbowlls* [rolled bowls] in 1501. Another synonym was *portbowlis*, the game played at one of the ports or gates of

Elgin. The Town Council recorded in 1654 an 'Act anent playing bowls and bullets at the portes. It is ordained ... that none cast either of them at the east porte bewest the subchanter's wynd and at the west porte be east Thomas Andersone's house'.[22] *Portbowlis* was thus distinct from *bullets*.

The most common term for the short bowling game was *allay bowlis*. A sixteenth-century English manuscript shows an alley with a surface of clay or sand, in which bowls are directed towards a feather stuck upright in the ground.[23] Alternatively, an *allay* may have been covered with grass – Sir John Foulis bought clover seed for 'the aleys in the little yard' at Ravelston in 1698.[24]

A bawbee she kyles (1). Beside Ravenscraig Castle, Kirkcaldy, two games were played under this name on Auld Hansel Monday, and later on New Year's Day.[25] In the one which is relevant here, an iron ball was rolled towards an iron ring which was upright on the ground, and players and spectators wagered on whether the ball would go through it. The game was played thus:

> Not more than six players at a time took part. Each player would begin by shouting, 'A bawbee she kyles!' and would throw a bawbee [halfpenny] on the grass near the Mark. The ball was rolled by each player in succession until one player 'kyled' the ball. If no one succeeded on the first round, each player threw down another bawbee and the game went on. When a player 'kyled,' he took all the money. At this stage anyone could retire and another take his place at the end of the row of those waiting to play.[26]

Cuting. This was the earlier name for *curling*. Sheriff Smith has pointed out the first reference to curling – a wager at Paisley in 1540/41 – uses the word *cos* (genitive *cotis*) for the stone.[27] This is a Latin version of either *cuting* or *quoiting* – if, indeed, these are different words. Although the word *curling* first appeared in 1638, a curling stone was still known as a *quoit* or *cute* in the west of Scotland at the beginning of the nineteenth century. A letter in the *Glasgow Herald* in 1833 said that *kuting* was still the word used by the older Lanarkshire curlers.[28] Since the earliest curling stones, *loofies*, were much smaller than later ones, it is at least possible that the same stones were used for *pennystanes* on dry land and *cuting* on ice.

Curling is one of the most distinctively Scottish sports, and is discussed separately later in this chapter.

BOWLING OR THROWING AT KYLES OR SKITTLES

The song 'Sheriff-Muir', concerning the battle in 1715, describes the Duke of Argyll leading his men into the fray:

> They houghed the clans like ninepin kyles.[29]

Kyles or skittles games occur in many different forms all over Europe, varying in the size of the ball, whether it is a ball or a 'cheese', the size and number of the skittles and whether one was larger than the rest, the *king*. The two kinds which were common in Scotland involved small skittles, a foot or so high. They differed in the size of the ball. As well as the nature of the implements, the rules varied and could be complex.

The Scots word *kyles* comes from the French *quille* and it first appears in Scots in *Ratis Raving*, a long poem which dates from no later than the end of the fifteenth century.[30] The English form *kayles* is known from *c*. 1325, suggesting that the game came from France via England to Scotland. *French kylis* were forbidden at Glasgow Grammar School in 1630.[31]

Ritchie Girvan, the editor of *Ratis Raving*, noted that an early set of kyles had been found on Ironmacannie Moor, Balmaclellan, in 1835: this set was presented to the National Museum of Antiquities of Scotland in 1860.[32] It appears to be of pine. It has not yet been possible to subject the wood to Carbon-14 dating, so its date remains uncertain. There is a possibility that the set is medieval, and it is difficult to imagine that it was made later than 1650. The kyles are quite crudely fashioned and the ball is distinctly sub-spherical: they were made by the players themselves, and not by men with the tools and skills of the joiner.

The Ironmacannie ball is seven inches in diameter, just small enough to be held in one hand. The use of a small ball has been recorded in Scotland. There is a painting by Sam Bough (1822–78) of a game on the shore road between North Berwick and Dunbar:

the kyles are a foot tall, perhaps a little more, and are thickest in the middle.[33] A small ball was probably also used in Strathaven where the game was called *coils* and may have given the name to the *Ballgreen*; in poor weather it was played in the ruins of the Castle.[34]

The use of a large ball in England was described as *Dutch-pins*.[35] This form was played in central Scotland in the nineteenth and twentieth centuries. The ball was about a foot in diameter. The technique was for the player to stand with his legs apart, and swing the ball between them, ending by throwing himself forwards so that he landed on the ground on his front. This delivery is illustrated in a photograph taken in Hamilton about 1890. This game is still played in one or two places, notably the Sheep Heid inn at Duddingston, on the south side of Edinburgh.

Rowley-powley was a game in which a stick was thrown at a number of pins or skittles. It was common at fairs and races in the eighteenth and nineteenth centuries. Thus at Thornhill in Dumfriesshire in 1844: 'We had a routh of shows of different kinds, shooting for nuts, rowley powleys, &c., &c'.[36] *Aunt Sally*, in which a single skittle is the target, is known in pubs in England, almost exclusively in Oxfordshire.[37] Where it is found in Scotland, for example at Boddam at Aul Eel, and at Irvine at Marymass, it had been imported by travelling showmen.[38] It was also known in Scotland as *molly dolly*, and in Renfrewshire as *rowley-powley*, where in 1934: 'A weaver's pirn, embedded in the clay, was set up, with a button the top, and the participant in the game threw another pirn at the 'rowley-powley' in hopes of upsetting it'.[39]

King's men was a simpler form of kyles 'in which three large stones are set on end near each other and a player, using another stone, tries to knock down as many as he can'.[40] It was recorded in Aberdeenshire in 1910.

Cock throwing. Hugh Miller records that at Cromarty, after the Fastern's E'en cock-fighting, the defeated birds and those which would not fight were stoned to death. Each throw cost a halfpenny.

A bawbee she kyles (2). The second New Year game at Kirkcaldy was originally played on the Castle Green, then in the adjacent public park. Nine holes were dug in the ground, each 6 inches in diameter, about a yard apart, and the 'mark' from which the ball was rolled was some ten yards away. The ball was 5 inches in diameter. This was a unique survival into the twentieth century of the ancient and widespread game of *nine holes*. It was last played in 1951. It is first recorded in England in 1573. Both the game and the name occurred all over England and Lowland Scotland, as at Mouswald where in 1640 there was a prohibition of 'Playing at nyne hollis, pennie stane or any such lik idle pastymes,'[41] and Dundonald in Ayrshire where 'IX holes' was played in the uninhabited Castle.[42]

In East Anglia *nine holes* was played both on the ground and also, on a smaller scale, on a board. It was thus a form of the game which was later imported from France as *trou-madame*, which is more often known as *bagatelle*.[43] *Trou madame* was known in Scotland in the seventeenth and eighteenth centuries. *Bagatelle* was first recorded at the beginning of the nineteenth century: initially the table had nine holes.

BOWLING AT A MOVABLE TARGET

Bowls developed a new level of sophistication with the introduction of bias bowls. The first reference to balls with a small bias is *The Castle of Knowledge* (1556) by the English mathematician Robert Recorde. In the Middle Ages, however, half-bowls had been used. These were, as their names suggests, hemispheres: they had a very large bias.[44] The first use of the word *bias* in relation to bowls occurs in 1570, and *jack* meaning a small ball used as a target occurs first in 1601, a development from using a fixed target which brought a new complexity into the game. That bias bowls were in use in Scotland in the seventeenth century is proved by their purchase for a bowling green laid out at St Andrews in the 1680s.[45] At the same time the Town Council of Edinburgh passed an Act 'dischargeing the keepers of biliards tables kyle alies and bouling greens and shoola [shovel] boards' to limit the length of time students were playing these games.[46] There was also a bowling green at Aberdeen in the late seventeenth century.[47]

The Burgh of Haddington laid out a green in 1662 and on this basis the claim has been made that it has the oldest club in Scotland. The green, however, soon fell into disuse.[48] The honour of being the oldest club belongs to Kilmarnock (1740). In the eighteenth century

3. Bowling in the Italianate manner: the eighteenth-century green at Chatelherault, the Duke of Hamilton's house near Hamilton.

there were bowling greens in several other burghs: Aberdeen, Stirling, Edinburgh and Glasgow in the eighteenth century.[49] One of these was mentioned by Allan Ramsay about 1720:

> Driving their ba's frae whin or tee
> There's no ae gouffer to be seen
> Nor doucer folk wysin a-jee
> The byas bowls on Tamson's green.[50]

The site of this green was behind the house at the west end of the Cowgate inhabited by Thomas Hamilton, otherwise *Tam o' the Coogate* or (from 1627) first Earl of Haddington. After his death it was let to a man named Thompson. The green was south-east of the Magdalene Chapel: the site lies beneath George IV Bridge.[51]

Historically, the most important of eighteenth-century bowling greens was the one south of Heriot's Hospital, where the Edinburgh Society of Bowlers played. They acquired a twenty-one year lease of the land in 1768, and the following year the Town Council granted them a Seal of Cause, thus giving them a permanent status similar to that of a guild. The Club's aim was to ensure continuity of

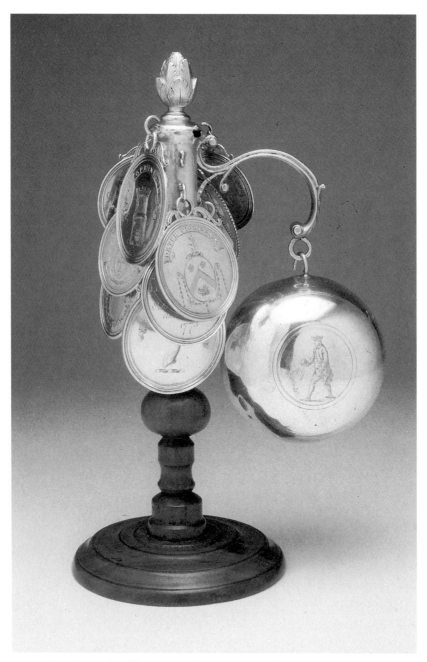

4.   The Silver Jack of the Edinburgh Society of Bowlers, 1771, with the medals added by the winners. This is the oldest bowling trophy in the world. *National Museums of Scotland.*

occupation of their newly-laid turf. In order to gain the Seal of Cause, their laws had to be approved: to this administrative requirement we owe the first laws of bowling. Among sports in Scotland, only golf has older rules. The rules themselves are unremarkable, save for a surprising concern for interference with the bowls in play.[52] The first bowling trophy was made for the Society, a silver jack to which medals were added by winners in the same way as balls were added to the silver golf clubs and medals to silver arrows.[53]

There were probably many more bowling greens beside private houses. There was 'a fair bouling graine before the Palace gate' at Hamilton in 1668, and Lady Grisel Baillie had one at Mellerstain in 1710.[54] A century later Henry Cockburn had a bowling green at Bonaly on the edge of the Pentland Hills. Around 1830 the game was still played largely by country gentlemen: urban greens were rare. An exception was the one by Tom Bicket's inn, where the 'gentry of Kilmarnock' played. 'Curling in winter, and bowling in summer, have, time out of mind, been their favourite pastimes': they were enjoying the profits they had made during the Napoleonic Wars.[55]

Bowling flourished in eighteenth-century Edinburgh: there were five greens on Edgar's map of Edinburgh (1742). At the beginning of the nineteenth century, however, there were fewer greens in the cities and the author of a history of Aberdeen felt that he had to explain the game to his readers.[56] In the nineteenth century the Scots then took a leading part in the development of bowling. They introduced the use of sea-marsh turf laid with great care. It had long been the practice in Scotland to lay good quality turf. In 1657 the Earl of Rothes employed men 'for casting the feall' for a bowling green, and the green at Cowan's Hospital, Stirling, was laid with 'salt faill' in 1738.[57] In the second half of the nineteenth century the *Scotch green* was used all over Britain. At its lowest level was subsoil with clay drains set in it. Then followed a layer of clinker, ash and broken stone; another of fine ash; and finally sand. The turf itself came from the flats at the mouth of the River Irvine and from the Solway Firth coast, and later from Forres.[58]

The growth of modern bowling started in Glasgow: the Willowbank Club was active early in the nineteenth century, and it

5. The flat ground at the mouth of the River Irvine in Ayrshire: the sea is to the left. This area was important for the supply of turf for bowling greens in the nineteenth century.

was joined by the Albany (1833), Wellcroft (1835) and Whitevale (1837) clubs: there were 15 clubs in 1864.[59] William Mitchell, 'The Solon and Nestor of Bowls' said that one reason for the increase in the number of greens was that, after a cold second decade, the third and fourth decades of the nineteenth century were much warmer. We may also see the expanding urban middle class copying the Lowland laird, taking advantage of the opportunity to bowl on summer evenings which were longer than those in the south of England, where cricket, a game which consumed at least a full afternoon and early evening, was rapidly increasing in popularity. For much of the nineteenth century bowling was a sport for small tradesmen. For example, when Kilmarnock Bowling Club was reconstituted in 1855 it issued 50 shares of 40 shillings each, and when Newmilns B.C. was organised in 1861 the founding members were a butcher, two grocers, a cabinetmaker, a weaver's agent, two drapers, a banker, mason, seed merchant and publican.[60]

The first great patron of the sport was the 13th Earl of Eglinton, who provided a green in every village on his estate at a rent of one shilling – to be paid every November 'when asked for'. He presented the Eglinton Trophy for an annual match between the Bowling Clubs of Ayrshire and those of Glasgow. It has been claimed – probably justly – that the area within a 1¼ mile diameter circle from Queen's Park in Glasgow has more bowling greens than anywhere in the world. In the late 1940s there were 45,[61] and the figure in the 1860s had only been a little lower. The area included part of the Earl of Eglinton's estate in Glasgow.

Although the growth of bowling took place through private clubs whose members subscribed to buy land, lay out turf and employ a greenkeeper, there are instances of entrepreneurs laying out their own greens. It was common for the licensed trade to lay out quoiting rinks, and it is through a quoiting match that we know of one commercial bowling green, Warren's in the Gallowgate of Glasgow.[62] The location of the other is significant: Port Eglinton Street, also in Glasgow, where James Wilson had an inn on Lord Eglinton's land.[63]

Although the Edinburgh Society of Bowlers had written down their rules in 1771, the first laws to be generally agreed and printed were not written until 1848/49. Their author was William Mitchell, a solicitor born in Kilmarnock, who was the most conspicuous individual in the development of bowling during the early period of its growth, as law giver, historian, song writer and teacher. The laws of the game issued by the World Bowls Board still bear the subtitle 'as originally formulated by the Scottish Bowling Association', and though the SBA was founded after Mitchell's death, their laws were a reworking of his.

CAICH OR HANDBALL

Caich or *cache* was the Scots name for a game which was found over most of Europe and still exists as *handball* in Ireland and America and in more developed forms such as *pelota* in the Basque country. It was the progenitor of the various forms of *fives* and *rackets*. *Caich* was played between two individuals or teams of equal numbers, and the object was to drive the ball against a wall so that at the end of a rally the winners were those who had struck it furthest from the wall. It is a form of the *jeu de paume* which James I enjoyed at the Dominican Friary at Perth in 1437. He attempted to escape from his assassins by descending into a sewer:

6.   Barr Castle, Galston, Ayrshire, probably built in the fifteenth century. Until
1939 caich or handball was played on the wall facing the camera.

bot he maid to stop hit well iij dayes afore hand with stone,
bicause that whane he playd there at the paume the ballis that
he plaid withe oft ranne yn at that fowle hole.[64]

A linguistic argument has been produced by Gillmeister which
points to the diffusion of the game from Picardy.[65] The word *cache*
is first found there in the late thirteenth century; by the end of the
fifteenth it was in the Low Countries (as *caetse, caetspel*) and
Scotland, and in the following century it appeared in Germany
(*katzenspil*) and Spain (*chaza*). In Scotland it was played in a
cachpoole or *cachpule*, the second element of the word coming from
the German or Dutch *spiel*. *Caich* had other names in Scotland such
as *handy, han-an-hail, guff-the-ba, caich-ba* and *hand-catch*.

Simple games tend to be diffused quickly: why did *caich* take
centuries to cross Europe? The answer may lie in the ball, for it is
not easy to make one which bounces using only organic materials.
Surviving balls usually have a stitched leather cover, tightly stuffed
with feathers or rags, sometimes with a core. They have usually split
along the stitching of the seams. An early account of making

feather-filled golf balls provides the likely answer, showing that they were under pressure. The cover, made of 'stout leather', was soaked in boiling water and sewn together, and then tightly stuffed. 'The leather being yet wet, it contracts into a ball of dimensions stated'.[66] This explains why surviving *caich* balls have split.

In essence, *caich* is a simple game, needing no more than a wall, a flat hard surface in front of it, and a ball which bounced. However, these requirements were not easily met in the Middle Ages. A flat wall had to be of finished masonry or plaster, and the ground beside it of beaten earth or stone flags. Thus at first it was played in monasteries, and later it tended to be an urban game. In one place in Scotland there is a record of a catchpull in an ecclesiastical setting. The commendator of the Priory of St Andrews was authorised in 1597 to feu out the 'girnells, orcheardis, yardis, doucaitts, kaithspell, cloistour, and haill office' which had become ruinous.[67] In Glasgow there was a cachpoole in Isle Toothie, near the Rottenrow, owned in 1554 by Thomas Forret. In Edinburgh there was one just outside the Watergate. There were catchpules at Dundee, Linlithgow, Stirling and Aberdeen,[68] and the game was also played in Lanark and Elgin.

Most cachpooles were probably blank walls with areas of paving or beaten earth in front of them. Thus at Perth about 1800:

> the best place was the south side of the square of Gowrie-house. In that wing the windows faced south, whilst on the north side they were all built up. There was then a spacious square, with a wall about 40 feet high.[69]

There is evidence which suggests that *caich* was played by the common people as well as by gentlemen. Church walls were used at Forres in 1586 and at Elgin where the play was 'vpon the queir [choir] of this kirk' in 1592 and again in 1727 when it was banned because 'it destroys the glass windows' of the kirk:[70] this implies the use of spaces that were accessible to all. There is a reference to the game in the satirical poem 'Women's Truth' which appears in the Bannatyne manuscript (1568). It lists impossible sights that will be seen when women are true, including:

> Ane handles man I saw but dreid
> In caichpule faste playane.[71]

For this to have been an effective image, caitch must have been common, and there are several references to it in Edinburgh in the 1580s which suggest that it was played with enthusiasm.[72] After James Melville went to study at St Andrews in 1569 his father gave him 'bow, arrose, [golf] glub and bals, but nocht a purss for Catchpull and Tauern' – associating caitch with gambling and probably with drinking.[73] Melville became a leading exponent of reform in the church and a thorn in the side of James VI: he was more sensitive to moral issues than most lairds' sons.

Caich was later known as *handball*. It makes few appearances in the written record in the seventeenth century or the first half of the eighteenth. The increasing use of dressed stone both in buildings in towns and in farm steadings meant that there were more flat walls: the opportunities for play multiplied. Nevertheless, the references to the game are few and suggest a limited distribution focusing on Ayrshire and Perthshire. Handball was forbidden in schools in Ayr in 1774 and Kilmarnock in 1784. It was played not by the boys –

7. Quoiters, as represented in a stained glass window at Neilshill, Ayrshire, *c.* 1890.

or perhaps not only by them – but by adults who were damaging windows and slates, and hurting the boys.[74] In 1819 the windows of Irvine Academy were broken by weavers playing 'at the ball',[75] almost certainly handball.

Between the middle of the nineteenth century and its demise in 1939, the centre for handball in the West of Scotland was Galston. The north wall of Barr Castle, a 15th-century tower house, was used: it was known as *Baur Alley*, so it may also have been used for kyles. An annual meeting was held there at which teams of three competed for senior and junior belts and medals.[76] Given the popularity of handball in Ireland, it is possible that immigrants contributed to the survival of the Galston competition. However, the names of some of the players in 1861 have been recorded, and they are Scots: Allison, Nisbet, Parker, Paton, Watson, Wilson.[77] There was also a 'handsome ball alley' at Hurlford where a handball match was arranged in 1851.[78] Around 1870 the sport was popular in Ochiltree, and played either two-handed or two-a-side.[79]

Handball was described at an unknown Lowland Scottish location by an anonymous author:

A glorious game was 'handy', or hand-in-hand-out ... and no fool's play either when all its conditions were complied with. Given only a good blank wall, a ball somewhat smaller than a cricket one – of tightly-rolled worsted covered with sheepskin – two teams of six, eight, or ten each, and then look out.

I have seen the last round of a twenty-one game of handy played out between two rival districts ... The game ... was for one man of each team alternately to strike the ball back to the wall with his hand, and the team which first failed to send it back lost one, which the other gained. And don't run away with the idea that this was the innocent play it looks on paper. There were creases right and left perpendicularly, and above and below horizontally, outside which the ball could not strike to count. There were clever fellows who could make it rebound from the wall thirty or forty feet as neatly as if cut; and there were sometimes cleverer ones who could send it back all that distance low enough to touch the wall just inside the lower crease, and leave the opponent's wall-keeper time to save himself by the skin of his teeth, if he saved himself at all. Men stripped to the work, and rolled up their shirt-sleeves on their stout arms, and swung and sweated over it obedient to a discipline as exacting as any which prevails on the cricket-field or amongst football players; and to be the best handy player of a district was to be a hero. It tested a fellow's stamina as effectually as any game I know, while it made the strictest temperance necessary, and developed a love of fair play and good-humour in all.[80]

Real or *royal tennis* was brought from France by King James V, who built the court at Falkland in 1540/1. It is still used, and is by far the oldest sporting structure in Scotland.[81] There was also a tennis court at the King's Wark at Leith, and it is possible that one or two of the cachpooles were in fact built for real tennis. Tennis used costly implements, rackets and balls which had to be imported, so when the royal court left Falkland the tennis court was used for the obvious purpose and the Synod of Fife recorded in 1643 that 'it was commonlie reported that men played at the catche on the Sabbath day, in the catchpell in Falkland'.[82]

An unusual derivation from real tennis was the Rattray handball game,[83] for which a trophy of a silver ball was given in the reign of James VI. In this Perthshire village, the play was started by striking the ball onto the Church roof, just as a service in real tennis is made on to the penthouse. The play thereafter was backwards and forwards, not against a wall.[84]

CURLING

> When chitterin birds on flichterin wing
> About the barn doors mingle
> And biting frost, and cranreuch cold
> Drive coofs around the ingle;
> Then to the lochs the curlers hie
> Their hearts as licht's a feather
> And mark the tee wi mirth an glee
> In cauld, cauld frosty weather.[85]

FIGS. 10, 11, 12, 13, 14. FROM THE BLAIRGOWRIE AND DELVINE CLUBS.

8. Late eighteenth-century channel stanes from Blairgowrie and Delvine, from
Kerr's *History of Curling* (1890).

These are the words of the verse of what was, in Victorian
Scotland, the most famous curling song – 'In cauld, cauld, frosty
weather' by the Reverend James Muir (1771–1831) of Beith. Although
he was an Ayrshire minister, Muir was a member of the Duddingston
Curling Society, which curled just outside Edinburgh, and it was in
their honour that he wrote the song, and at one of their dinners he
first sang it.

In Britain, the coldest winters of modern times were in the Little
Ice Age of the seventeenth century – when small glaciers may have

formed on the Cairngorms. In the nineteenth century, winters were colder than they have been in the twentieth. They were most severe in the second decade of the century. Charles Dickens was born in 1812, and six of the first nine Christmases of his life were white with frost or snow in London – where white Christmases have always been rare.[86] In 1815 Mount Tambora on the Indonesian island of Sumbawa erupted, and its dust distorted the world's climate for several years. In England the winter of 1823 was the coldest of the nineteenth century. It is possible that the growth of curling in this period owes something to a volcanic event on the edge of the Flores Sea, a few miles south of the equator.

Curling was increasingly popular between 1780 and 1880 and during this period it was played by more people in Scotland than any other sport. The minister of Dryfesdale (in Annandale) said it was 'the principal diversion or amusement' in 1793, and his colleague in nearby Wamphray wrote in 1799 that it was 'the one general amusement'.[87] In 1823 one issue of the *Ayr Advertiser* reported parish matches between Ayr and Coylton, Old and New Cumnock, Loudon and Tarbolton, Dalmellington and Straiton, Irvine and Kilwinning, Kirkoswald and Maybole; and between the married men and bachelors of Straiton and of Catrine. At the head of the column the editor said, 'The following and many other communications on this subject have been sent to us by our persevering Correspondents. If they be of little interest to the world in general, they appear of much consequence to the parties concerned'.[88] At Muirkirk in Ayrshire:

> The chief amusement in winter is curling, or playing stones on smooth ice; they eagerly vie with one another who shall come nearest the mark, and one part of the parish against another – one description of men against another – one trade or occupation against another; – and often the whole parish against another, – earnestly contend for the *palm*, which is generally all the prize, except perhaps the victors claim from the vanquished the dinner and bowl of toddy.[89]

In other words, it was not a gambling game. An English traveller observed in 1850 that:

FIG. 29.
" THE STAR," FROM PENICUICK HOUSE.

FIG. 30.
" THE HORN," FROM PENICUICK HOUSE.

FIG 31. TAM SAMSON'S STONE.

9. Mason-dressed curling stones dating from the first half of the nineteenth
century, from Kerr's *History of Curling* (1890).

People who talk about the Scotch as phlegmatic would alter
their note if they saw them at curling time ... Inn stables near
the favourite ponds were so full that it was a mercy we could
get a stall for our mare at all. If we passed a cart at about 10
a.m., we generally found it full of the paraphernalia of the game
instead of ordinary produce ... At night we heard desperate
discussions on the events of the day ... the Old Cumnockites ...
disregarded their ale and their toddy, they stood up and held
each other by the coats, and cross-pumped into each other's
systems their curling observations and criticisms. Almost from
day break telegrams were flying about as to the state of the ice,
and the very farm lads looked as if they contemplated suicide
when the thaw came softly stealing from the south.[90]

Some curlers were so keen that they would often go out before they went to work: thus the name of the Kilmarnock Morning Star club.[91] At the other end of the day, was the practice of curling after dark – by moonlight, or lanterns, or in the case of the Carron and Stenhouse Club, by the light of blast furnaces. At Bridge of Allan in the 1850s, Major Henderson lit his pond by gas.[92]

Curling was a game of passion. As the Reverend John Kerr wrote of the Dunblane Club:

> Every oath cost 1d. If repeated, the price was doubled; and the doubling process went on with each new offence, so that an ill-tempered member might swear himself out of a large fortune in a small space of time.[93]

At Sanquhar, an irate curler under the eye of the minster addressed an opponent who had angered him: 'It's a gude thing ye're gaun where *there'll be nae ice*'.[94] Further down Nithsdale, James Hogg farmed at Tynron – and curled. One bitterly cold day his herds repeatedly brought news of sheep stuck in the snow, but Hogg saying 'Skin them, skin them,' played on. Soon he was himself skint, went bankrupt, and retreated to Edinburgh to become a literary lion.[95]

We have already seen that traditional sports fitted into the social pattern by being part of annual festivals. They were looked forward to, prepared for, for weeks ahead. With curling, the excitement was different. Curling could be hoped for, but not planned. Curlers had to wait not for ice on the loch or the mill dam but until there was a positive answer to the often-asked question 'Is the ice bearing?' Curling related to forced inactivity. The opportunity to curl occurred, as the Regulations of Peebles Curling Club said in 1821:

> At a season of the year when the Plough is arrested in the furrow, when masonic & many other handcraft employments are laid aside, and when the Mill wheel refuses to revolve on her axis.[96]

Curling is simple in concept but the reality of the play is complex. A Penicuik curler explained:

> Every keen and true curler ... knows full well that every skip

10.   The badge of Duddingston Curling Society, 1803, with the Kirk behind.
National Museums of Scotland.

is expected to possess the virtues that ought to be found in every Prime Minister of Britain, – keeping a watchful eye upon the tricks and tactics of the enemy, having the light and heavy artillery always in good and efficient order, and, in the event of any real blockade, being able to ... clear the decks and open the ports.[97]

The last word is a pun, standing both for a gunport and the gap between two curling stones.

Curling stones before about 1700 were *loofies*, flattish stones which had one or more notches for the fingers. A number survive and in the absence of any preserved pennystanes one is inclined to regard the *loofies*, or at least the smaller ones, as having been used for curling in winter and pennystanes when there was no ice. Stones were boulders lifted from the river bed – *channel stanes*. Henry Adamson, writing of the first quarter of the seventeenth century, addressed his curling stones in mock-heroic fashion:

And ye my *loadstones* of *Lednochian* lakes
Collected from the loughs, where waterie snakes
Do much abound . . .[98]

In other words, Perth curlers used stones from Glen Lednock, above Comrie. Later stones were more highly worked, but still made by hand by a local mason. Here the Reverend George Murray (1812–81) of Balmaclellan addresses his favourite stone, and describes the way in which it was made:

Wi' mony a crack he cloured your crown
Wi' mony a chap he chipped you down
Fu' aft he turned ye roun' and roun'
    And aye he sang;
A' ither stanes ye'll be aboon
    And that ere lang.

Guided by many a mould and line
He laboured next, with polish fine
To make your mirrored surface shine
    With lustre rare –
Like lake, reflect the forms divine
    Of nature fair.

A handle next did Rab prepare
And fixed it with consummate care –
The wood of ebony so rare
    The screw of steel –
Ye were a channelstane right fair
    Fit for a spiel.[99]

Stones varied in size and shape, and in the period before they were machine-turned, they were highly individual. Some of these enormous stones had their own names – *Whirlie* at Penicuik, which when struck would spin but not move from its spot, and at Coupar Angus *Cog*, *Fluke*, *Black Meg*, and the extraordinary *Saut Bucket*, which weighed 116 lbs.[100] The same parish had the *Suwaroff*, named after Alexander Vasilievich Suvárov (1729–1800) of whom *Britannica* observed, 'In an age when war had become an act of diplomacy he

11a and b.   The medal of Muirkirk Curling Society, 1823. The inscription – 'An ice stane and a guid broom cowe [broom] / Will warm us like a bleezing lowe [fire]' – refers to the warmth produced as the curler sweeps the rink.

restored its true significance as an act of force'. He may also have attracted sympathy because he lived the life of an ordinary soldier and after retirement donned a smock and worked in the fields with his peasants.[101] East Kilbride had the *Cheese* of 70 lbs – used for tests of strength and for weighing oatmeal and cheese – *Sleepin Maggie*, *The Door Hinge Handle*, and nearby Jackton had the *Whin Boulder*.[102]

Curling changed enormously between 1770 and 1840 in equipment, venue, rules and organisation. It ended the period as the first modern sport played widely in Scotland.

Around 1770 three devices were introduced to make it easier to deliver heavy stones; indeed, it is difficult to see how the heaviest stones could be delivered without their aid. *Crampits*, also called *cramp-bits* and *tramps*, were iron grips worn over the shoes, like alpinists' crampons of a later age. Their disadvantage was that the wearer mutilated the ice as he went up and down the rink, yet they were still in use in Dumfriesshire at the beginning of the twentieth century. *Trickers* or *triggers* were fixed in the ice either singly or as a pair, and the curler placed his foot or feet in them. Both of these devices were made by the local blacksmith, as stones were hewed by the mason, and so they appeared in a range of different forms. In the Kilmarnock area a different source of security from the effects of gravity was deployed. Carpet weaving was begun in the town about 1780: curlers had their boots covered with carpet.[103] The most widely-used utensil for remaining upright during delivery was the *foot-iron* or *footboard*, later and confusingly called the *crampit*. It was invented by John Cairnie of Largs, about 1820. He explained:

> it consists of a piece of strong sheet-iron, three feet nine inches in length, and nine inches broad. The iron is to be punched or well frosted on both sides, and turned up about one inch at the end.[104]

This enables us to envisage a footboard – and a blacksmith to make one.

However, the crucial development in the material culture of curling was the development of the circular stone, which made it possible to predict the directions in which they would rebound off one another. As in bowling, the role of chance and 'the rub of the green' were diminished and consequently the player's skill and ability to think tactically became more important. Until about 1860 they were fashioned by masons, and after that by machines.

At the same time as the apparatus of curling was changing, two administrative developments took place: the first rules were written in 1804, and the Grand Caledonian Curling Club was organised in 1838.

Edinburgh curlers had played on the Nor' Loch, and later on Canonmills Loch, to which the magistrates marched behind a band when the ice was bearing. This élite moved to Duddingston in the 1790s, and the Duddingston Curling Society was formed on 24th January 1795, in the coldest single month which Britain has experienced in the last three or four centuries.[105] At its first meeting the third resolution entered in its minute book was:

> That to be Virtuous is to reverence our God, Religion, Laws

& King: And they Hereby do declare their attachment to the same.[106]

Ministers and officers in the armed services were among its members, and so were lawyers, particularly after 1800. We may infer that they understood the advantages of written rules, and were a force on the committee which drafted them.[107] They included the requirement that 'all curling stones to be of circular shape'. The rules were approved on the day that John Cairnie joined the Duddingston Society, and were printed in 1811. Thus made accessible, they spread, partly because of the authority of the Society, which was regarded rather as the Marylebone Cricket Club was in its own sphere in London. The Society's members came from all over the Lowlands, and included well-known west-country figures such as Sir Alexander Boswell of Auchinleck, and James Muir of Beith.

John Cairnie (*c.* 1769–1842) is the most significant figure in the history of curling. Born at Dunipace near Stirling he served as a surgeon in India from 1792 to 1805 when he retired to Largs, built a house called Curling Hall, sailed and bowled in summer and curled in winter. We have already met him as the inventor of the footboard. Even more important was his artificial rink, first made in 1827. This had a level base of beaten clay on which a thin skin of ice was built up by watering from watering cans: the result was to multiply several fold the number of days on which curling was possible.[108] News of Cairnie's invention spread through enthusiastic notices such as those in the *Dumfries Courier* and *Glasgow Herald* in 1829 and in his *Essay on Curling and Artificial Pond-Making* (1833).[109] Perhaps he was removing a recognised difficulty, for in 1795 it had been said that 'the progress of improvement' – that is, better drainage – had removed the small lochs and ponds which had been used by curlers.[110]

Cairnie and others advocated the establishing of a national curling club. It came into being as the Grand Caledonian Curling Club in the summer of 1838, and achieved royal patronage in 1842. It aims were to provide competitions between clubs and to improve the skills of curlers by encouraging the points game in which points were accumulated by each player individually by attempting to play predetermined shots.

The Royal Caledonian Curling Club (RCCC) is of some significance in the history of sport in Scotland. The first national sporting association of any kind was the Royal Caledonian Hunt Club, whose membership was restricted to the aristocracy and the upper levels of the gentry. The RCCC was the first national association of clubs, 35 years before the Scottish Football Association. It organised Grand Matches, national bonspiels in which the North played the South. The first one, at Penicuik House in 1847, was played with only 12 rinks on each side, but there were 35 in 1848 at Linlithgow and 127 at Lochwinnoch in 1850 as well as several thousand spectators. Its activities encouraged the formation of more clubs, and by 1850 roughly half of the sports clubs in Scotland were curling clubs.

Part of the importance of curling is the way in which it involved all kinds of people. For example, the *Hamilton Advertiser* of 1856 said, speaking of the Upper Ward of Lanarkshire:

> In a rural and thin populated district ... the laird might be seen mingling not only with his farmers, but his cottagers, interchanging the broad jest at his own failures, and giving applause whenever it was due. The minister might also be seen driving his stone with as much anxiety of eye as any one, and occasionally, perhaps, envying the good fortune of an unlettered peasant, whom, on another occasion, he would have to chide for his backwardness in the Single Catechism.[111]

'We are brethren a'' says the medal of the Polmont and Westquarter Club, giving a biblical flavour to the image of a top-hatted, frock-coated land owner shaking hands with one of his tenants in 'bunnet' and plaid. The evening was as much part of curling as the day, for 'players usually conclude the game and day with a good dinner, drink, and songs'.[112] The customary meal was *beef an greens* – salt beef and kale, washed down with whisky toddy. At Crawfordjohn in the Upper Ward of Lanarkshire 'Curling is a favourite diversion among the commonality; and even the gentlemen sometimes join in it.'[113] In 1838 dinner followed a match at Roslin, 'bringing together both on the ice, and at the social board, the landlord and tenant, farmer, tradesman and manufacturer ... no slight advantage in times of turmoil, combination, and crime ..'.[114]

12. Curling at Windyedge near Perth, from the *Illustrated London News* of 23 January 1843.

In other words, curling was not always for all of the people, and in some places at least the farm labourer did not play.

A snuff box in the National Museums of Scotland emphasises the social side of curling. It is a typical piece of Mauchline boxwork, and painted on it is:

> Take a pinch and send me roun
> There's nothing like me in the Town
> I'm nae Sheep shank you may think
> I'm snuff box mind to Logans Rink.[115]

– 'I'm nae Sheep Shank' meaning 'I'm not important'.

Curling fitted into the established framework of society. Before clubs were organised the parish was the basis for larger matches, and within the parish games were sometimes played on the basis of where men lived – thus the Queensberry Street medal from Dumfries

(1831), to be played for by the inhabitants of the street from Queensberry Square to St Andrew Street, one side of the street against the other.[116] In Dumfries there were matches between masonic lodges, between different trades and between the officers of a trade incorporation and its ordinary members.[117] Curling was also the focus for charity. It was quite common to play for a boll of meal or a load of coals for the poor. Occasionally, a collection for the poor was held at the end of a match, as at Crossmichael in 1813.[118]

Ministers have been prominent in curling. The great historian of the game, John Kerr (1852–1920), was minister of Dirleton in East Lothian. John Somerville (1774–1837), minister of Currie, was a notable improver of curling's hardware. It was he who invented the *Currie crampit*, and nearly anticipated Cairnie as the inventor of a practicable artificial pond. He also made improvements to sporting guns and was the preacher of the sermon on the laying of the foundation stone of the National Monument on Calton Hill. And James Taylor, a Doctor of Divinity, was the great collector of curling anecdotes.

Here is one, in Taylor's own words. It is a sample of Victorian humour, but it also illustrates the strength which was needed on a rough outdoor rink, as compared with the smooth ice indoors to-day. In mid-Victorian curling it was an established tactic to drive a well-placed stone off the ice with a maximum of force. The skip would call out 'A' the pouther i' the horn' or 'Come doun like a vera judgement and clear the hoose,' and it was then time for 'a thunnerin' cast':[119]

> The late Sheriff Burnett of Peebles, a worthy man and keen curler, was playing in a rink with a well-known Peebles char- acter, a stone-mason by trade, a first-class curler but a noted river poacher. Indeed, the Sheriff had nearly every winter to send him to prison for illegal fishing. On the present occasion the poacher was skip, and the Sheriff was about to play, when the former addressed him thus:- 'I say, Shirra, dae ye see that stane?' 'Aye, Jock', answered the Sheriff. 'A' weel, Shirra,' says Jock, pointing to the stone with his kowe, 'just gie that ane sixty days'.[120]

One form of evidence for the active prosecution of an activity is a rich material culture associated with it. Curling produced medals and other prizes: no other sport in Scotland can compare with it for quantity in the period 1800–1870. The oldest curling prizes are the medals of Coupar Angus and Kettins Curling Club, dating from 1772 and 1774. The next in age are the gold medal of Duddingston Curling Society (1809) and the silver medal of Tarbolton Curling Society (1814), the latter being the oldest which is still the subject of competition. For the remainder of the nineteenth century the medal was by far the most common curling prize.

These early curling medals, engraved, not struck, have a great charm. Perhaps surprisingly, few appear to be copies of others or of engravings as is so common with the images on medals: each one is an independent piece of folk art. Typically, they show a curler or some of the apparatus of curling. One of the most handsome of all is the medal of New Abbey Curling Club, dated 1830 and still in the possession of the Club. On one side it shows Loch Kindar, where they curled. Conspicuous on the skyline is the Waterloo Monument. The motto is PALMAM QUI MERUIT FERAT: let the man who deserves it bear the palm. On the reverse is a splendid and accurate view of Sweetheart Abbey itself. Thomas Ferguson, Minister of Kirkbean had written:

> Come, cheer up, my lads, to Loch Kindar we steer
> To strive for those laurels we all hold so dear.

Laurel and bearing the palm: Olympic language had reached curling.

Medals point us to the awareness of the Scottishness of curling. The thistle and Highland costume appear from time to time, as on the medals of the Muirkirk club (1823) and Ardrossan Alma (1855). The most assertive statement was made on the badge of the Duddingston Society: SIC SCOTI: ALII NON AEQUE FELICES, 'This is the way the Scots play: the rest of the world isn't half so lucky'.[121] When Auchinleck played Sorn in 1820 on the Whirr Loch, 81-a-side, it was described as the 'Ancient Scottish game' and the accompanying '*baiks* and whisky' were food and drink to the Scots.[122] The favourite toast of Durham Weir, president of the Bathgate Club, was 'Scotland's ain dear game o' curling' and the health of Robert

Burns was drunk at the Club dinner, which was always held on Burns's birthday.[123]

Curling has a rich language of its own, and examples of its vocabulary have already been mentioned. Some of it has a Scots etymology, emphasising the Scottish character of the game.[124] The word *rink* comes from the Old Scots *renk*, a combat area, a race, and is thus an area of play for curling, bowls, or quoits. In curling it is also used to denote a team. The eight and four-foot circles round the tee, the target, are sometimes called the *broughs*, from the Old Scots *bruch*, a ring or halo. *Wick* occurs in curling and in bowls: it is a shot in which the stone or bowl is aimed at another so that one or other is moved towards the tee or jack. The struck stone or bowl thus moves at an angle to the path of the striker. *Wick* is often found in the compounds *inwick* and *outwick* dating from the beginning of the nineteenth century. It comes from the Old Norse *(munn)vik*, the corner of the mouth. In Scots the word *drive* has the general meaning of to throw with force. It is first recorded in golf in 1642.[125] In both bowls and curling it is the phase of the play where a bowl or stone is removed by playing the shot with force, and without concern as to where the two bowls or stones finally lie.

There are more terms which are used both in curling and in bowling. In view of the small number of quotations available before 1850 it would be unwise to speculate which of the two was influencing the other. In curling *trickers* are the small metal platforms, usually triangular in shape, set on the ice on prongs, on which the curler placed his foot when delivering the stone. In bowling the bowl is delivered from the *tricker*: in both sports the word comes from the *trigger* of a gun. In curling to *draw* is to play a stone so that it lands on a spot indicated by the skip at or near the tee; in bowling it is the same kind of shot in relation to the jack. A curler lays a *guard* when he places a stone so that it protects another, or the tee. There is also the *deid guard* which completely covers a stone and the *double guard* which is composed of two stones. *Guards* are also used in bowling, and William Mitchell explained, 'in the Glasgow district, [guards] are denominated *Paisley* and *Kilmarnock*. A *Paisley* guard is one which lies from one two three yards short of the jack; and a *Kilmarnock* guard does not run over mid-way to it'.[126] To *break an egg* is to play a stone so that it strikes a nominated stone gently, with just sufficient force to crack an egg. Mitchell records the word having been used in the past by bowlers in Kilmarnock.[127]

Even after the invention of artificial ponds, much curling was done on mill dams or on water which naturally collected in low-lying land. When parishes met, before the rise of clubs, they often chose what might be seen as a neutral venue, and equally distant to two groups of men, most of whom would be on foot: a loch which straddles the parish boundary. Thus in Ayrshire Maybole and Kirkmichael met on Drumore Loch, and Coylton and Dalrymple on Martnaham Loch.[128]

The artificial pond enabled curling to remain an urban game. Before the nineteenth century ponds and boggy areas were common in and around towns, and towns themselves were small. As they grew these stretches of water were filled in, and the number of water mills fell. At Perth the shallows of the Tay were used for curling until about 1800, but 30 years later 'the fishers lay hold of the ice the minute it is formed' and curlers had to go to the country for their sport.[129] In Edinburgh there were a number of artificial rinks, but in Glasgow only a few are to be found on nineteenth-century maps.

There is some evidence for an uneven distribution of curling. In the seventeenth and eighteenth centuries it was found over most of the country south of the Highland line: it is impossible to say more. But at the beginning of the nineteenth century there were two areas where the game was becoming much more popular: around Edinburgh, and in Ayrshire and Galloway. At the time of the second Great Match it was said that it was appropriate that it should be held at Lochwinnoch because curling was particularly associated with the western counties.[130] The sport was introduced into Kincardineshire in the 1840s. There was a very cold period in January 1841, but the local newspapers reported no curling despite a temperature of 10°F at Montrose. Nine years later it had reached Fettercairn and Montrose though it was still 'of recent introduction into this part of the country'.[131]

GOLF

Golf, along with whisky and people, is Scotland's great export. Yet the extent to which it is Scottish has been challenged. Whatever doubts there are about its origins, it is certain that between the seventeenth and the nineteenth centuries it became completely Scottish in character. It was played almost exclusively in a few places on the east coast of Scotland. Geographically, golfing was skin deep, because it was rarely seen inland. Yet it inspired deep devotion in its players: if golf did not penetrate far into Scotland, the Scots profoundly affected the character of the game.

Golf grew on the Scottish links. Their undulating sandy soil and often coarse grass are common on the east coast and present in a few places on the west coast. It was natural for there to be short grass on the fairway (to use a modern term) accompanied by rougher grass, patches of sand, and topographical and botanical hazards – though no trees. These features introduced new phases of play such as (again, to use modern words) chipping and hitting the ball low into the wind which had not had great significance in previous stick-and-ball games. The English traveller who saw golf at Montrose and tried to explain it as a giant species of billiards was utterly mistaken.[132]

A modern historian, David Hamilton, has captured the spirit of the play:

> The links had from the start their 'fairways' – the fisherman's term for a safe passage. Golf was a serious journey out and back, as unpleasant but rewarding as the winter deep-sea fishing of the towns. It was a voyage out and back in rough weather, and full of hazard.[133]

The eighteenth-century expression was *fair green*, but Hamilton is right in spirit. In the 'Address to the Unco Guid' Burns imagined the individual as a ship:

> Wi' wind and tide fair in' your tail
> Right on ye scud your sea-way;
> But in the teeth o' baith to sail
> It maks an unco lee-way.

13.   The Goffields on the south side of Irvine (Ayrshire) are thought to have been
known by this name since the seventeenth century: they are one of the earliest
locations of the game in the West of Scotland. The building on the left was a
powder magazine.

Playing golf on the open links with feather-filled balls was similar.
Burns used sailing to give a moral message, and in Calvinist Scotland
the metaphors within golf must have been clear to the player, and
have been part of the experience of playing the game. Golfing
precepts such as *never up, never in* can be applied more widely than
on the links.

From near the beginning golf had two forms: the aristocratic,
which used craftsman-made clubs and balls stuffed with feathers,
and the people's, which used pieces of bent stick and any ball which
was available, typically one of solid wood.[134] The first we meet often
in histories of golf. The second has left fewer traces in the historical
record. It was probably played with a range of implements including
cast-offs from the more formal game, and with far greater variety
in rules and local conventions. Most of the players were boys. At
Inveresk in the 1790s the minister said that:

Children are trained to it in their earliest days ... excited by
the example of their parents.[135]

Tom Morris (1821–1908), the giant of Victorian golf, remembered his childhood:

> as soon as I could gang I and the other laddies would be doon on the links with any kind of a club we could get, and any old ball, or even a bit of one ... You ken a' St Andrews bairns are born wi' web feet an' wi' a golf-club in their hands.[136]

By the seventeenth century the golf club and ball were already sophisticated objects. Whilst they were not widely distributed, they were made in quite large numbers. Donald Blaine, 'bower burgess' of Edinburgh left 'clubheids and clubschaftis ane thousand made and unmade' when he died in 1635.[137]

The earliest reference to the nature of the ball suggests that it had been at least partly made of leather for centuries: in 1554 the golf ball makers of North Leith were mentioned at the same time as cordiners [shoemakers]. In his *Vocabula* (1636) the Aberdeen schoolmaster David Wedderburn referred to the golf ball as a 'pila calvaria', a skull-like ball.[138] Hamilton reasonably comments that this may refer to the pattern of stitching which is similar to the junction of the bones on the dome of the skull, and in addition we may see the bone of the skull paralleling the cover of the ball, and the goose down or other soft filling as being the equivalent to the brain. In 1687 Thomas Kincaid described balls as made of thick leather, being ambiguous as to whether they were solid or stuffed.[139] In the eighteenth century the feather-filled ball was certainly the standard type.

In 1691 Professor Alexander Monro wrote from St Andrews to John Mackenzie of that Ilk, who was in Edinburgh, sending 'ane sett of Golfe Clubs consisting of three, viz. ane play club, ane scraper, and ane tin fac'd club'.[140] Thus there were already different types of club, and the *putting club* is first known from another letter of 1690.[141] The clubs themselves were complex, using different woods for the shaft and head, and horn for the sole.

Golf grew throughout the eighteenth century, though the pace of expansion varied. In the 1740s, and specifically in years 1743 and 1744, the game suddenly seems more conspicuous. The first silver trophy was made, the rules written down, the first piece of literature

THE GOLFER'S LAND.

14. Golfer's Land in the Canongate, Edinburgh, now demolished, said to have
been built by John Paterson with the money he made as the Duke of York's partner
at golf in 1681/82.

devoted to the game was printed, and there is evidence of the export
of quite large quantities of golfing equipment.

The Edinburgh Silver Club was made in 1744 on the instruction
of the Town Council as a prize for a competition open to 'As many
Noblemen or Gentlemen, or other Golfers, from any part of Great

Britain or Ireland'. The only formality was to enter one's name a week in advance in a book at Lucky Clephane's tavern beside Leith Links. The founding of the Honourable Company of Edinburgh Golfers followed the establishment of the competition. At first, it was a completely open event though there was a selection based on wealth caused by the cost of equipment. Not until 1764 was competition restricted to members of the Honourable Company. The silver club at St Andrews dates from 1754 and the one at Glasgow from 1787.

Thomas Mathison published the first golf poem in 1743, *The Goff*. In it, he gave the first clear description of the manufacture of golf balls. They were:

> The work of *Bobson* [Robertson]; who with matchless art
> Shapes the firm hide, connecting ev'ry part
> Then in a socket sets the well-stich'd void
> And thro' the eyelet drives the downy tide;
> Crowds urging Crowds the forceful brogue impels
> The feathers harden and the Leather swells;
> He crams and sweats, yet crams and urges more
> Till scarce the turgid globe contains its store.[142]

The English naturalist and traveller Thomas Pennant visited St Andrews in 1772 and described 'an iron rod, with a wooden handle, pressed against the breast' which was used to force the feathers into the ball.[143] In this period, there is not complete agreement as to the method of manufacture. Some say that the leather skin was boiled before stuffing, but others that there was no boiling. The two are not irreconcilable if we regard the original method as boiling, superseded by the use of the tool which Pennant described, but still used by some conservatives in conjunction with it.

Golf in the eighteenth century, though a minority sport, was taken abroad when Scots spread over the globe. They played it in Ireland, Virginia, South Carolina, and the West Indies. In 1743 the *Magdalen* sailed from Leith with 8 dozen clubs and 3 gross of golf balls in its cargo.[144] When in the same year the sloop *Matty* sailed from Port Glasgow, Jamaica bound, she took over 8000 yards of linen, '20 Dozen Gowf Balls 13 Gowf Clubs'.[145] By 1753 golfing equipment was being sent to Russia.[146] A Swedish botanist went up the Sierra Leone

15. The Edinburgh Silver Club (1744) being carried by the Town's Officer, supported by the Town's drummers, in an engraving after a drawing by David Allan.

River in 1773 to visit a slaving and trading station. He found the Scots had laid out a two-hole course: they went to and fro dressed in Indian cotton before retiring to drink Madeira and smoke Virginian tobacco. Their caddies, local boys, wore tartan loincloths woven in Glasgow.[147]

The oldest rules of golf are those for the first competition for the Edinburgh silver club. There is thus a civic context for these rules, for they were written to ensure a fair competition for the prize, the gift of the town. The silver jack of the Edinburgh Society of Bowlers (1771) has the same background. These early rules were for clarification rather than codification: they set out points which might be disputed, but left out the most basic assumptions, such as the convention of playing the ball where it lies.[148]

The rules of the Honourable Company of Edinburgh Golfers were in 1775 the first to be printed and so became the models for others elsewhere, but not in the way that the Duddingston rules for curling were followed all over Scotland. Golf clubs adopted their own variations. Golf in the Edinburgh area, however, fell into a decline in the period between 1820 and 1840. At St Andrews the Royal and Ancient grew in comparative importance, and when in 1897 one set of rules was adopted for all golfers, it was that in force in St Andrews.

Golf in 1800 was almost identical to the game two hundred years earlier, played with similar implements by similar people on the same small number of courses. Perhaps the skill of the club makers had increased. Certainly, some of them went to great lengths to ensure a quality product. One of the most gifted of them was Douglas MacEwan (1809–86) of Bruntsfield and later Musselburgh. Sir Guy Campbell, the distinguished golf historian, explained how he prepared to make the heads of his clubs:

> They were made out of small 'cuts' from the hedge-thorns. These thorns were planted horizontally on sloping banks, with the result that the stem of the tree or bush grew at an angle at the root, giving a piece of wood with a natural bend for the neck of the head.[149]

In some places there was a dip in the amount of golf played in the first quarter of the nineteenth century, just as other sports were laid aside during the Napoleonic Wars. At Perth, golf went into decline in the 1790s, but revived thirty years later: one consequence was the founding of the Royal Perth Golfing Society in 1842.[150] In general, however, the number of glof clubs active in Scotland in-creased steadily from six in 1800 to 19 in 1830 and well over 50 by the end of the 1860s.[151] Perhaps the most signifcant addition was Prestwick Mechanics (1851, now Prestwick St Nicholas) whose name

16.   The medal of New Abbey Curling Club, 1830. The curlers are on Loch
Kindar. *National Museums of Scotland.*

indicates the nature of its membership. The first instructional text
was published in 1857. In 1860 the first Open Championship was
held at Prestwick and won by Wille Park (1834–1903) of Musselburgh.
In that year it was open only to professionals, but amateurs were
soon allowed to enter: it was the first national competiton which
was held every year.

Expansion was made possible by the invention of a new kind of
ball. The feathery ball was replaced rapidly by a solid ball made out
of gutta percha, the *gutty*. It was imported first from Singapore, then
from Indonesia and Malaya, and it had great commercial importance
as the insulating substance for submarine telegraph cables. The gutta

17.   Sweetheart Abbey, accurately depicted on the New Abbey medal. *National Museums of Scotland.*

percha ball was probably first tried in 1845, and was certainly widely used by the summer of 1848. On 1st September that year a song was sung at the dinner of the Innerleven Golf Club at Leven in Fife. It explained some of the difficulties of playing with the feathery:

> And though our best wi' them we've tried
> And nicely every club applied
> They whirred and fuffed, and dooked and shied
> And sklentit into bunkers.

The gutta percha ball was better:

> At last a substance we hae got
> Frae which, for scarce mair than a groat
> A ba' comes that can row [roll] an' stot –
> A ba' the most transcendent.[152]

The gutty ball, though cheap and long-lasting, brought disadvantages. The necks of light and elegant wooden clubs broke when they struck the resilient mass of the new ball. Club makers produced less elegant and more solid products, using softer woods such as apple, pear and beech. Iron play with the old ball was no more than a means for escaping from an awkward lie: with the new one it was extended by the St Andrews professional Allan Robertson, and then developed in sophistication and control by 'Young' Tom Morris (1851–75), the first great golfer who did not begin his career in the era of the feather-filled ball.

Golf, though a minority sport, had its own language and in the nineteenth century much of it was Scots. This can be illustrated by looking at some of the names for the equipment of the game.[153] The *putting club* had become the *putter* by 1743. These words come from the Scots *putt* or *putt*, to push gently or nudge. The *spoon* (1790) was named after the club's concave face. The *cleek* (1842) was a narrow-bladed iron club. The word's more general meaning in Scot is a hook, which would of course be made of iron, but it can mean more specifically a walking stick with a crook at the end. The *niblick* (1857) with its short nose probably comes from *neb* or *nib*, meaning a bird's beak or the human nose. Thus:

> Strath, having laid his ball by his 'teed' shot in the cart track,
> Tom [Morris] played a beautiful shot out with his nibby iron.[154]

The -y ending indicates a diminutive in Scots, which may either be a physical diminutive or a mark of affection. Early irons had a face scarcely bigger than a golf ball.

The *baffing-spoon* (1862), later the *baffy*, was a wood with a steeply-lofted face used for approach shots. A *baff* is a blow, often with something soft. Thus the contact of a club with the turf just behind the ball is a *baff*. Finally, before the language of golf became part of global English, the *mashie* appeared (1881), a lofted iron, its name deriving from *mash*, a heavy hammer for stonebreaking. The spliced joint which united the wooden head to the shaft of the club was the *scare* or *skair*. The word first appears in print in a golfing context in 1857, but as it was used by craftsmen rather than golfers it had probably been applied to clubs for centuries.

In the latter part of the nineteenth century English holidaymakers golfed in Scotland: *Punch* published a cartoon of a flock of them drifting along together, captioned 'The Golf Stream'. It was a cheaper version of shooting on Scottish grouse moors. In England, golf remained the Scots game in language and in the employment of Scots professionals who, if A. G. Macdonnell's novel *England, their England* (1933) is to be believed, exaggerated their Scottishness because their clients expected it. The dilution of the Scots character of golf took place only when it spread to America.

REFERENCES

1. Burke (1978), 28–9.
2. Quoted in *DOST*, s.v. boull.
3. *KWP*, 26 June 1858.
4. Wodrow (1842), i, 73.
5. Cunningham (1887), 36.
6. Central Ayrshire Archives, CO 3/5/33, 162.
7. Murray (1927), 427.
8. Hardy (1843).
9. Alexander (1952), 23.
10. Douglas (1934), 358.
11. Matheson (1905), 155.
12. Anon (1898); Banks (1937–41), ii, 121–2; McNeill (1957–68), iv, 213–15; Simpkins (1914), 150–1.
13. Barbour (1980–85), iii, 137.
14. Anon (1927), 63.
15. Gillespie (1939), ii, 330.
16. I am heavily indebted to James Winters, Secretary of the Scottish Quoiting Association, for his advice.
17. The history of quoiting is given by Tranter (1990 and 1992).
18. *AA*, 24 July 1834.
19. *AA*, 4 August 1842.
20. Tranter (1987b).
21. *AA*, 15 July 1841.
22. Cramond (1903–8), i, 296.

23. Bodleian Library, Oxford, Ms. Douce. f. 276 f. 12r, reproduced in Reeves (1995), 90.

24. Foulis (1894), 228.

25. Banks (1937–41), iii, 116; McNeill (Glasgow, 1957–68), iv, 215–16.

26. McNeill (1957–68), iv, 216.

27. Smith (1981), 4.

28. *GH*, 23 August 1833.

29. MacQuoid (1887), 96.

30. Anon. (1939), 35.

31. Grant (1876), 177.

32. Ibid., 120; National Museums of Scotland H. MP 92 (the ball) H. MP 93 to 99 (the kyles). Girvan's 'Tronmacannie' is a misprint.

33. Wingfield (1988), 235.

34. Downie (1929), 283.

35. Strutt (1841), 273.

36. *D&GS*, 5 July 1844.

37. Finn (1975), 79–84.

38. Macleod (1964–89); *A&SH*, 31 August 1867.

39. Quoted in *SND*.

40. *SND*.

41. Mouswald Kirk Session minutes, 1 July 1640, quoted in *DOST* s.v. penny-stane.

42. Gillespie (1939), ii, 330.

43. Gordon (1893), 60.

44. Strutt (1841), 274.

45. Fleming (1969), 221.

46. Armet (1962), 174. Act of 22 May 1695.

47. Kennedy (1818), i, 256.

48. Gray & Jamieson (1944), 124.

49. Fraser (1905), 58; Armet (1956); Dalgleish (1990), 189–200; Durand (1936–37).

50. Ramsay (1944–74), i, 223.

51. Pretsell (1908), 34–5.

52. Printed in Pretsell (1908), 31–2.

53. National Museums of Scotland H. MEQ 1594, Dalgleish (1990), Armet (1956).

54. Lauder (1900), 186; Scott-Moncrieff (1911), 251.

55. Mitchell (1864), 4–6.

56. Kennedy (1818), i, 256.

57. Fraser (1888), iii, 102; Fittis (1891), 202.

58. Evans (1988), 19–28.

59. Ibid., 12.

60. Kilmarnock Bowling Club (1867), [1]; Morton (1962), 3.

61. Mackintosh (1946), 6.

62. *DT*, 2 August 1841.

63. *GC*, 21 September 1848.

64. Shirley (1837), 56.

65. Gillmeister (1981).

66. Blaine (1840), 116.
67. Quoted by Murray (1899), 78.
68. Murray (1927), 430. For the location of Isle Toothie see Murray (1924–32), i, 77.
69. Penny (1836), 115–16.
70. Douglas (1934), 358; Cramond (1903–8), ii, 22 and i, 427.
71. Maidment (1868), 4.
72. Anon (1882), passim.
73. Melville (1839), 23–4.
74. Grant (1876), 177–8.
75. Strawhorn (1985), 109 and (1989), 129.
76. *AA*, 26 August 1862.
77. *KWP*, 10 August 1861.
78. *AA*, 21 August 1851.
79. Murdoch (1920), 203–4.
80. Anon. (1873), quoting from 34–5.
81. Butler & Wordie (1989).
82. Anon (1837), 137.
83. Rodger (1992).
84. Baxter (1898), 150; Burnett (1998b).
85. The full text is given by Smith (1981), 20.
86. Lamb (1982), 238–9.
87. *OSA*, ix, 432; xxi, 457.
88. *AA* 13 February 1823.
89. *OSA*, vii, 613.
90. Dixon (1865), 248–9.
91. Taylor (1884), 74.
92. *FH*, 29 January 1852.
93. Quoted by Kerr (1890), 215.
94. Taylor (1884), 30.
95. Kerr (1890), 204.
96. Quoted by Kerr (1890), 202.
97. Cowan (1878), 113–14.
98. Adamson (1774), 18.
99. Murray (1882), 44.
100. Taylor (1884), 108, 157–8.
101. *Encyclopedia Britannica*, 11th edn, s.v. Suvárov.
102. Niven (1965), 288.
103. Smith (1981), 82–8.
104. Quoted by Smith (1981), 88.
105. Lamb (1977), ii, 569.
106. Quoted by Smith (1981), 31.
107. The rules of 1804, as printed in 1811, are reprinted by Smith (1981), 216–17.
108. Smith (1981), 67–9.
109. *GH*, 16 January 1829.
110. Robertson (1795), 47.

111. *HA*, 6 December 1856.
112. *OSA*, ix, 433.
113. *OSA*, vi, 277.
114. *EA*, 26 January 1838.
115. National Museums of Scotland, H. NQ 390.
116. In Dumfries Museum.
117. *DWJ*, 28 January 1823, 1 January 1826.
118. *DWJ*, 23 February 1813.
119. Kerr (1890), 404.
120. Taylor (1884), viii–ix.
121. As translated by Smith (1981), 31–2.
122. *AA*, 13 January 1820.
123. *FH*, 8 March 1849.
124. The following remarks are based on *SND*; see also Smith (1981), particularly 198–200.
125. Davies (1993), 52.
126. Mitchell (1864), 470.
127. Mitchell (1864), 54.
128. *AA*, 20 January 1820.
129. Penny (1936), 115.
130. *EEC*, 12 January 1850.
131. *MS*, 15 January 1841, 4 January and 13 December 1850.
132. Burnett (1995), 39.
133. Hamilton (1999).
134. Hamilton (1997) and (1999).
135. *OSA*, xvi, 28–30.
136. Tulloch (1907), 30.
137. Hamilton (1999).
138. Reprinted by Hamilton (1985): see especially 16.
139. Lewis (1995).
140. Darwin (1952), 64.
141. Grant (1912), 65.
142. Quoted by Johnson & Johnson (1993), 197.
143. Pennant (1790), iii, 198.
144. Henderson & Stirk (1982), 316.
145. Port Glasgow exchequer records E504/28/1.
146. Henderson & Stirk (1982), 337.
147. Hancock (1996), 1–2.
148. Gardiner-Hill (1952).
149. Campbell (1952), 71.
150. Penny (1836), 115.
151. Personal communication from Peter Lewis, 1997.
152. Quoted by Henderson & Stirk (1982), 317.
153. This paragraph is based on *SND* and Davies (1993).
154. *SND*, s.v. nibby. The quotation dates from 1869.

CHAPTER FIVE

Sports and Traditional Holidays

The annual pattern of the year, and its formalising through the device of the calendar, was at the heart of pre-industrial life. The year was one of the three cycles upon which social life was constructed, along with the predictable day and the unchanging pattern of life and death. In Scotland the calendar combined Celtic and Latin Christian elements: in the Lowlands the latter predominated, whereas in the Highlands the former were more important. The holy days of the year were of more than religious significance, for they also marked turning points in the agricultural cycle or in the astronomical pattern, particularly the two solstices, the shortest and longest day, midwinter and midsummer.

Many of the traditional games of the British Isles, as we become aware of them as the mist of the Middle Ages clears, were held on religious and other holidays. There is insufficient evidence from medieval Scotland to be sure about the picture, but in the Lowlands it is unlikely to differ much from that in England. However, the post-Reformation pattern of sports was different in the two countries. The Scots Calvinists stopped elaborate public festivals at Easter and Whitsun, and gave less weight to Christmas. Although saints' feast days were removed from the ecclesiastical calendar many remained as secular local holidays, such as St Inan's Day at Beith in Ayrshire and St Patrick's Day at Kirkpatrick Fleming in Dumfriesshire, which were still celebrated three hundred years later.

The Gregorian calendar was introduced by Pope Gregory VIII in 1582. It replaced the Julian calendar in Scotland, England and Ireland in 1752, when the London mob rioted in protest at the adjustment: 'Give us back our eleven days'.[1] Some areas of Scotland, particularly the East and more particularly the North-East, continued to celebrate Yule according to the old calendar, *Auld Yule* or *Aul Eel*. After 1800, which was a leap year in the Julian but not the Gregorian system, *Aul Eel* was twelve days after Christmas Day, and so coincided with *Uphalyday* or Twelfth Night.[2] In Old Scots, *up* means an ending: it was the last day of *yule*. The change of calendars did not affect movable feasts such as Fastern's E'en, but in some places patron saints' days were kept according to the old style. There were a number of local festivals in early July which may have originally been Midsummer in the Julian calendar.

Whenever events took place, they expanded far beyond that day in the year. As Scott put it:

> A Christmas gambol oft would cheer
> The poor man's heart through half the year.[3]

Similarly, folk looked forward for months to the Dumfries Siller Gun, 'expectation was certainly on tip-toe' before the Royal Company of Archers arrived in Montrose in 1850.[4] The festival was the central act in long periods of anticipation and remembering.

The Traditional Year

Rather than describe only the days on which sport was played every year, we need to see the whole pattern of the traditional year.[5] This forms a prologue to the discussion later in this chapter of two sports which were played all over Scotland on holidays, usually Fastern's E'en, football and cock-fighting; and to horse races and other burgh sports in later chapters.

Yule. Christmas (25th December) is an English, but not Scots, quarter day, though it was a term day in Shetland.[6] In North-East Scotland football was played on Christmas Day down to the eighteenth century, and the *Christmas baa* survives at Kirkwall in the Orkneys.

The word *Yule* means both Christmas Day and also a longer period which ran to New Year's Day, Uphalyday or even the beginning of February. Before the agricultural revolution holiday activities were spread through this period. In different places and periods different activities were carried out on particular days: there were religious services and guising, special foods were cooked and eaten – as well as sports and games.[7] Many social practices were transferred from one holiday to another. For example, cock-fighting began on Fastern's E'en but somewhere in Scotland it was found on each of the principal winter holidays.

New Year's Day was in most parts of the Lowlands the major winter festival. Christmas must have been more important before the Reformation: when New Year's Day became more prominent, it drew in rituals and social practices from other winter holidays. Its sports were various. For example, there was cock-fighting in a few places such as Boharn on the border of Banffshire and Moray.[8] In Fife *a bawbee she kyles* was played at Kirkcaldy. On the Aberdeenshire coast home-made model ships were raced.[9] In the Highlands and the Western Isles, huge shinty matches were played on New Year's Day, often on ice or on a large beach, and the small amount of information available on shinty in Lowland Scotland suggests that this was once the case there too. For example, a match at *camack* – the word is a Scots form of the Gaelic *camanachd* – was recorded in Edinburgh on New Year's Day 1821.[10]

A group of holidays, at least one of them celebrated in most places, fell in the first week of January. **Hansel Monday** was the first Monday of the New Year. The English equivalent was *Plough Monday*, the first Monday after Twelfth Day.[11] **Auld Yule** and **Auld Hansel Monday** were holidays according to the old calendar: they survived longest in north-east Scotland, and a range of games was enjoyed on them. At Boddam, on the Buchan coast, the men walked inland for 'the sailin o the shippies on Den Dam' – sailing model boats on a reservoir – on the morning of Auld Yule. In the afternoon there was general hilarity based on an absence of teetotalism: shying at Aunt Sallies, the blind wheelbarrow race – reputedly no one ever reached the finishing post – and climbing the greasy pole for a currant loaf or fruit cake.[12] Cock-fighting took place on Hansel Monday at Queen Anne of Denmark's House in Dunfermline until its demolition in 1797 and on Old Hansel Monday at Gallatown (Kirkcaldy).[13]

Wad shooting was particularly associated with New Year's Day and Auld Yule. Every entrant paid a stake, in the nineteenth century typically a shilling, for the right to fire at a target. The guns were muzzle-loading fowling pieces or blunderbusses, or other highly inaccurate weapons: it was less a game of skill than of chance. The organiser, usually an ale-house keeper, would provide the prizes –

18. An ancient sport: climbing the greasy pole at the Marymass Races, Irvine, 1994.

a plough, or the carcase of a young bullock which could provide several prizes – and keep the stakes. The competitors supplied their own powder and lead bullets melted in a crusie lamp, and they even had to find the use of a gun. At Monifieth, for example, the sport continued until 1856 or 1857,[14] and there is little suggestion of wad shooting elsewhere after this date.

Imbolc (1st February) was the first day of spring in the Celtic calendar, in the period when the lactation of ewes began. It was associated with the Celtic Brigid and later with St Brigit (d. 524) who founded a convent at Kildare. In some places in the *Gàidhealtacht* there was cock-fighting.[15]

Candlemas (2nd February) is a Scots quarter day. It was the feast of the Purification of the Virgin Mary, which from the Dark Ages had been celebrated with a great display of candles. Candlemas was not an important day for sports, though in a few places such as Lanark cock-fighting was on Candlemas rather than Fastern's E'en.[16]

Fastern's E'en is the Scots name for the English Shrove Tuesday, or the French Mardi Gras. The name first appears about 1375 and comes from the Old Northumbrian *faestern* and West Saxon *faesten*, a fast, especially at Lent. Fastern's E'en is the last day before Lent, a day of feasting before weeks of self denial. It is the first Tuesday of the first Moon in spring. James IV held tournaments with jousting and swordplay, and in the evening dancing.[17]

In Scotland, as in other countries, it was an important day for sport, but its relative stature was greater than elsewhere because of the absence after the Reformation of sport on days such as Easter and Whitsun. Cock-fighting and football or handball were widespread in the Lowlands, and there is extensive evidence of cock-fighting in the Highlands.[18] The strongest evidence for football and handball comes from the Borders and Aberdeenshire, but as in England they were probably played in many places, conceivably in every parish.[19] There was a Fastern's E'en foot race at Kilmarnock.

Easter (**Pasch**) In England Easter was the most important holiday for sport, along with Christmas and Whitsun, and football, quoiting and cock-fighting were widespread.[20] After the Reformation, however, it was not a significant festival in Scotland.

Beltane (1st May) was the second most important festival of the year when the Celtic year was divided into two parts, before the introduction of *Imbolc* and *Lughnasad*. Like *Samhuinn* it related to a pastoral economy: it was the time when cattle were driven to open grazing. Fires were lit, and cattle driven between a pair of fires to protect them from disease. Like *Samhuinn* the night before the Beltane was as important as the following day, for the Celtic calendar counted nights, not days. At some point, perhaps in the late seventeenth century, the quarter day was moved from Beltane to Whitsun, though the quarterly terms for paying school fees remained Candlemas, Beltane, Lammas and Hallowmas until late in the nineteenth century. Beltane was also the day of the Roman *floralia*, the celebration of the beginning of summer when, as at Dumfries, green branches were brought into the town.

Beltane appears to have been a major Lowland festival until the Reformation. One Beltane festival, that at Peebles, continued to be held until 1766. It was revived – or perhaps it had never really stopped – in the second half of the nineteenth century. The particular sport at the Peebles Beltane was horse-racing.

Whitsunday (15th May) is a Scots quarter day.[21] It is fixed no matter on what day the religious Whitsunday falls. Along with Martinmas it is one of the two Scots rent days. Whitsun was consequently the day for moving from one rented property to another. After the adoption of the Gregorian calendar in 1752 there was a confusion which was resolved by giving fourteen days' grace, 28th May became *Flitting Day*, the day when people moved house, and 28th November had the same function, though more people moved in summer. Some continued to recognise Old Whitsun on 25th May.

Midsummer (24th June) is an English quarter day. It was also the birthday of John the Baptist and was celebrated in Scotland as **Johnsmas**. It was preceded and followed by summer festivals in many places – perhaps every parish once had one. Those in the first week of July, especially between the 5th and the 7th, may owe at least part of their origin to Midsummer, the date having moved when the Gregorian calendar was introduced. Many summer sports were enjoyed on and around midsummer, especially during the long reign of George III (1760–1820), whose birthday on 4th June was loyally taken up as a holiday by some burghs.

Lammas (1st August) is a Scots quarter day. The name comes form the Old English *hláfmaesse* meaning loaf mass: the first element is also found in *lady* (loaf kneader) and *lord* (loaf ward or keeper, that is head of the household). It was the time of the consecration of the loaves made from the first corn to ripen. The idea, widespread

in the past, that the festival is *Lamb's Mass*, is erroneous. **Lugnasad**
(1st August) was a Celtic quarter day. Its name comes from *Lug*,
the Celtic God of *Lugudunum* (Lyons), Laon, Leiden and other
places. His cult probably reached Ireland in the first century AD,
when the Gauls were driven out of France by Caesar. Lug is said to
have founded a festival in honour of *Tailltu*, a nature goddess, at
Teltown in Co. Meath, and it was she who was the focus of
Lugnasad, not the god. From this came the *Aonach Taillteann* or
Taillteann Games in honour of the dead.

Michaelmas (29th September) is not a Scottish quarter day, though
the election of burgh and other councils took place on it: thus it
was the beginning of their administrative year. It is an English quarter
day. It was the traditional day for horse-racing in the Scots
Gàidhealtachd, but Michaelmas races, or indeed any kind of sport,
were not found in the Lowlands on this day. Michaelmas – and
other festivals in early autumn – were widespread in England,
occurring after the corn harvest had been gathered and at a point
when harvesters and servants who had reached their term day had
a little money to spend. It is also linked to the Highland *kirn*: these
harvest games were one of the origins for the Highland Games which
became conspicuous in the nineteenth century.

Samhuinn (1st November) was the most important day in the
Celtic year, the end and the beginning of the year and the beginning
of winter. It was a pastoral rather than an agrarian turning-point,
when the stock was slaughtered at the end of the grazing season: it
was thus an opportunity for feasting. This was done the previous
night, later known as *Hallowe'en*, for the Celtic day ran from sunset
to sunset. *Samhuinn* was intensely magical: on the night before, fairy
troops issued from caves and mounds and travelled everywhere. This
led to the idea that witches fly at Hallowe'en. It is thus linked with
All Saints' Day or **Hallowmas** on the same day of the year. This
festival had originally been set on 1st May, but it was moved to
November in the year 837.

Martinmas (11th November) is a Christian equivalent of *Samhuinn*,
and a quarter day in Scotland. It is the festival of St Martin of Tours
(d. 397): St Ninian (d. 432) dedicated the church at Whithorn to
him. From the festival came the word *mart*, found in Scotland and

the north of England for a fat ox or other animal to be slaughtered for salting. Like *Samhuinn* it was a day for killing the animals which could not be fed through the winter. This was neither a day nor a period of the year which was associated with sport.

From this description of the traditional year an important generalisation emerges. In Lowland Scotland sport was not played on the significant days of the Celtic year – the absence of sport from Beltane and *Samhuinn* is striking – but rather on those of the Christian year: on Fastern's E'en, on the feast days of patron saints, and on Yule and *Aul Eel*. To an extent, this is a simplification, for some of the significance of Fastern's E'en had been transferred from Imbolc, and the celebration and rites of the winter festivals were a complex mixture of practices drawn from one another and Celtic tradition was incorporated in them. Nevertheless, Lowland sporting tradition was by the Reformation largely based on customs which had been brought from Continental Europe by the Normans.

BA' GAMES, FOOTBALL AND SHINTY

Folk football was popular in Ancient Rome. It was a game which people played, however, rather than one they watched in the Roman arena or circus. Football must have reached Scotland with the Romans, but it probably did not survive their departure. In the north of France it was reinvented as *la soule*, an imitation by the people of knights jousting, potentially involving large numbers of men.[22] Although evidence for the game in Scotland does not appear until the fifteenth century it had probably arrived for the second time with the Normans. Gaelic football, though deeply ingrained in modern Irish life, did not appear until the sixteenth century and also seems to be descended from *la soule*.

In this chapter the word *handball* is taken to mean the team game, akin to football, in which the one rule is that kicking is prohibited. Here it is not, as it is elsewhere, a more modern name for *caich*. The various occurrences of *ball* and *football* in the sixteenth century give few clues as to the nature of the game, or the way in which it must have varied from place to place and time to time.

In some places there is a hint of a pagan ritual in which two groups of men contest for fertility in the coming year. Thus at

Kirkwall it was a contest between men who drew their livelihood from the land and from the sea, or at Jedburgh between the two ends of the town. There was also a tradition of playing football on the North and South Inches at Perth, usually the married against the single men.[23] At Crieff it was the custom until 1830 for a bride to give a football.[24] In three places cock-fighting and football were linked. At Westruther the cock-fighting 'king' had to give the ball for the football match, and in the Lammermuirs the fight was followed by football. At Selkirk:

> The 'king', or owner of the best bird, had to provide a hand-ball, and carry it to a certain distance out of the burgh without being overtaken by those pursuing him. Of course he got an 'archcap', or start. While he was at the Haining Gate, the other boys stood at the West Port, both waiting for the signal. This given, they set off, through Mill Burn, up Muiriston's Hill, straight through Lauriston, along by the Scaur-heads, until they reached the Woody Path. If the 'king' could throw the ball over the burn to Howden Haugh before his pursuers gained on him, he was considered to have added to his laurels; but if not, the royal honours obtained at cock-fighting were considerably dimmed.[25]

The race was about 1½ miles long.

Finally, there is a charming tradition at Scone in Perthshire that their football game had started after an Italian had travelled through the country, challenging each parish to a match: every one except Scone declined. Scone beat him, and instituted the annual match to commemorate the feat. We need not examine the improbabilities here: after all, some have believed that the MacCrimmon family of pipers came from Cremona.

From a number of literary references we can be certain that football was a common game in pre-Reformation Scotland. Gavin Douglas (1474–1522) was almost certainly the author of the allegory *King Hart*. In it, the ageing king, having attained a life of perfect goodness, and knowing that death is fast approaching, bequeaths parts of his body to various figures. To Deliuerance or Bodily Activity he gives a shin and arm, both broken 'at the ball':

19.   Throwing up the ba' at Lilliesleaf, Roxburghshire, about 1930. *National Museums of Scotland, Scottish Life Archive.*

Deliuerance hes oft tymes done me gude
Quhen I wes young, and stede in tendir age.
He gart me ryn full rakles [reckless], be the rude
At ball and boull. Thairfoir greit weill that paige:
This brokyn schyn, that swellis and will nocht swage
Ye beir to him – he brak it at the ball –
And say to him that it salbe his wage.
This breissit arme ye beir to him at all.[26]

In a description written in 1568 of the political manoeuvring before the Reformation, the bishops were said to have 'the ball at thair fut'.[27]

The violent nature of the game is clear; indeed, it was central to the play. In Aberdeenshire:

The heroes of the field were those who could stand the roughest usage. They cuffed and kicked all within reach, devoting themselves, apparently, more to the hearty kicking of the enemies' shins than to kicking of the ball. 'It was a feat worth boasting of to be able to make a man's "harn pan" [skull] ring ...'[28]

It is little surprise that Inverurie burgh banned the playing of football by adults in 1615.[29] John Skinner's poem 'The Christmas Bawing of Monymusk' (1738) describes a series of bruising incidents. He revels in the onomatopoeic possibilities of the Scots language:

> Like bumbees bizzing frae a bike
> Whan hirds their riggins tirr
> The swankies lap thro' mire and slike
> Wow! as their heads did birr:
> They yowph'd the ba' frae dike to dike
> Wi' unco speed an' virr
> Some baith their shouders up did fyke
> For blythness some did flirr [grind]
>   Their teeth that day.[30]

Skinner gives us thirty-five stanzas of joyful violence: skulls are cracked, eyes blacked, blood and tears flow. Many of the players are named: Francy Winsie, Taylor Hutchin, and so on, and the young 'inset [substitute] dominie' – Skinner himself. He is so much focused on the action that he gives us no indication of the reasons for the game being played, or the cause of its extreme physicality. What is clear is the local nature of the game, the absence of anyone from outside the parish, the revelling in the incidents of the game. Skinner's poem brings us as close as we can ever be to the end of the play when:

> The pensy lads dosst down on stanes
> Whopt out their snishin-millies [snuff mills]
> And a' were fain to tak' their einds
> And club a pint o' Lillie's
>   Best ale that day.[31]

– and describe to one another the dramas of the day. It must have happened everywhere the game was played.

Football was played in schools. David Wedderburn, master of the Grammar School at Aberdeen, published a Latin grammar in 1636. He interested the boys in the language by giving them texts on familiar subjects. Here is one, in translation:

Come! choose sides; Pick your first man; Those on this side come here; those on the other side stand yonder; Toss the ball that we may begin the game; Come! kick it here; You keep the hail or goal; Snatch the ball from that fellow if you can; Throw yourself against that man; Run to that other one's assistance; Kick back the ball ... The game is theirs ... He is a good ball-man; Had he not been, we had won; Come on, take heed and serve me; We have yet the likeliest of it.[32]

Wedderburn's staccato prose gives a good idea of the breathless excitement of the play. He mentions the traditional method of ensuring an equal contest – picking players alternately; the throw-up, still used in ba' games as the way of starting the action; and that at least one player had a specialised role. Ba' games were kept alive by schools, and were still held at Forfar, Cupar (Fife) and Closeburn (Dumfriesshire) in the 1870s.[33] Boys who played often together in the same field are likely to have developed conventions about the play, and being under the eye of the schoolmaster would have played in a less boisterous way than in the parish game, in order to limit casualties. Football also survived in the English public schools in which soccer and rugby were devised in the middle of the nineteenth century.

Of the handball game at Scone, the *Old Statistical Account* says that 'the custom being attended with certain inconveniences, was abolished a few years ago'. Although we know far more about the Victorian suppression of traditional sports because of their association with heavy drinking and violence, it is clear that much had been quietly done away with in the eighteenth century. Perhaps the key word in the last quotation is *abolished*: someone in authority took the decision and enforced it. Perhaps it was the minister, the Reverend Robert Thomas. He wrote the following in 1796:

Every year on Shrove-Tuesday, the bachelors and married men drew themselves up at the cross of Scone on opposite sides. A ball was then thrown up, and they played from 2 o'clock till sun set. The game was this. He who, at any time got the ball into his hands, ran with it till overtaken by one of the opposite party, and then, if he could shake himself loose from those on the opposite side, who seized on him, he ran on: if not, he threw the ball from him, unless it was wrested from him by the opposite party; but no person was allowed to kick it. The object of the married men was to hang it, i.e. to put it three times into a small hole in the moor, the *dool* or limit on one hand; that of the bachelors was to drown it, i.e. to dip it three times into a deep place in the river, the limit on the other. The party who could effect either of these objects, won the game. But, if neither party won, the ball was cut into two equal parts at sun-set. In the course of the play one might always see some scene of violence between the parties; but, as the proverb of this part of the country expresses it, all was fair at the ball of Scone.[34]

Thomas was wrong to write in the past tense: the last match was held in 1835 and young men continued to play a more informal match for some years after that.[35] At Monzie in Perthshire the football game was ended by William Chalmers, minister from 1691 to 1702, and at Kippen by Michael Potter whose charge ran from 1700 to 1740.[36]

We have already mentioned football at Scone, Monymusk, Aberdeen and Wigtown; to this we can add Fife in general in 1611, Dundonald in Ayrshire in the seventeenth century and in Lanarkshire at Carstairs in 1628 and at Wiston at the end of the eighteenth century,[37] Glasgow in the sixteenth century, Edinburgh in 1659,[38] Banff and Deeside,[39] and at several places in the Borders including Peebles in 1570, and Foulden and Westruther at the end of the eighteenth century.[40] In Perthshire it is recorded at Perth, Dunning, Cargill, Auchtergaven, Dunblane, Blairgowrie and Kirkmichael.[41] Football matches were played on holidays in the calendar: on Auld Yule, as at Monymusk or Elgin,[42] or New Year's Day, as at Kirkwall or Wigtown, but most were played on Fastern's E'en. The surviving Border ba' games are now played in the week of Fastern's E'en.

Football has a long history in Ireland, and there is a record of immigrants playing in Scotland. This was a match held on St Patrick's Day in Queen's Park, Edinburgh. It was first held in the late 1830s, and comes to notice because policemen interfered in 1840 on the ground that it was a riot: one suspects that traditionally vigorous play close to Holyrood was unacceptable. The footballers turned on the police, who made four arrests.[43] For several years in the early 1850s Irishmen in Perth played football on Saturday afternoons.[44] However, association football stemmed neither from the Irish nor from the Scots tradition, but from events involving men who were educated at English public schools. That their invention should almost immediately become the preoccupation of men in industrial Scotland is one of the less explicable twists of history.

Shinty was the other sport which was played by large groups of people on holidays of the year, and also on some other days. As *chow* or *chew* shinty was prohibited at Elgin 'within the burgh or outwith neirhand' four times between 1600 and 1607.[45] It appears all over Scotland among the frequent censures of sports and games on the Sabbath in the middle of the seventeenth century: for example at Markinch in Fife in 1633 and North Berwick in East Lothian in 1671.[46] It was mentioned in a list of Ayrshire sports around 1780.[47] Shinty was played in parts of England. The *English Dialect Dictionary* records *shinham* in the north of England in general, *shinnins* and *shinnop* in Yorkshire, and *shinny* and *shinty* in the north of England, and as far south as Lincolnshire, Nottinghamshire and Gloucestershire. It survived in the Scottish Lowlands into the nineteenth century, largely as a boys' game.[48]

COCK-FIGHTING

According to legend, cock-fighting came to Greece from Persia in the time of Themistocles in the fifth century BC. When marching to war he saw two cocks fighting and told his men to take them as an example of the determination never to be beaten. Cock-fighting was popular in Ancient Greece and Rome, and the Romans brought it to Britain. Strutt says that it became particularly popular in England during the reign of Edward III, and that both Henry VIII and James VI were enthusiasts.[49] The cock is a symbol of dawn, and at some point it became associated with the dawn of spring and in time this was recognised all over Europe as Shrove Tuesday. On this day, the cocks fought for sport and died as a sacrifice.[50]

In Lowland Scotland cock-fighting took place on Fastern's E'en, but in the Highlands and Islands on Candlemas. Neither Fittis nor the present author have been able to find pre-Reformation references to cock-fighting in Scotland,[51] but its very strong association with traditional festivals, and the fact that it re-appeared on Fastern's E'en in 1661, confirm that it is an ancient practice. When a young man was found dead at the roadside near Dunfermline in 1846, his friends said he had gone into the country to get some cocks to fight on Hansel Monday.[52]

Cock-fighting took place all over Scotland and descriptions of it are remarkably consistent. It was held in the school – in the church, if the school was held there. At Dunblane it took place in the 'vasterie', probably the eastern part of the Chapter House, and certainly in the precincts of the cathedral.[53] A minister who was educated in Wester Ross in 1831–33 wrote:

> It was in a General Assembly School (which was the church) that the cockfight took place. The fight was held in the Elders' square seat at the foot of the pulpit, and the great thing was to get into the pulpit for the best view ...[54]

In Aberdeenshire at exactly the same time:

> We yees'd tae hae cockfechtin' on Brosie [Brose Day, i.e. Fastern's E'en]. When I wuz at the skule, I hae seen as mony as a score tae'n tae the skule that day, an' we daurna tak yin that wasna oor ain, nor yin that wasna brocht up in oor ain biggin. The best fechter a shune as it beat yin had anither pit doon till't, an' the cocks that widna fecht the maister got. The yin that had the cock that focht best was King.[55]

Mrs Macleod Banks quotes several good accounts of cock-fighting.[56] Here is one which has not been noticed before, from a novel by Alexander Whamond which describes north-east life. The scene is as usual the parish school:

> A few days before [Fastern's E'en], all our conversation was about cocks, and where we would get one for the fight ... On the day before, all the boys who were to bring forward cocks gave in their names to the master, who counted the number of

names. Suppose there were twenty, he wrote the figures from one to twenty on slips of paper, and put them in a bonnet; we then drew the figures ... [at the end of the fighting] ... the last two were declared – the victor, king, and the last vanquished, queen. A little bell about the size of a thimble was hung round the king's neck, and red ribbon was put round the queen's, but *she*, or rather I should say *he* (for the queen was a cock), got no bell. If we had not a cock of our own, we set out to the different farm houses in search of one, and there was not a farmer's wife in the parish who would have refused us one, if it was not previously bespoke by some of our schoolfellows.[57]

The title of *king* for the owner of the winning cock seems to have been used everywhere. The schoolmaster controlled the fighting, received payment from the boys and had a right to the *fugies*, the cocks which were defeated or refused to fight. Fastern's E'en cock-fighting in schools disappeared rapidly after 1820, as its cruelty was recognised.

The strangest of the material survivals of cock-fighting is a crown from the parish of Dyke in Moray.[58] Its form is the skeleton of a royal crown, 150mm high. It is made of tinplate. At the front are painted two cocks addressing one another, with the words GALLORUM REX. There is an unmistakable echo of the sign REX JUDORUM which was placed on the cross on Calvary: Luke tells us that the inscription was in Greek, Latin and Hebrew.[59] Christ sacrificed himself as men sacrificed cocks. He was raised from the dead, and the life of the year was resurrected from the dark and cold of winter.

In England there was a separate tradition of cock-fighting as a sport for adults to gamble on and watch, free from the constraints of the calendar. Henry VIII built a cockpit in Whitehall. The first known pit in Scotland was established in Leith in 1683: the presence in Edinburgh of the Duke of York, later James VII, was probably not an accident. In England cockpits beside, or even within inns, were built in several places. The *Cockpit* in London retained a viewing gallery until the twentieth century and names such as the

Fighting Cocks at St Albans, the *Turf and Feather* at Padgate near Warrington and the *Gamecock* at Hereford commemorate the sport.[60] These names are not found in Scotland.

In Scotland, cock-fighting by adults was seen as a disreputable sport in the latter part of the eighteenth century: a 'famous' main, or series of fights, in 1785 took place in the kitchen of the half-built Assembly Rooms in George Street, Edinburgh. The use of such an odd venue implies that there was no regular site at which 'the Fancy' could watch fights, such as an arena attached to an inn, as in England or Wales. The main in the Assembly Rooms was between East Lothian and Lanarkshire. The sporting gentry were there, as was Deacon Brodie and Kay the caricaturist – who made an engraving of the scene. He shows two men in the ring superintending a fight, one a butcher and the other an Englishman, indicating that sporting cocking (as against Fastern's E'en fights) had only a limited presence in Scotland.[61] Matches outside the schools appear only rarely in print. It may be significant that one of the few known was held on 25 February 1795 at the George Inn, Dumfries, quite close to England.[62] The cockpit at Leith was still in use in 1801 when John Ramsay of Ochtertyre said that one of his neighbours had been there 'and was astonished at the mixture of peers and sharpers, lawyers and pick-pockets'. The *Scots Magazine* said it was vulgar and cruel.[63] It continued in many country districts until the 1830s, but an attempt to establish it in Glasgow about 1835 failed.[64]

By the middle of the nineteenth century it had vanished from polite society but continued underground: there was, for example, a long-remembered match about 1860 between Tranent and Fife miners. Elphinstone Fair in East Lothian became known as Pate's Fair after a famous breeder of cocks. Some weeks before the Fair breeders from the surrounding area met to challenge those from further away, from the country stretching from Dalkeith to Macmerry. Then birds were 'closeted' – placed in a dark room or a deal box to make them 'wild for the fight'. Their combs were cut, heels pared, metal spurs made and applied. At the last Elphinstone main before cock-fighting was banned by Parliament, 50 birds were entered. Cock-fighting was not the only sport at Elphinstone: as at Leith races, there was a free fight afterwards.[65] In some places, such as West Lothian, the character of the sport on Fastern's E'en changed and the cocks were owned by adults who gave them to the boys on the morning of the fight. The men attended the fight and gambled on the results. Cock fighting was thought to have died out in Kilmarnock shortly before 1898, and at Auchterderran in Fife about 1900.[66] This is the period when it was in rapid decline in mining communities. There is informal evidence, however, that it continues clandestinely to the present day.

OTHER ANIMAL SPORTS

As a tailpiece to cock-fighting, some other cruel sports may be briefly mentioned. At Haddington, Kelso, and St Andrews a cat was ritually killed.[67] At Haddington:

> a cat was confined in a dryware cask containing soot, and hung at the end of a beam fixed to the top of the cross. Each rider armed with a wooden mell, and rode at full speed under the barrel, and gave it a blow which operation continued until the barrel was staved. The poor frightened cat, on its release, was pursued by the assembled crowd, and was very often trampled to death.[68]

A similar sport was conducted in the Netherlands in the middle of the nineteenth century. It is probably the origin of the inn sign of the *Cat in the Basket* which was used for booths on the frozen Thames in 1740 and 1789, and north of Dublin there was the *Cat and Cage* at Santry.[69] The killing of cats on the Feast of John the Baptist (24 June) was practised in France: in Paris they were burned by the sackful.[70] The event at Haddington was held at the end of the carters' races in May, so the place in the calendar of this dark ritual is not clear.

Neither is there evidence for the origin of the *goose race* at St Andrews. The goose's neck was plucked and greased, and the bird hung at a height at which riders could comfortably try to pluck off its head. At Newton-on-Ayr horse races a similar feat was required of the rider of the winner: if he missed, the next competitor might take it.

The practice of thus claiming the prize is paralleled by the placing of the prize on the winning post, as in James Ross's painting of *The Meeting at Clifton and Rawcliffe Ings, York, September 1709*,[71] in which a silver punchbowl is shown thus: a jockey *could* have lifted it as he passed. A later development was to place the judges in a crow's nest on top of the winning post: this was shown in a woodcut on a handbill advertising Nottingham Races in 1765, and it is probably a generic image.

Bull-baiting was practised in Scotland before the Reformation,[72] and the Bull Stone on the green at Leslie in Fife is said to have been the tether for the bulls. Later references are rare, though we can point to a baiting at Kelso in 1700, and in the 1830s at Dumfries, where a family at Maxwelltown who bred bull terriers set them on animals which had been brought to the slaughterhouse for the winter's beef.[73] It is likely that in both these cases the English tradition had briefly crossed the Border.

REFERENCES

1. In Scotland, the beginning of the year was moved from March to 1st January in 1600.
2. Since 1900 the difference between the two calendars has been 13 days, and both regard 2000 as a leap year so the gap will not increase to 14 days until 2100.
3. Scott, *Marmion*, introduction to Canto VI.
4. *MS*, 3 May 1850.
5. A description of the English sporting year at the beginning of the nineteenth century is given by Brailsford (1991), 1–15.
6. Banks (1937–41), ii, 19.
7. Banks (1937–41), ii, 25–128, iii, 199–244.
8. Banks (1937–41), ii, 71.
9. Banks (1937–41), ii, 117.
10. Macdonald (1932), 56, quoting *EEC*, 22 January 1821.
11. Malcolmson (1973), 28.
12. McLeod (1964–89), 24–5.
13. Henderson (1879), 179, 536, *FH*, 15 January 1848.
14. Malcolm (1910), 232–4.
15. Banks (1937–41), ii, 156.
16. Robertson (1974), 167.
17. Banks (1937–41), i, 28–9.
18. Banks (1937–41), i, 11–15.
19. Banks (1937–41), i, 15–27, Hole (1995), 272–5.

20. Malcolmson (1973), 29.
21. Banks (1937–41), i, 48–9.
22. Gillmeister (1996), 269.
23. Penney (1836), 115.
24. Baxter (1898), 61.
25. Craig-Brown (1886), 175–6.
26. Douglas (1967), 169. See also Magoun (1931).
27. Lindsay (1931–36), i, 398.
28. Allardyce (1913), 28.
29. Allardyce (1913), 28.
30. Crawford (1987), 103.
31. *Ibid.*, 113.
32. Translated by Murray (1927), 432–3.
33. Grant (1876), 41.
34. *OSA*, xviii, 88–9.
35. Baxter (1898), 37.
36. Tranter (1987a).
37. Anon (1837), 21; Gillespie (1939), i, 330; Anon (1839), 6; Tranter (1987a).
38. Baxter (1898), 11, Robertson (1967), 201.
39. Robertson (1967), 204, Fittis (1891), 164.
40. Baxter (1898), 11; Tranter (1987a).
41. Baxter (1898), 150–2; Robertson (1967), 204.
42. Cramond (1903–8), ii, 86.
43. *EA*, 20 March 1840.
44. Baxter (1898), 146.
45. Cramond (1903–8), ii, 79, 88, 100, 151.
46. Simpkins (1914), 182–3; Maclennan (1995), 50.
47. Mitchell (1939), 287.
48. Burnett (1998b).
49. Strutt (1841), 281–3.
50. Maclagan (1901), 87.
51. Fittis (1891), 161.
52. *FH*, 8 January 1846.
53. Barty (1944), 187–8.
54. Quoted by Banks (1937–41), iii, 13.
55. Quoted by Banks (1937–41), iii, 14.
56. Banks (1939–41), i, 11–15.
57. Whamond (1895), 36–7.
58. Highland Folk Museum, NS 5.
59. Luke 23.38.
60. Dunkling & Wright (1994), 57, 90, 274.
61. Kay (1842), i, 96–7.
62. *DWJ*, 24 February 1795.
63. Ramsay (1966), 43, 115–16, *Scots Magazine* 63 (1801), 207.
64. Kay (1842), i, 97.

65. McNeill (1883), 169–71.
66. Smellie (1898), chapter XL; Houston (1924), 313–14.
67. Hall (1805), i, 165.
68. Martine (1883), 100–1; see also Banks (1937–41), ii, 252–3.
69. Larwood & Hotten (1866), 198.
70. Darnton (1984), 75–104.
71. In the National Horse Racing Museum, Newmarket.
72. Fittis (1891), 32–3.
73. Kelsall (1986), 90; Elder (1897), 83–4.

CHAPTER SIX

Horse-Racing

Horse-racing was uncommon in England in the late Middle Ages, and the first known race which had a long future was run on the Roodee at Chester in 1540. Queen Elizabeth had no interest in the sport: it did not grow rapidly in England until her successor arrived from Edinburgh.

Horse-racing grew out of the wish of hunters to judge whose horse was fastest: to own the fastest animal was to have a certain status. Thus the value of a horse was affected by its success in racing: from the beginning horse-racing had a commercial aspect.[1] There was also a military background to racing, and something of jousting and the tournament.

In Scotland, élite horse-racing first appears as a royal pastime in the reign of James IV. After his great-grandson James VI moved to London more races were established in Scotland. The sport achieved great popularity after the restoration of the monarchy in 1660. In the eighteenth century, it declined with the departure of the aristocracy to London following the Union of 1707, rose to a new peak after the Napoleonic Wars, and by 1914 had assumed roughly its modern form, involving only a small number of first-class courses. There were, however, other forms of horse race.

The *broose* was a horse race which might be held almost anywhere in Lowland Scotland. Thus Burns addressed his horse, Maggie:

> At Brooses thou had ne'er a fellow
> For pith an' speed.

The *broose* was a marriage custom. After the Reformation weddings were often performed in private houses: by the latter part of the eighteenth century, when horses were present in increasing numbers, the young men rode after the wedding to the house where the couple were to live – where the groom's mother waited for them. It was a race, and the winner was given a handkerchief or a bottle of whisky by the groom's mother: he returned with it to the married pair and drank their health. This custom died out in the nineteenth century: a late instance was in the 1850s on the remote moorland east of Cumnock in Ayrshire.[2]

Wagers between individuals might be organised as part of a race meeting, but more often farmers would boast over the punchbowl and settle the matter on the high road. Formal horse-racing was recorded in the newspapers, but casual matches only become visible when there is a special reason. For example, in 1840 a case was heard in the Sheriff Small Debt Court at Montrose. Two farmers had bet £5 on a race between their ponies on the turnpike from Montrose to the Lower North Water Bridge, now the A92. One failed to appear, and the other walked over and was awarded the stakes by the umpire on whom both parties had agreed. The first then claimed that the bet was void because racing on the turnpike was illegal. The Sheriff declined to intervene.[3] In 1792 the Marquis of Huntly and other sporting noblemen held a horse race up Edinburgh's Royal Mile, from the Abbey Strand to the gate of the

20.   Some of the crowd at Leith Races, *c.* 1810, an etching by Walter Geikie. In the middle is a game of rowley-powley (see Chapter 4).

Castle.[4] Alcoholic stimulus may be inferred, but the event was remembered because a marquis was involved.

There were three widespread forms of horse race, and to them we will now turn. First, there were the élite races each of which attracted runners and spectators from a handful of counties, and which after 1773 appear increasingly in Weatherby's *Racing Calendar*, published in London. Next, there were local races where farmers and town people matched their animals against one another. Between 1700 and 1850 these were most common in the West of Scotland and in the Borders. It is striking that races were very rarely associated with major horse fairs in Scotland – just as there was no race meeting, for example, at the great horse fair at Ballinasloe, Co. Galway – or with other major livestock markets such as Falkirk Tryst. Finally, there was the racing of draught horses, as part of celebrations which were strictly local and organised by the men who worked with the horses but were not in all cases their owners.

ÉLITE HORSE-RACING

When Mrs Calderwood of Polton, bound for the Low Countries in 1756, met a young English corn factor on the Harwich packet and observed, 'he seemed to understand a horse-race or a cock-match much better than the price of corn',[5] she was pointing to the sporting world of the eighteenth century: it centred on horse-racing, and though many respectable men were connected with it, it was not itself quite respectable. The world of horse-racing was well developed in England, with numbers of inns with racing connections and knowing ostlers, aristocratic owners and sporting gentlemen, horse nobblers and other disreputable individuals seeking an advantage or a half crown wherever they might find it. Near the margins of racing were dishonesty, cock-fighting, prostitution and a little thuggery. These things were largely absent in Scotland, though on the road to Leith Races:

> Some chaises honest folk contain
> An' some hae mony a whore in.[6]

The names of horses suggest that racing had an amorality of its own: *Sweetest When She's Naked* ran at Leith in 1760, and at Aberdeen in 1845 the Broadhill Hack Stakes were won by *Ellen (late Fanny Hill)*.[7] In the latter instance, one can guess that only a few racing men would have heard of Cleland's erotic novel (1749); but the former is a real surprise in Calvinist Scotland. So is the name of the winner of the gold cup at Kelso in 1813, *Agnes Sorel*, once the mistress of the king of France. Brechin Castle, the seat of a great racing enthusiast, William Ramsay Maule of Panmure, was 'not a house to which mothers would take their daughters'.[8] Conventional opinion must have been shocked by horses called *Martin Luther* and even *John Knox*.

The culture of racing was not Scots: its values were those of the English sporting world which in the seventeenth century was as immoral as the court of Charles II, in the eighteenth was tinged with hellfire, and in the nineteenth produced the very English figure of Mr Soapy Sponge and was often straightforwardly crooked. In Scotland, the patrons who put up the prizes and the stewards were noblemen and gentlemen who had half an eye on London life as the model for their behaviour. Some of them inhabited two worlds, one of moral correctness north of the Border, and mistresses, copious drinking and cruel sports south of it. An example who shows some of these features was James Merry (1805–77), the ironmaster and racehorse owner, who supported cock-fighting and pugilism in England, and employed a retired bruiser as his stable watcher. Also in his service was a Glasgow wine merchant, Norman Buchanan, 'little better than a sponger, parasite, and a tricky gentlemen to boot'. He was Merry's 'commissioner': he laid Merry's bets. Merry's first stay in parliament ended when he was found guilty of corrupt electoral practices. He habitually referred to himself as 'a plain Glesca bodie', another of his deceits. The Earl of Glasgow (1792–1869), owner of a large string of horses, was a brute. He is said to have thrown a waiter out of a first-floor window, breaking his leg, and snapped, 'Put him on the bill'.[9] If his horses were unsuccessful, he had them shot.

During the seventeenth century the quality of racehorses improved through careful breeding and the import of bloodstock from abroad. By the end of the century the racehorse was well on the way to being a specialist whose only roles were to run fast and procreate –

but even then one of the three foundation fathers of the thoroughbred racehorse, the Byerley Turk, saw action at the Battle of the Boyne (1690).

In the reign of James VI and after the Restoration the burghs had been the patrons of horse-racing. Whilst we can be sure that racing continued intermittently during the first half of the eighteenth century, it left few remains and even the meeting at Leith may have been discontinued for a few years after 1741. When the sport becomes visible again at the end of the eighteenth century patronage came first from the aristocracy – for example, the Duke of Hamilton at Hamilton, William Ramsay Maule, son of the Earl of Dalhousie, at Montrose – and then from other landed gentry.

Leith races, like most other metings, were for the poor and the gentry, but the people in the middle were less enthusiastic. Farmers, when they did attend, did so in order to meet other farmers and ride over improved fields. They did not gamble, and this distinguished them from their English equivalents.[10]

Leith races were under both royal and burghal patronage. The town gave a prize in cash which was carried to Leith in a purse on top of a pole borne by one of the town's officers. Members of the town council attended in their official capacities. The town controlled the running: it was their drummer who gave the drumrolls which started each heat.[11] The races were run from the starting point, out to a distant mark or stoup at which the horses turned, and back: at Lanark in 1719 the magistrates appointed themselves the judges of 'turneing the stoups'.[12] The practice related to the frequent use of the high road as the site of the race. In it there is a distant echo of the shape of the course for Roman chariot races, with a sharp turn at each end.

The King's Plate, first given by Queen Anne about 1710, was one of a small number of royal prizes, in most years about a dozen, awarded at leading meetings over the whole of Britain. Leith races had the only one in Scotland, with a single exception in one year at Kelso. The winning owner commissioned a piece of his own choice and the crown paid £100 of its cost. If he chose to add to the £100, the prize could be on a lavish scale. Those which survive include silver teapots, a silver salver and a quite staggeringly useless object

– a gold teapot. Only three Leith race prizes of any kind have come down to us from the whole of the period between 1660 and 1815. The growth of thoroughbred racing in Scotland began in the 1770s, and towards the end of the century the largest crowds were seen at Leith. Other things were being modernised too. The Industrial Revolution was beginning to generate new wealth and to produce easier communication. A woman observed the improved roads in Ayrshire which were paid for by the Earl of Dundonald and engineered by John Loudon MacAdam: 'odds theyll hae the hail coonty whamellin doon intae the Atlantic'. It was possible for large crowds to reach major race meetings.

Robert Fergusson's poem 'Leith Races' was written during the races of 1773, and it shows the crowd at its largest and liveliest. It begins with the poet meeting a young woman, the personification of Mirth, who tells him that since he has already written about Hallow-Fair, he should turn his attention to the Races. Thus Fergusson emphasises their importance in the people's calendar. Boys went through the old town in Fergusson's time – the New Town had yet to be built – selling handbills:

> Here is the true and faithfu' list
> O' noblemen and horses;
> Their eild [age], their weight, their height
>   their grist
> That rin for plates or purses
>   Fu' fleet this day'.[13]

By coach and foot the crowd make their way down Leith Walk, past 'Stands . . . Decked out by slee auld jaudies'[14] to Leith, drink, and loose money at *rowley-powley* and dicing. Most significantly – for Fergusson is writing from the point of view of the ordinary citizen – he did not describe the races themselves. He ends instead with drunken altercations and fighting: 'Their skins are gaily yarkit [bruised]'. He refers to the arguments as 'Robinhood debates', and although this is a reference to a contemporary Edinburgh club, it is also a reflection of inversions of status at the pre-Reformation May Day festival.

People came to Leith Races from a wide area. Fergusson mentioned Buchan folk being present, and an anonymous poet described:

> Vulcans, an' cartwrights, drouthy pairs
> Come frae the country clachans
> While sturdy herds, whave cleared hale fairs
> Come rowed in plaiden raughans.[15]

Leith races were last held in 1815. The Harbour Commissioners planned to build docks on the site of the races. It was suggested that they might move to Bruntsfield Links, on the other side of Edinburgh and uncomfortably close to it. Instead, they reappeared at Musselburgh, six miles along the coast and at such a distance from Edinburgh that the journey deterred people from going there. Crowds were smaller and more sober. The change did not meet with universal approval. An anonymous poet complained:

> And why should siccan sports be stopt
> For any whey-faced canters
> Wha fain would hae our Scotch lugs cropt
> And mak us rigglin ranters!
> Deil nor their greedy hands were chopt
> Wha toom their braw decanters
> And yet wad hae puir bodies snopt
> O' a' their pranksome banters
>   On sic a day.[16]

Alexander Campbell, a Leither, baxter by trade and historian in his leisure, praised Leith races, then turned to the organised running which had replaced them in 1816:

> the Musselburgh races are utterly and wholly destitute of any portion of that reckless and thorough-going spirit of hilarity, which never failed to attend those of Leith. The former … are the coldest and most heartless things imaginable; and what they have gained in elegance and refinement, but indifferently sup-plies the place of the obstreperous interest, which the rough and round skelping on the plashy sands of Leith was wont to excite.[17]

The anger of Campbell and the anonymous poet stems from a

feeling not of loss but of theft. Though the races were organised by the Town Council, and despite the fact that wealthy people owned the racehorses, the folk believed that the races belonged to them, and that they were being deprived of their tradition.

Horse-racing in eighteenth-century Scotland was a rather haphazard, disconnected business: the founding of the Hunters' Club in 1777, soon to become the Caledonian Hunt Club, was the first stage in creating a consistent organisation. The Club was exclusive and aristocratic. Initially its membership was set at 45, though it was later increased to 80, then reduced to 70. In 1814 the annual subscription was ten guineas, in 1818 the entry money forty guineas. It was said that when a vacancy occurred there was 'almost incredible competition', and that Scots noblemen and gentlemen, hearing of an impending election, would race home from 'the most remote parts of Europe'.[18]

The Club held annual race meetings. The first was at Hamilton and went on for a fortnight, and subsequent ones lasted a week. These meetings were only at the best courses, and as the number of courses decreased it was the ones which were patronised by the Club which survived. Significantly, it held only one meeting at Leith. The value of the prizes at other race meetings totalled between £200 and £800, but at the Hunt Club races they were much higher. For example, at Kelso in 1840 they amounted to £1600. Their meeting was held near the end of the season – that year the last race on the last day was run in the dark – and moved from one course to another, dispensing patronage as it went. The landlord of the Cross Keys at Kelso, having laid out 'Ordinaries' for 60 to 130 on four consecutive nights, must have been a happy man.[19]

The Club was not merely sporting, for during its meetings there was a ball every night. It also exercised cultural patronage and was Caledonian in more than location. It subscribed for one hundred copies of the Edinburgh edition of Burns' poems, and from 1787 employed the fiddler Nathaniel Gow (1766–1831) and during the last four years of his life, when he was too old to play, payed him an annuity of £50. The Club also erected a monument to him in Greyfriars' Churchyard in Edinburgh.[20]

The Hunt Club, however, did not become the controlling body

in Scottish horse-racing. In the nineteenth century the Jockey Club, based at Newmarket, established and enforced rules which were essential if gambling was to be fair and the sport competitive. As part of the strategy, thoroughbred racing was defined so that it was distinct from the ungoverned and ungovernable local races. Some meetings briefly crossed the line and achieved the higher status, and some struggled to retain it.

Horse-racing thus took place at several levels, and the definition of these levels was slowly changing from the seventeenth to the early twentieth centuries. Thoroughbred racing and the thoroughbred racehorse evolved into a separate species of sport and an aristocratic class of animal. In the eighteenth century strength was as much a virtue in a racehorse as was speed: on a long, heavy course such as Leith sands, endurance was vital, particularly because most events were run in three heats. Racing was still close to hunting, through the stamina required and through the organisers of events. A description of the Borders explained the results of better breeding:

> Instead of gentlemen, as formerly, priding themselves upon the *bottom* of their horses, by running them against each other for small sums, *blood* alone is now consulted; heats abolished, great bets made and lost in a twinkling; and mean arts resorted to protect one set of betters, and fleece others.[21]

At the same time the pace of horse-racing was increasing. The existing longer races for fully mature animals were being joined by shorter ones for three-year-olds: the first of these was the St Leger at Doncaster (1776). These new races were less certain in their result, which made betting more interesting.

Kelso races illustrate the development of the sport. There were meetings around Kelso in the first half of the eighteenth century before, in the 1760s, a fixed site was adopted on Caverton Edge, four miles south of the town. It was accessible both to Scots and English spectators, and in 1793 achieved the distinction of a Royal Plate, the only course apart from Leith (and later Musselburgh) at which such a prize has been offered. Despite this, the fragility of Scots racing, dependent on a small number of patrons, was shown the following year when there was no racing at Kelso. One practical problem was that only a few owners would race their horses on Caverton Edge: on one occasion only three appeared for four days' racing. In 1821–22 the meeting was held on another course on high ground, at Blakelaw between the Tweed and the Bowmont Water. The crucial development which saved Kelso races was the laying out of a genuinely flat course on the edge of the town, at Berrymoss – the moss had just been drained. This is the present course. The move was made by the Duke of Roxburghe, again emphasising the role of landed patron in racing.

The new course was described just after it had opened:

> The ground on which the course is formed was originally a morass, which was imperfectly drained twenty years ago, and the idea of forming it was treated as chimerical. His Grace, however, who united in his character promptitude and decision, with acute penetration, gave orders for the work ...[22]

There is something of the Industrial Revolution in this conscious domination of nature: in the same decade Chat Moss was being packed with brushwood so that the Liverpool and Manchester, the first genuine railway, could run over it. After the Napoleonic Wars race crowds increased in size all over Britain as working people flocked to the entertainment, and this produced resentment among those who thought of ordinary folk as unruly muscle-power. At Lessudden (St Boswells) in 1820 an observer said that the race 'brought all the labouring class of people from their work'.[23]

Horse-racing was the first sport to operate on a national (British) basis, with events being co-ordinated and horses moved from one meeting to another. In 1808 the Ayr meeting was moved by a week because the chosen date clashed with the one chosen for Pontefract. George IV's visit to Scotland caused the meeting of 1822 to be cut to two days, and the *Ayr Advertiser* said 'we expect neither sport nor company'.[24] By 1840 horse-racing was a national sport which was locally organised. Only the best horses were walked from one place to another: this took time and the horse had to be allowed to recover after the long journey. But it *did* happen, and spectators were mobile, provided they could afford to own or hire a horse to carry them to fixtures.

Horse-racing is historically important because it has provided sources for practices which have affected other sports. It was the first sport since the time of Byzantium to attract large crowds. It was a sport for all social classes. Some meetings, such as Kelso, might have been exclusive, but Leith and Paisley were very popluar. Leith may have, and Paisley certainly did, attract crowds of 100,000 before the railways. The success of horse-racing in the 1820s can be seen as fulfilling a demand for sport, in that over the whole of Britain more spectators went to the races than before. But at the same time, most meetings were annual and the demand for sporting entertainment was not fully met. Other sports were able to take up this challenge over the next half century and more.

Horse-racing was the first sport to become highly competitive. It was also the source for betting and wagering on sport, and for the prize which is the victor's to keep, rather than the trophy which is to be returned. The burgh's bells were replaced by plates and cups. The cup itself, after 1850 the predominant form of trophy or prize for all sports, was first used widely in racing.

PAISLEY RACES

Paisley was described by Alexander Smith in 1865 as 'A third-rate Scotch town' in which the largest building was the jail.[25] Smith was travelling to Skye: one might suspect the comparison was less with other industrial burghs than with the Sound of Sleat and the bare serrated ridge of the Cuillin. Nevertheless, Paisley was unpleasant, suffering from extremes of poverty, pollution, filth and overcrowding. It was also a focal point for Irish immigrants, many of whom passed through the town on the way to Glasgow, and a large number stayed in Paisley.

Paisley had two medieval fairs, dedicated to St Mirrin and St Marnock. Both fairs have pre-Christian origins. The Town Council of Paisley agreed in 1608 to hold a horse race with the prize of a silver bell, but the first race was not held until St Mirrin's Fair in 1620. This fair was moved in 1665 to St James's Day (20th August), and the horse race moved with it.[26] Paisley Races were held approximately on St James's Day until their demise in 1907.

One pagan tradition continued until the nineteenth century. At

St James's Fair bonfires – *tawnles* – were lit on artificial islands in the River Cart. They were still being prepared in 1825 when the newly-established *Paisley Advertiser* said:

> we do not recollect of having ever witnessed more splendid Tandles than what gleamed on the Cart on Wednesday night. To children it had formed the occupation of many weeks, to construct the circular mounds or little islets in the middle of

21.   The larger of the two Paisley Bells, 1620. It bears the arms of the burgh, and is preserved in Paisley Museum.

22. The Lanark Bell of 1608–10, made by Hugh Lindsay of Edinburgh. *National Museums of Scotland.*

the river where the Tandles are lighted ... these immense fires with myriads of children dancing round them had altogether a grand and imposing effect ...[27]

They continued until the late 1820s when alterations to the River to improve water supply to the mills made the flow too fast.

In the eighteenth century Paisley Races were a minor event. When in 1746 the race was advertised in one of the Glasgow papers, the council was advertising its loyalty to the Hanoverian succession as much as its race: life was going on as usual in Paisley despite the fugitive Prince still being in Scotland. Runners were required to be booked on the day before the race at the Town Clerk's office.[28]

The races remained a local affair until after the Napoleonic Wars, but then they expanded rapidly. This can be seen in the description in the new *Paisley Advertiser* of the profusion of entertainers who now found it worthwhile to be present. In 1825 there were tumblers, fiddlers, equestrians, fire-eaters, jugglers and rope-dancers.[29] By 1833 an even wider range of shows was present, mostly from the south: Wombwell's menagerie, fifteen Waterloo flys and merry-go-rounds, Mumford's Theatre of Arts, the Pavilion of Novelty, Steel's Minor Theatre, Scott's Royal Pantheon, glass-blowing and working in miniature, scriptural and historical paintings, Wallace the Scotch Gigantic Youth, the Surprising Giantess, and the astonishing child born without hands or arms.[30]

The races, too, were developing. For the first time, horses were recorded as having been brought from England in 1834.[31] Two years later the *Paisley Advertiser* trumpeted: 'This year ... begins a new era in Paisley racing'.[32] 'Ascot and Doncaster must take care, otherwise Ayr and Paisley will throw them under an eclipse'.[33] The races had been held on the Greenock Road, but now they were moved to open ground north of the road. With a purposely laid-out track and vastly increased prize money they attracted better horses and for the first time appeared in Weatherby's *Racing Calendar*. In the early 1830s the prize money was typically £35 for the whole meeting. In 1836 it was £80, and a week after the races £320 had been subscribed for the following year.

The crowd in the early 1830s had grown to 40,000. In 1836 it was said to number 50,000, and the scene was compared with Liverpool and Manchester races. Those present included the Earl of Eglinton, Lord Kelburne, Sir James Boswell of Auchinleck, and many other West of Scotland gentry; literature was represented by Professor John Wilson (Christopher North) and Thomas Campbell. Also at Paisley Fair were others who sought any large crowd: pickpockets and preachers, as in 1839 when 'a gentleman ... addressed his audience on spiritual matters for several hours'. 'Two tents erected on the non-inebriating principle, had ample employment'.[34] There were fifty tents erected on the inebriating principle. Suddenly the crowd grew larger: in 1837 the figure of 110,000 to 115,000 was given on the authority of John Orton of York, a professional race official who had been employed for the first time that year. A new and handsome box was provided for the Bells: it records the change in the Races, according them greater status but also recognising the depth of tradition, and valuing it.

Some elements of tradition were abandoned. Traditional sport was only in a qualified sense competitive: other qualities such as unpredictability, participation and the opportunity to indulge in violence were sometimes equally important. The spectacle of horse-racing included the possibility of accidents, and the smooth operation of thoroughbred racing placed an emphasis on safety, partly to minimise the element of luck in gambling. This did not please some members of the Paisley crowd:

> At our next St James's Day, therefore, we must calculate on losing the patronage of our friend of the shuttle, who having visited Bogside on one occasion, returned home utterly dissatisfied, because 'there was na' a tummil in the hail races' for should so *interesting* an event occur on our new course, it must be from some cause other than the fitness of the ground.[35]

A level playing field was required.

In this period St James's Fair was still an important livestock market for the west of Scotland and beyond: in 1836, for example, Highland black cattle, milk cows and pigs from Ireland were particularly noted.[36] Soon, its commercial function became less conspicuous as the racing moved into the foreground. By the 1840s St James's Fair was becoming increasingly an event for Glaswegians. 'That which Musselburgh races are to Edinburgh, those of Paisley are to Glasgow'[37] – the Musselburgh meeting being the most important one in Scotland. In the 1850s Paisley Races had had a bad name: 'There was as usual a good amount of drinking, thieving and fighting, especially in the after part of the day'.[38] They were 'a Saturnalia of ruffianism'.[39] This cannot have encouraged families to attend the races. Increasingly, Paisley people tended to go to the coast. For example, from the Thursday morning of the Fair to Friday afternoon trains leaving Paisley in 1860 were heavily laden.[40]

Paisley Races had reached their peak in the late 1830s. In the next twenty years, as the population of the industrial West of Scotland

increased rapidly, fuelled by immigration from Ireland, crowds at
the Races remained buoyant in number and spirit. But they were
subject to only limited policing and feeling against the Catholic Irish
was growing. After the Races of 1857 there was a sectarian riot. The
Renfrewshire Independent observed:

> Bowling-greens and cricket-grounds are as necessary as Mech-
> anics' Institutes and Athenaeums ... [but] The Crystal Palace
> at Sydenham cannot supersede the sports of the ice – curling,
> skating, sliding, and the glorious old game of 'shinty' ... the
> sight of a regatta, or a horse race, stirs the blood and interests
> the soul.[41]

This radical journalist realised that the Free Kirk and the Town
Council were not prepared to recognise the emotional appeal of
sport in general and horse-racing in particular – the excitement and
emotional release which they produced.

In the second half of the century St James's Fair slowly split into
a holiday for Paisley people and the Races chiefly for visitors from
Glasgow. The commercial side of the Fair disappeared. It was still
a time for heavy drinking, when abnormal standards of policing were
applied: insensible drunks were simply left in doorways to sleep.[42]

There was also increasing competition from new racecourses, and
some courses which had once held a single meeting each year began
to exploit their facilities by increasing the number of racing days.
Paisley, with a badly drained course, awkward corners, and a poor
reputation, was at a disadvantage. The Jockey Club, by this time
grown into the authority over British racing, threatened to close the
course; the Jockey Club acted, and the last race for the Paisley Bells
took place in 1907.

LOCAL HORSE RACES

As the number of local newspapers increased in the middle of the
nineteenth century, minor races make fleeting appearances in the
printed record. Most of them probably began in the late eighteenth
century, when improved agriculture was making farmers wealthier
and so more likely to own a good horse. In Ayrshire, in the period
between 1820 and 1870 there was racing at Sorn, Cumnock,

Mauchline, Kilmarnock, Kirkoswald, Ardrossan, Muirkirk, Whitletts, Helenton, West Kilbride, Tarbolton, and Dalry. In Renfrewshire, there are records of horse races at St Inan's fair at Beith; and at Eastwood, Eaglesham, and Lochwinnoch.[43] These events are in addition to the more formal races at Paisley – which in 1758 'would have furnished a fine piece for the pencil of Hogarth or Teniers'[44] – Ayr, Irvine and Bogside. No other area of Scotland shows a similar concentration: the image of Habbie Simpson, piper of Kilbarchan, playing the pipes at horse races is more local than one might expect. Few of these west-country meetings survived into the last quarter of the nineteenth century.

A few of these races started in the seventeenth century or perhaps earlier. In 1858 Mauchline Race was said to be five or six hundred years old – dating from 1250 to 1350.[45] In the absence of more information one is inclined to reject this out of hand; but if it was first a *play day* and only later a race, then a link with a medieval religious festival is more likely. Mauchline Race was held on 30th April, the feast of St Catherine of Siena, and although the parish church was dedicated to St Michael, it was not unusual for a holiday to be held on a day other than that of the patron saint. At nearby Cumnock there was a fair on St Matthew's Day (21st September), though the church was St Conal's. Mauchline Race is probably a post-Restoration event: it was first recorded explicitly in 1674, and some of the others may also have begun in the period after the Restoration, though at nearby Old Cumnock the race had started before 1610 when a quarrel took place there.[46]

One Ayrshire horse race, of a very particular kind, has achieved worldwide celebrity. In the frantic gallop at the end of *Tam o' Shanter* we can see the way in which Burns takes the Ayrshire tradition of local horse races at fairs, and inverts every aspect of it. Certainly, the action takes place after a predictable event, a market, but the race is not something which has been looked forward to for months, it happens unexpectedly. There are no spectators, instead of the whole community being present. Or one could say that whereas an ordinary race had a few hundred spectators, millions have relished the poem; and a horse race was ephemeral whereas *Tam o' Shanter* will last for centuries. There is a long period of socialising and heavy drinking before the race, but it is completely over before Tam starts on his journey home. When he reaches Alloway Kirk he sees that the Devil is master of the revels, not some local hero who would once have been dressed as the Abbot of Narent. It is the main competitor, Tam himself, who starts the race by crying 'Weel done, Cutty-sark'.

The lines at the beginning of the pursuit of Tam:

> As bees bizz out wi' angry fyke   [fuss]
> When plundering herds assail their byke

are an adaptation of lines from another play-poem, John Skinner's 'The Christmass Bawing of Monimusk, 1728'. In it, the footballers rush after the ball:

> Like bumbees bizzing frae a bike
> Whan hirds their riggins tirr.

These lines link Tam with traditional country sports. The winning of a race by tearing off the head of a living goose hung from a pole is mirrored by the loss of Meg's tail. And in the end, Tam wins nothing, only retaining what he began with – his horse and his life.

William Aiton, a solicitor, wrote *A General View of the Agriculture of the County of Ayr* in 1811. He was a statistician and moral critic and he assessed races and fairs thus:

> There are not less than 200 fairs in the county of Ayr, every year, and, on average, there cannot be fewer than 100 people at every fair or race; supposing the half of these to have no necessary business, and that, on an average, their loss of time, and expenses at the fair, were not to exceed ten shillings each, the aggregate loss to the public, in Ayrshire alone, must not be less than £50,000, per annum. To this, a very considerable sum must be added, as lost every year, by people attending weekly markets and county roups, without having interesting business …[47]

Country races were organised by change-house keepers, and they and the proprietors of dram shops were the only beneficiaries. Aiton's point is valid, though he overstates it: he criticises also the consumption of tobacco, spices, onions and gingerbread. He moves from argument to vituperation, condemning in lurid language the excessive consumption of spirits and giving a long account of the use of alcohol in seduction, until:

> about midnight ... the *lads* and *lasses* begin to pair off, and return to the fair one's home, where they generally spend an hour or two by themselves, in the barn, byre, or the cart shed, talking over the events of the day ...[48]

Or, perhaps, doing things which did not fit into Aiton's view of the human race as rational, driven only by economic imperatives, and controlled by the kirk's authority.

By contrast, Aiton approved of the thoroughbred races at Ayr and Bogside. His phrases glitter: excellence of the horses, brilliancy of the company, rank and fashion, fashionable amusements, urbanity of manners. He recognises that at the race meeting there were thieves and prostitutes, but 'it is not the races, but the depravity of human nature, that gives rise to such worthless characters'.[49] The wealthy can afford leisure and the occasional moral slip: the poor cannot. Aiton was a modernist: Walter Scott and Thomas Love Peacock would have distrusted his sentiments. Of all the authors of county reports on agriculture, Aiton is the only one to mention horse races, which again indicates that they were more common in Ayrshire than elsewhere.

The other area in which there was a group of horse races was the Borders, where they were held on high moorland. At Kelso races took place successively at two hilltop sites south of the town: on Caverton Edge and at Blakelaw. Hawick races were at Pelmanrig, and Selkirk at Gala Rig: a *rig* is a ridge. Lamberton Races, just over the Border from Berwick, were held on top of a moor with wonderful views both inland and out to sea. At Jedburgh, races were held on Jedburgh Edge: this site has not been identified, but it is obviously another hilltop.

The explanation for the use of moorland is that it was not under crop, or even enclosed, and sheep could be herded out of the way for a few days. The open hill was already a social place in the Borders: cattle droving from the great markets in central Scotland, and the earlier movement of stolen beasts, took place not along valleys but over high ground where there were fewer obstacles. At Selkirk a drove road passed one end of the racecourse. Border horse-racing contained a memory of flight and pursuit with the possibility of victims and thieves watching one another over miles of moorland.

With the exception of Kelso, the Border races were relatively local in the nineteenth century.[50] For example, at Hawick in 1858 the runners had names such as *Aytoun Castle* and *Annandale*; an event explicitly restricted to the counties of Roxburgh and Selkirk; a maximum prize of 20 sovereigns and 'great numbers of people from the town and neighbourhood'. All indicated a restricted geographical range, though the meeting was reported in the Edinburgh papers.[51]

The local nature of some of the Border race meetings can be seen from two further pieces of evidence. The names of the races – the Operatives' Purse, the Town's Subscription Purse, 'the London Silver Cup presented by Hawick men in London, to be run for by horses belonging *bona fide* to the district within 20 miles of Hawick' – emphasise the burgh and its surrounding country. For one race the prize was a whip given 'by the Cornet and his lads' – the Cornet being the principal actor in the Common Riding – linking this race very closely to burgh traditions.

The evidence for local races is uneven. None have been discovered in Aberdeenshire before 1850, despite the example of good-quality racing at Aberdeen. They scarcely appear in Angus or Perthshire and were uncommon in Fife. In the Lothians, they take the unusual form of draught horse races, which we will examine later: these events were modelled on the races of the gentry.

MARYMASS AT IRVINE [52]

Irvine was one of the three large burghs in Ayrshire, along with Ayr and Kilmarnock. By the 1820s it had changed completely from the sleepy little burgh in which Galt had set *The Provost* (1822), and was surrounded by coalmines and ironworks, and was an important port for the export of coal to Ireland.[53] Irvine was, incidentally, the birthplace of Edgar Allan Poe. There is a strong but erroneous local belief that Marymass races are the oldest in Europe, and F. Marian McNeill accepted this extraordinary idea.[54]

There is no doubt, however, that the festival is medieval in origin. In 1372 Robert II granted the merchants of Irvine the right to form a guild and the exclusive right to trade within the baronies of Cunningham and Largs, and it is likely that they organised miracle or mystery plays in honour of their patron, the Virgin Mary, on the feast of her Assumption, 15th August.[55] The phonetic spelling of *Merrymass* was sometimes used.[56] In the sixteenth century it was known as the *first Lady Day*, for Irvine had a *latter Lady Day* fair a few weeks later.[57] By the nineteenth century the Marymass festival was no longer held on a fixed day, but had been fitted into the pattern of commercial fairs, and was held on the Saturday after the third Monday in August, as it is now. In the nineteenth century the organised part of Marymass extended from the Wednesday before the races until race Saturday, and drinking continued on the Sunday and Monday. It was the main holiday in Irvine. Quite separately from Marymass, a horse race had been started at Irvine, probably in the first half of the seventeenth century, and perhaps in 1601.[58] At some point – maybe after the Restoration, when many horse races were restarted, but perhaps later, even as late as the end of the eighteenth century – the race was moved to Marymass.[59] One possible date is 1753, when the responsibility for riding the marches of the burgh passed to the carters.

At the beginning of the nineteenth century Marymass and its races fade somewhat from view – they appear only as entries in the Town Council Minutes, recording the payment of small prizes. From later practice, we can infer that there was a procession round the burgh, out to the Town Moor, and horse races. Marymass was unusual in that it was under the patronage of both the burgh and the Earl of Eglinton, by far the largest landowner in north Ayrshire, and when local newspapers begin to report Marymass, he is present every year. Local landowners and farmers entered their horses in the races, which were different from the thoroughbred racing a few hundred yards away at Bogside, where the Earl laid out a course in 1808. To begin with most runners came from the West of Scotland, but later they came from all over Lowland Scotland and the North of England. From the start Bogside appeared in Weatherby's *Racing Calendar* – Marymass, emphatically, did not.

Bogside Races were in abeyance between 1824 and 1836, when the young 13th Earl of Eglinton revived them.[60] Irvine Town Council stopped supporting Marymass Races at this point, giving money instead for prizes at Bogside.[61] The Town Council revived its financial support in 1851.[62]

At the same period crowds at Marymass Races grew rapidly in size. In 1852 'the number of publicans' tents and carts, and dealers in sweetmeats, toys &c., was ... great – more resembling an Eglinton Park [i.e. Bogside] meeting than the cadgers' races'.[63] It seemed possible that the races might reach the status of a first-class fixture, and become integrated into the national racing scene. But soon the gentry ceased to attend the races: they became rowdier and the quality of the horses declined.

Marymass was at its most flavoursome between 1850 and 1869. On the day of the races the town crier's drum preceded the announcement that all carters should meet at their Captain's house, dressed in their best blue coats and bonnets. There was another 'anti-musical roll', and onlookers learned that 'potatoes are to be sold at the Tron for fourpence per stone'. Marymass races took place in the midst of burgh life. The people were proud of them: the Irvine Flute Band and the Irvine Rifle Brass Band marched round the town and walked in the procession to the racecourse. In 1852 the brass band had too few instruments but rather than ask strangers to join them they borrowed instruments from other towns and made what they could of them.

On the Town Moor in 1865:

> There are 17 tents for the sale of – well, say liquor, 6 ovens warming cold pies, about 20 tart and biscuit carts, beside fruit barrows, shooting saloons, and other etceteras too numerous to mention. Aunt Sally shows her ugly head here and there.

This reporter estimated the crowd between 14,000 and 17,000, some of whom were incapably drunk. Although he felt sorry for the 'poor inebriates lying by the roadside', there is not the same direct criticism of drunkenness which coloured other accounts. He went on to list the shows which had arrived: the diorama, half a dozen photographic booths, hobby horses, fly boats, a fat lady, a

23.   Marymass Races, 1994, on Irvine Town Moor. There was a crowd of some thousands on the other side of the course.

dwarf, a boa constrictor, and so on. Every stall seemed to have a monkey on it:

> On looking at the group outside, monkeys and all, we thought for a moment that there must be some truth in 'Darwin's theory', but dispelled the idea as we moved along with the proverb, 'Birds of one feather flock together'.

The Origin of Species had been published six years earlier. It is only at the end of the evening that this account becomes more clearly critical:

> Drunkenness now is having full swing; the public houses are vomiting forth the reeling, shouting, roaring, swearing, singing, yelling, fighting inmates.[64]

Even then, the reporter admits that there were only a few fights: the real source of fear was the noise.

By the 1860s, the crowd at Marymass had grown to between 10,000 and 17,000, depending on the state of the harvest and the weather. Landowners and most of the members of Irvine Town Council avoided it. Its function as a hiring fair had disappeared: 'Our

Bridgegatehead, which used to be thronged with Highlanders and Irishmen offering themselves for the harvest, now scarcely presents a Celtic-looking physog'.[65] Marymass was a festival of heavy drinking for industrial Ayrshire and Renfrewshire, and for Glasgow. In 1865, 700 gallons of whisky were delivered to Irvine on the Monday before Marymass.[66] Publicans from Ayr, Kilmarnock, Paisley had four hours to recoup their expenses in their stalls on the Town Moor, and they did so by selling cheap whisky as fast as they could. There was a continuous stream of complaints about drinking, violence and swearing. Marymass was becoming more disordered at a time when standards of public behaviour were increasingly emphasising self-discipline. One commentator described 'the sober portion of the community disgusted with the various brutal exhibitions, and wondering what is the use of such "a carnival" as our Marymass fair'.[67] The possibility had arisen that the fair might be suppressed.

So Marymass horse-racing, which gave much of the character to the festival, continued because it was capable of being reshaped, and drunkenness was restricted to the middle of Irvine, where it could be more easily controlled – and where the profits went to voters for the Town Council. In the 1890s the Captain of the Carters was no longer a carter, but the landlord of the Commercial Inn. Crowds grew smaller and better behaved, and in 1891 the *Ayr Advertiser* said 'while Marymass Saturday is still a holiday, there is none of that boisterous merriment which was so common in by past years'.[68] The commercial aspect of Marymass had disappeared several decades earlier: the horse fair on the preceding Wednesday, for example, had declined in the 1860s. By 1913 the procession was described as 'quaint'.

Yet Marymass survived. It gained new life in 1927, when many local gala days were being created to foster civic identity. The invented pageantry pretended that the name of Marymass referred to the Queen of Scots and not the Blessed Virgin. The carters and their processions gave continuity. The festival thrived in the 1980s with the encouragment of Irvine Development Corporation, and the races are still held on Town Moor.

RACING DRAUGHT HORSES

Draught horses were raced in a number of places in Scotland from the seventeenth to the nineteenth centuries. The sport was most widespread in the first half of the nineteenth century, when the Clydesdale breed spread rapidly over the country: enormous animals whose running was delightfully comic, yet with a docile disposition which limited the danger from half a ton of horseflesh at an unaccustomed speed.

The first such race emerged in 1662 when the Dumfries town council ordered a silver bell for a race on the second Tuesday in May, 'according to auncient custome' – it had probably started in the reign of James VI. The date was linked to the practice of collecting boughs from a birch wood outside the town – bringing in the summer. It was called the *Muck Race*: by implication the horses belonged to the Burgh's scavengers. The trophy was the *Muck Bell*. At this date the draught animal of the countryside was the ox. The Town Council abolished the race in 1716, though it continued to be held less formally until the middle of the nineteenth century.[69] A similar race was held at Lanark in the eighteenth century, where the prize was a pair of spurs.[70]

As the country grew wealthier, more farmers could afford horses, replacing their oxen. At the same time the quality of roads was improving: more wheeled agricultural traffic meant an expansion in the trade of the carter. Better roads were also better for racing.

The Whipmen's Society of Newton and St Evox [or Quivox], a friendly society which paid burial costs and supported widows, was founded at Newton-on-Ayr in January 1830.[71] However, their race of 1842 was said to be the 96th running, and that of 1864 the 118th, implying that it had first been held in 1747.[72] The preciseness of this statement gives it some weight, and in 1799 the Town Council had discussed 'the old custom of having a race at Lammas'.[73] Its origin lay in the trade of the carters who carried kippered salmon inland, and Kipper Fair was held on the first Friday after the end of the salmon-fishing season, 12th August.

Newton Races were a modest local event. They caused most of the people in Newton, and many in Ayr, to take a half-holiday, but only once is there evidence of outsiders being attracted, when in 1852 a special train was run for spectators.[74] In one year when 'the day was a beautiful one' the crowd reached five thousand.[75]

Race day began with an action which benefited the whole population: the streets were cleaned for the only time in the year.[76] The cadgers assembled in front of the Captain's house, where the flag of the corporation was unfurled and the prizes of bridles, saddles and spurs were mounted on poles, and carried at the head of the procession to the sands.[77]

After the races the procession returned to the centre of the burgh, calling at the inns and being fed kippered salmon, or after the early 1850s, mackerel, while they drank. The Captain performed a sword dance at Newton Cross,[78] just as the Captain of the Kilwinning Archers, after shooting the papingo, danced a reel at Kilwinning Cross every year down to 1869.

The races themselves were shaped by the unpredicatable behaviour of the horses. For example, in 1872:

> No. 2, a likely-looking racer took a fancy to be over among the stones at the foot of the sea-wall, where his jockey was still engaged unsuccessfully endeavouring to convince him he had no business to be after that heat had been won ... in the second heat ... [he] looked dangerous till ... he suddenly remembered that he had not completed his investigations among the stones.[79]

Horses might also pause to drink, or simply rush off to the sea with excitement. The state of the tide and the sands also created inconsistencies.

Despite their lively character, Newton Races were part of the burgh tradition of horse-racing, adapting it to the small size of Newton-on-Ayr and to its trade of carting fish. It was also a matter of pride, separating Newton from the large burgh on the other side of the River Ayr. Ayr races were called the Western Meeting, just as Dumfries was the Southern, and Inverness the Northern Meeting.[80] Newton ignored the rest of the country: if the Western Meeting was at Ayr, the Northern Meeting was at Newton.

Races which were similar to Newton in their practice were held in the Lothians, but their origin was different for they did not have links with burghs. They were *carters' plays*. The Kipper Fair was

24.   The box made in 1836 for the Paisley Bells.

the celebration at the end of a season, a kind of harvest, and the fair was a form of harvest festival or *kirn*. Carters' plays were modern, for they did not have such a close link with the activities of the year, even if they did have a fixed place in the calendar.

CARTERS' PLAYS IN THE LOTHIANS

Horse-racing with draught or plough horses was the central event at a carters' play. There was a group of nineteen plays in Mid and East Lothian, Peeblesshire and Lanarkshire. They began in the late eighteenth and early nineteenth centuries, and most of them ended between 1850 and 1870, though two survived in modified forms into the twentieth century.

On 23rd July 1802 the young James Hogg – not yet 'the Ettrick Shepherd' – was riding from Ettrick to Edinburgh. On the moor at Pomathorn, over the North Esk from Penicuik, he found a crowd who shouted at him to get off the road: a horse race was about to begin. The race was won by a galloway – a farm horse. He asked a gentleman spectator about the origin of the races:

He said they were put out by a club of boys, each paying so

much annually to a box or common stock, for the support of such members as should be reduced by sickness or misfortune, that this was a holiday with them (the anniversary of their club he supposed), that they would spend the evening in foot races and dancing, that these were the members so fantastically dressed with ribbons which they had got from neighbouring girls whom they, in return, would treat at their ball in the evening; that there had lately been another day of diversion by the whipmen – another and stronger club – at which the farmers grudged, as it took all their servants from work.

After another race:

They then rode off with a sort of regularity, two men at rank preceded by the drum; the members were all most all on horses, some of which were very lean. I never in all my life saw ribbons more unfitly matched than on some of the riders; they seemed to have only one suit of clothes and, the day being warm, many of them had left their stockings and shoes behind them. I would not have given forty shillings for man, horse raiment and furniture – one half of which I rate as the value of the ribbons.[81]

Hogg had witnessed a carters' play.

The striking fact about the carters' plays is their limited distribution. Apart from those at Biggar (Lanarkshire), West Linton and Peebles (both Peeblesshire), all of the plays were in Mid or East Lothian: two at Dalkeith, Langlaw [Mayfield], Cousland, Pathhead, Leith, Corstorphine, Gilmerton, Lasswade, Penicuik, Musselburgh, Tranent, Prestonpans, Aberlady, Haddington, and East Linton. Guthrie refers to a play at Liberton, but he means in Liberton Parish, in other words Gilmerton.[82] The carters' plays were concentrated round Edinburgh. A search has been made for comparable events in West Lothian and Fife, but none has been found: the origin of the horse race at Ceres in Fife, for example, is quite different.[83] The focus on Edinburgh is clear. The statement that carters' plays were 'once common throughout Scotland' is questionable.[84]

The fifteen plays listed above are an average of 10 miles from Leith, with Peebles the most distant at 23 miles. The distribution of carters' plays is explained by the focus on Leith. The horse-racing was in imitation of the racing on Leith sands. The prelude to Leith Races was the procession from the Old Town to the Sands behind the Town's Purse, carried on top of a pole.[85] Similarly, at Lasswade:

> Their prize is hooked on a pole
> > A gude stout new cart saddle
> And by the truth, upon the whole
> For it they run and padle [move with short quick steps]
> > Gay sair that day.[86]

The names of the Friendly Societies emphasised carters, such as the Haddington Carters' Friendly Society, and the Prestonpans United Society of Carters. The title of the New Society of Carters and Others in Musselburgh and Fisherrow was more accurate since the only exclusions in the articles of the societies were fishermen and miners whose lives were thought too dangerous, and so likely to impose an extra burden on the funds. Elsewhere most of the members were probably, as at Pathhead, ploughmen.[87] In Haddington anyone aged from 18 to 40 from the 'labouring and trading part of the community' could join provided they were 'not engaged in any occupation or trade ... particularly dangerous or detrimental to health'.[88] Most societies had arrangements for suspending, rather than withdrawing, the membership of men who went to sea or down the pit.

The dates on which the carters' plays took place were scattered from May to July. Haddington held one on 22nd May, and there were three in the third week in June: Prestonpans on the Wednesday, Tranent on the Thursday, and Corstorphine on the Friday. The Cousland play was on the first Friday in July, West Linton on the second Tuesday, the two Dalkeith plays on the second Friday, and Peebles on the last Friday. Gilmerton play was at first on 6th May, but later on the last Friday of July. It may be that they were deliberately held on separate days to enable stall-holders to travel from one to another, and people to attend more than one. This implies that the organisers of one play were aware of others. It also suggests that the plays were not based on older festivals, with the possible exception of the group at the beginning of July which are around the time of Old Midsummer Day.

THE BEGINNING OF THE CARTERS' PLAY DAY

The formal part of the play day was the annual meeting of the Friendly Society. This was held first, as at Prestonpans, or after a parade through the town to gather members, as at Gilmerton. The Whipman Society of Peebles was unusual in that its membership included men from adjoining parishes. Its procession started from the Preses' house at 9 a.m: members with horses were to be there, though those on foot were allowed to appear at whichever town the procession had reached an hour later.[89] At West Linton and Pathhead the procession called at various 'leading houses' for 'monetary recognition'. The West Linton Society had their banner painted in 1807 by a professional artist, James Howe, who specialised in horses, as the Biggar Whipmen had four years earlier.[90]

At the meeting 'My Lord' and his two 'Bailies' were elected, as well as the formal officers of the Friendly Society. The offices of the Societies passed from year to year among the members: as well as being an honour, it was also a time-consuming burden to visit the sick, or those reluctant to pay their dues. The play was an event separate from the Friendly Society in as far as My Lord and his Bailies were not officers of the Society and might be re-appointed year after year. At Cousland, for example, Jock Cockburn of Airfield was My Lord for many years.[91] My Lord led the procession to the race, and acted as judge. The Bailies were the starters. The printed Articles of the Tranent Carters' Society, dating from 1813, required members to parade at 9 o'clock on penalty of a fine of one shilling. Article XXI named a similar fine for quarrelling, making a disturbance or 'raising a mutiny' at the race.[92] 'My Lord' needed considerable strength of character to exert control, whatever written rules existed.

After the formal meeting there was a procession to the site of the race. The flags or banners were an important part of the procession. Here they are at Aberlady:

> The hinds their banner bore on high
> Wi' mony a lood triumphant cry
> What 'Speed the plough' we could descry
>   Their motto for the Race.[93]

25. 'A laddie and auld meer', a pen and ink drawing by James Howe (1780–1836). *National Museums of Scotland.*

There is a clear implication that there were ploughmen among the membership. The horses were adorned with ribbons 'till even [they] themselves seemed vain of their trappings'.[94]

David Macbeth Moir (1798–1851), essayist, novelist and poet, was born in Musselburgh and practised medicine there from 1817. In his novel *Mansie Waugh* (1828) he gave a description of the carters' races at Cousland, including the animals' decorations:

What a sight of ribbons was on the horses! Many a crame [a merchant's booth or stall] must have been emptied ere such a number of manes and long tails could have been busked out. The beasts themselves, poor things, I dare say, wondered much at their bravery, and no less I am sure did the riders. They looked for all the world like living haberdashery shops. Great bunches of wallflower, thyme, spearmint, and southernwood, were stuck in their button holes; and broad belts of stripped silk, of every colour in the rainbow, were flung across their shoulders. As to their hats, a man would have had a clear ee that could have kent what was their shape or colour. They were all rowed round with ribands, and puffed about the rim, with long green or white feathers; and cockades were stuck on the off side, to say nothing of long strips fleeing behind them in the wind, like streamers. Save us! to see men so proud of finery: if they had been peacocks one would have thought less; but in decent sober men, the heads of small families, and with no great wages, the thing was crazy-like. Was it not?[95]

At Haddington they rode in a body to the Sands at Nungate Bridge and on their way visited the public schools and asked the schoolmasters to give the schoolchildren 'the play' to see the races.[96] There was also a school holiday at Pathhead. In the procession to the races, and in the request – always granted – for the children to be allowed to join the procession and to watch the fun, we have a clear picture of the carters' play involving the whole of the working-class community.

THE CARTERS' RACES

The racecourse was usually a stretch of public road (as at Haddington, East Linton, Pathhead, Cousland, Dalkeith, Gilmerton), though the sands were used at Leith, and for a time a field at Cousland. It seems to have been generally understood that only 'common bred work horses' were to race, though this is only rarely stated explicitly.[97]

In 1835 Thomas Watson, a gardener, described the preliminaries at Lasswade in verse:

> Then they bouk in their horse to rin
>   Wi' many sair reflections;
> And for a while there's nothing done
>   For flyting in a' directions;
> Till forward speaks bald [bold] Johnnie Fox
>   His drink being gey weel in
> 'That horse is not into our box
>   And not a fit he'll rin
>   Wi' us this day'.[98]

In other words, the owner of the horse in question was not a member of the Lasswade carters' society, and so was not eligible to run in the race.

The most detailed accounts of racing are from Haddington:

The races were held on the public road to the west of the town. The carters on their horses lined the road for ¼ mile on each side from Smail's Pond, now part of the gasworks manager's garden, while the public ranged themselves behind fences. There were 6 or 8 races ... prizes were horse shoes, saddles, bridles. As might be expected, many of the riders were indifferent horsemen, and it was rare fun to see them lashing their horses to gain the races, and riding as it were, faster than the animals were going.

Then they passed on to the race field. The last race was run in Plum Park, just inside the road wall, and hundreds of on-lookers thronged the wall and roadway. There were three hurdles with brushwood to be jumped. Though cart horses, they were light-legged animals. Some may have had their day following the hounds. Others had dragged the Laird's coach. The last race was won by a big chestnut horse owned by a Rosehall carter, and ridden by the Carters' horse-coper quack-doctor. By this time there was scarcely a remnant of the hurdles left, and as the horse came on he crushed and plunged through them. Before he reached the winning post he was shouting 'Bat the drum! Bat the drum! Am furst! Am furst!' [99]

A certain amount is also known about the race at Dalkeith because of the involvement of the well-known character, 'Camp Meg', Margaret Hawthorn (d. 1827). She lived alone near the Roman camp on top of the hill between Gorebridge and Edgehead and travelled the area as a horse doctor. One of her horses, 'Snowball', was successful against an animal owned by a Dalkeith innkeeper named Cossar, and she made a song to celebrate. [100]

The course was from Croft's Park to Gallowshall Toll, Newbattle Toll, Benbught and back to the start, a distance of 1½ miles. This was unusual since most carters' races were run 'out and back'. Dalkeith races were defunct by 1860 when there was an attempt to revive them on the Saturday after the October fair.

Moir's quasi-fiction is more vivid than any historical account:

The race course was along the high road; and, dog on it, they made a noise like thunder, throwing out their big heavy feet behind them, and whisking their tails from side to side as if they had dung out one another's een, till, not being used to gallop, they at last began to funk and fling; syne first one stopping, and then another, wheeling round and round like peeries, in spite of the riders whipping them, and pulling them by the heads ... so back they came ... all the folk crying, and halloing, and clapping their hands – some 'weil done the lame ane – five shillings on the lame ane,' – and others, 'Weil run Bonaparte – at him, auld Bonaparte – two to one Whitey beats him all to sticks,' – when, dismal to relate, the limping-legged ane couped the creels [collapsed and died], and old white Bonaparte came in with his tail cocked amid loud cheering, and no small clapping of hands.[101]

The Carters' Society at Musselburgh insisted that on its annual meeting day 'the meeting of this Society shall be dismissed at an early hour; that this institution be noted for its regularity and not for dissipation'.[102] At Prestonpans the position was ambiguous: members were to be sober, and were not 'to stop and drink at public house doors' on penalty of one shilling.

At the racecourse were confectioners' stalls: at Aberlady the sale of sherbet drinks, lucky bags, and sugar-bools is mentioned, and at Pathhead it is known that travelling confectioners came from Dalkeith.[103] Only at Leith was there a complete fair with all the attractions including boxing and dancing booths, pints of gooseberries for sale, and 'paltry bands of music making din enough for a coronation'.[104]

AFTER THE RACES

At Haddington alone is there evidence of additional rituals after the races. A cat was killed: this was unique among the carters' plays although it did take place elsewhere in Scotland.[105] There is a strong suggestion at Haddington of a survival from before the Reformation. Even older, a vestige of sun worship, was the final act at Haddington:

the carters ... continued to ride their 'Bassies' for three times in a circle opposite the cross, which terminated the horseman-ship of the Carters' Race-Day.[106]

In some villages the Society's flags were auctioned to augment the funds. What was sold was not the flag itself, but the right to carry it the following year. The procession at Penicuik consisted of: 'the village band, then the president of the society ... after him followed the standard-bearer, who, at some financial cost to himself, occupied this coveted position.[107] At Gilmerton some of the sums paid for this distinction are known, and they vary quite widely: 3s 6d in 1803, 19s 6d in 1805.[108]

The two essential events after the races were the dinner and then the dancing, sometimes under the name of a ball. The dancing was led off by My Lord and his Leddy. The evening continued in dancing and drinking which is mentioned by historians but never described. Watson, however, went into affectionate detail:

> And ilka one that wants a lass
>   O lang he need na want
> For I am sure, if truth shall pass
>   This day they are not scant;
> They're here wi' curls baith broad and wide
>   There some drawn tight wi' laces
> And some wi' combs stuck at a side
>   And some gay weel-fared faces
>   Are here this day.
>
> Into the ale-house they are drawn
>   Wi' a' their braws sae gay
> To get a share o' what is gaun
>   And crack about the Play.
> They hand them aye the ither cap
>   And aye they press the tipple;
> And when they've gotten in their drap
>   They chew ginge'bread like apple
>   Fu' sweet that day.
>
> But night is bye, and mornin's in;

There's mony a weary frame
Ere these queer bodies do begin
To tak' the road they came.
When they get hame, they then, nae doubt
Amang the blankets creep
And there at last they ha'd it out
Beside auld daddy Sleep
Their friend that morn.[109]

THE END OF THE CARTERS' PLAYS

Most of the carters' plays ended around 1860. At Pathhead the last
play was in 1855, and the plays had come to an end at Dalkeith
before 1860.[110] At Penicuik the last Whipman Play was in 1864, the
same date as the last races at Tranent.[111] The last carters' races took
place at Haddington in 1858: the number of carters had fallen after
the opening of the railway ten years earlier.

In 1838 Leith races were revived without any thoroughbred events
and they had a disorderly existence, condemned by the Kirk Session,
until 1859. They were called 'Subscription' races – the subscribers
were the shopkeepers who had contributed money, in distinction to
the earlier Leith races which had been under the patronage of the
City of Edinburgh. The day began with the carters' procession behind
flags, banners, and a band. There were separate races for cart, van
and coach horses, 'a shabby display of horses, respectable in the
draught, but contemptible in the saddle'. These practices were
borrowed, both from the original Leith races, but also from the
carters' plays: the carters' imitation of Leith had been re-imported
there. At Leith there were also sack races, pig races, and donkey
races 'almost on the level of *Anster Fair*'.[112] These races were less of
a local event than the other carters' plays and attracted a range of
minor showmen with attractions such as the wheel of fortune, prick
the garter and rowley-powley. The last running of Leith Subscription
Races coincided with the vanishing of most of the other carters'
plays.

The middle-class view that the carters' plays were uncivilized was
the main reason for their being brought to an end. We have already
heard the views of the minister of Gilmerton, and South Leith Kirk

Session condemned the Subscription Races.[113] In 1858 the sale of liquor on the Leith sands was prohibited,[114] and commercial interest in organising the event disappeared. In 1859, the final year, a steamer 'accidentally' ran onto the sands and thirsty individuals climbed on board.[115] At Pathhead it was the road trustees who forbade the races. They were transferred to a field at Muttonhole Farm (now Whitburgh Mains), but crops were damaged and the farmer refused to give further help. Significantly, the carters' play was replaced as the local festival by the horticultural society show – static, decorous, open to control by the gentry for 'The Society is managed by an *Executive* consisting of three honorary presidents, president, vice-president, secretary, and a committee selected from the membership'.[116] This mild bureaucracy is quite different from the election of 'My Lord' on the morning of the race, who would be master of the revels like Robin Hood in the May Day celebrations in Edinburgh, or the Abbot of Narent in other Scottish burghs, a custom which had been suppressed with some difficulty after the Reformation. The substitution of the horticultural show can be compared with the collapse of the races at Newton-on-Ayr after they were displaced from their traditional site on the sea front: in both cases the genteel and the disciplined replaced the lively and the traditional. At Cousland the carters' dinner was held in the local school until a new building was built by the County Council: they did not allow the society to use it. Instead, a joiner's shop was used, and then the Cousland play was amalgamated with the one at Pathhead, and it soon came to an end.

The Gilmerton Play and the West Linton Whipman Play survived into the twentieth century because they changed: it was their derivatives, not the traditional plays, which continued. The traditional Whipman Play was last held in 1877.[117] Some years later it was revived by local gentlemen who transformed it into the local sports day. Gilmerton Play was able to continue after the horse-racing had stopped because the events were modified. In its last, respectable, phase, there were still memories of the 'Old Play', which had been far more rowdy.[118] It is not clear when the Old Play ended, though one writer speaks of it as being in the past in 1904.[119] At Aberlady also the Play continued after the racing had stopped.[120]

The names of the cart-horses at Leith Subscription Races show some aspects of the people's culture. Some referred to local place names (*Gala Water*), others to figures in popular literature (*Donald Dhu, Maggie Lauder*), and many were familiar names for women (*Jessie*). The names of military heroes were also used (*Blucher*). In contrast, the gentlemen's horses which ran in other events at the same meeting had names from the world of gambling (*Potluck*) or a different kind of literature (*Cynthia*).[121]

William Reid painted the last running of the Subscription Races, though since his picture shows stalls selling drink on the sands it is better to look at it as a composite image of the final years of the Races.[122] There are also card-sharpers, thimble riggers, Punch and Judy, and a fight. He shows in the centre of the painting a man lying on the sand yet still able to drink out of a bottle: this, in more than one sense, is the spirit of the picture.

The same flexible word was used in a description of the Kipper Fair at Newton-on-Ayr:

> grey morning saw many a one 'toddlin' hame' under the erratic guardianship of Sir John Barleycorn ... this makes us seriously question how far such festivities are in accordance with the advancing spirit of the age.[123]

REFERENCES

1. Mandell (1984), 136–41.
2. Warrick (1899), 309–11.
3. *EA*, 31 March 1840. The bridge is over the North Esk.
4. Seton (1896), i, 444.
5. Anon. (1842), 126.
6. Fergusson (1974), 178.
7. Fairfax-Blakeborough (1973), 41; *AJ*, 17 September 1845.
8. E. D. Cuming, 1926, quoted by Fairfax-Blakeborough (1973), 266.
9. Fairfax-Blakeborough (1973), 257.
10. Robertson (1795), 47.
11. Geikie (1841), 43.
12. Anon. (1893), 300.
13. Fergusson (1974), 176.
14. Geikie (1841), 42.
15. Geikie (1841), 42.

16. Geikie (1841), 43.
17. Campbell (1827), 184–5.
18. *GH*, 17 October 1828.
19. *EA*, 20 October 1840.
20. Rogers (1884), ii, 311–14.
21. Mason (1826), 66.
22. Mason (1826), 65.
23. From an anonymous journal: I am grateful to Professor Alexander Fenton for this reference.
24. *AA*, 29 August 1822.
25. Smith (1865), ii, 292.
26. Marwick (1890), 97.
27. *PA*, 13 August 1825.
28. *GC*, 4 August 1746.
29. *PA*, 13 August 1825.
30. *PA*, 10 August 1833.
31. *PA*, 2 August 1834.
32. *PA*, 23 April 1836.
33. *PA*, 11 June 1836.
34. *PA*, 13 August 1836 and 24 August 1839.
35. *PA*, 23 April 1836.
36. *PA*, 13 August 1836.
37. *GH*, 21 August 1840.
38. *AA*, 25 August 1853.
39. *GH*, 16 August 1858.
40. *GH*, 13 August 1860.
41. *RI*, 29 August 1857.
42. *GH*, 16 August 1870.
43. *NSA*, vii, 405, 110, 45.
44. Burrell (1997), 59.
45. *KWP*, 8 May 1858.
46. Warrick (1899), 308–9.
47. Aiton (1811), 570.
48. Aiton (1811), 574.
49. Aiton (1811), 576.
50. For qualification of this statement, see Fairfax-Blakeborough (1973), 213–22.
51. *EEC*, 15 June 1845.
52. More details are given in Burnett (1999).
53. The standard history is Strawhorn (1985).
54. McNeill (1957–68), iv, 115.
55. Salvio (1970), 7–8.
56. For example, *A&SH*, 1 September 1860.
57. Marwick (1890), 70.
58. *AA*, 27 August 1891.
59. Strawhorn (1985), 98.

60. Fairfax-Blakeborough (1973), 200.
61. Strawhorn (1985), 124.
62. Strawhorn (1985), 124.
63. *AA*, 26 August 1852.
64. *A&SH*, 2 September 1865.
65. *AA*, 20 August 1864.
66. *A&SH*, 19 August 1865.
67. *A&SH*, 27 August 1864.
68. *AA*, 27 August 1891.
69. McDowall (1986), 335.
70. McDowall (1986), 334; Robertson (1974), 191.
71. A Burgess (1830), 122–3. Strawhorn (1985) gives the date as 1838 but does not give his source (146–7).
72. *AA*, 18 August 1842, *A&SH*, 13 August 1864.
73. Carnegie Library, Ayr: Newton Council Book, 1794–1815, B6/27/3, 25.
74. *AA*, 19 August 1852.
75. *A&SH*, 13 August 1864.
76. *AA*, 21 August 1862.
77. Hugh L. Allan, *Ayr Half a Century Ago: and since*, a collection of cuttings from the *Ayr Advertiser*, c. 1889, 11 (Carnegie Library, Ayr).
78. *AA*, 21 August 1862.
79. *AA*, 22 August 1872.
80. These names date from the 1820s.
81. Hogg (1981), 17.
82. Guthrie (1885), 76.
83. McNeill (1957–68), iv, 60–2.
84. McNeill (1957–68), iv, 98.
85. Campbell (1827), 188; Irons (1897), i, 415–16; Banks (1937–41), iii, 32–3.
86. Watson (1835), 36.
87. Dickson (1911), 112.
88. *Rules and Tables of the Haddington Carters' Friendly Society* (1832). Scottish Record Office FS 9/3/19.
89. *Rules and Regulations of the Whipman Society of Peebles and Adjoining Parishes* (1829), 5–6. SRO FS 1/19/1.
90. Cameron (1986), 14–17.
91. Dickson (1907), 156.
92. *ELC*, 25 June 1965; Articles of the Carters' Friendly Society, Haddington Library A1–26S.
93. Martine (1890), 8–9, quoting J. R. Reid of Aberlady.
94. Dickson (1907), 156.
95. Moir (1828), 201–2.
96. *HC*, 26 June 1926.
97. *Articles of the Prestonpans United Society of Carters* (1829). SRO FS 1/9/8.
98. Watson (1835), 36.
99. *HC*, 7 August 1926.

100. Carrick (1907), 292–3.
101. Moir (1828), 206–7.
102. *Articles of the New Society of Carters and Others in Musselburgh and Fish-errow* (1841), 6. SRO FS 1/17/169.
103. Martine (1890), 9; Dickson (1911), 112.
104. Hudson (1910), 19–22.
105. Hall (1805), i, 165.
106. Martine (1883), 101.
107. Wilson (1981), 187.
108. Cash Book of Gilmerton Junior Friendly Society, Edinburgh Central Library.
109. Watson (1835), 38–9.
110. Dickson (1911), 113; Carrick (1907), 293.
111. Wilson (1891), 187.
112. *Scotsman*, 21 July 1838.
113. Robertson (1925), 146; Marshall (1976), 55–61.
114. *EEC*, 18 September 1858.
115. Hudson (1910), 22–3.
116. Dickson (1911), 119–20.
117. Clark (1987). See also McNeill (1957–68), iv, 194–6.
118. McNeill (1957–68), iv, 98–100.
119. Carrick (1904), 88.
120. Martine (1890), 10.
121. *EEC*, 3 August 1850.
122. In Huntly House Museum, Edinburgh.
123. *AA*, 21 August 1845.

CHAPTER SEVEN

Burgh Sports

There were a number of burgh sports which were held annually, or less frequently, and which were more closely associated with burgh life than were the horse races. The races involved landed patrons from the surrounding country, but burgh sports were typically restricted to the members of the incorporated trades, which was the collective name for the guilds, or to inhabitants of the burgh.

The oldest of these competitions are the two siller guns, at Dumfries and Kirkcudbright, both of which date from 1587–88 and they are described in detail below. The shoots for these prizes took place on the king's birthday. Other burghs established archery prizes soon after. These seem to have been open both to townsmen and to local men of property: the custom of the winner adding a silver medal to celebrate his victory suggests that only those who could afford to pay for a medal took part in the archery. Thus, by the time archery emerges as a sport rather than as practice for war, it is no longer an activity for all adult males.

Instead of horse races, some burghs had foot races. At Inverkeithing there was the Hat and Ribbon Race. The Fastern's E'en Race at Kilmarnock is described below, and there were also foot races in the small burghs up the Irvine Valley from Kilmarnock, and at Eaglesham, on the other side of Fenwick Moor.

All the events which are described in this chapter and the preceding one were to an extent special, being held no more than annually. The full picture of sporting activity in a Scots burgh between 1660 and 1860 would include the play on bowling greens, some paid for by the town council itself, games such as kyles in or beside inns or howffs, and boys playing shinty in the street.

SHOOTING COMPETITIONS
Hand-held firearms were first made on the Continent in the fifteenth

century and a culverin had reached Scotland by 1489. James IV used one to shoot seabirds from a boat – or more likely, he shot *at* seabirds. Given the cost of a gun in the sixteenth century shooting must have been a sport for a tiny minority, though in 1552 James Henderson asked the Town Council of Edinburgh for the ground between Greyfriars Port and the Kirk o' Fields (the area around the modern Chambers Street) to be set aside for shooting with the bow, crossbow and *culvering*.[1] *Culverings* were among the weapons which could be brought to wapenschaws, according to an Act of Parliament of 1540.[2]

Early shooting competitions were all associated with burghs. For example, in March 1557 Edinburgh Town Council made a payment to one of their own number, a goldsmith:

> Item, for twa silver culverings to Michael Gilbert to gif the young men occasioun to leir to schut with the culvering, price theirof XLs.[3]

Later, there are traces of shooting competitions elsewhere. In 1721, 55 'Residenters in Ayrshire' said they would support 'the Pryse of Irvine to be shott for with gunns'. The prize itself had been presented by Hugh Montgomerie of Hartfield: unfortunately its nature is not known.[4] There is a record of a shooting competition at Kilmarnock which came to an end about 1740, when the prize money was diverted to the construction of a bowling green.[5]

THE DUMFRIES SILLER GUN

The Siller Gun was a shooting competition held at Dumfries, named after its trophy. It is usually said that it dates from 1617 when James VI visited the Burgh while returning from Edinburgh to London. However, the initials on the gun are those of Roger Gordon, provost in 1588, and it was probably connected with the burgh's application in the same year for a new fair and other privileges.[6] The other surviving siller gun, that of Kirkcudbright, also bears the initials of a provost, Sir Thomas McLellan of Bombie, who held the office in 1587/88. 1587 was the year when James VI came of age in two senses: chronologically, and in that his mother was executed, and he became king of Scots without question.

The Dumfries Siller Gun itself is said to have been a cannon mounted on a wheel carriage, in total ten inches long, all of silver. In time, it was reduced to the barrel only – it was probably handled roughly on the day of the shoot – and according to McDowall the butt now present was added about 1810.[7] The competition at first was held as part of a wapenschawing, and was probably annual, although the dates of the sixteenth and seventeenth century shoots are not known. They were held on the Kingholm, a flat piece of ground on the banks of the Nith whose name indicates an earlier royal gift to the burgh.[8] The Kirkcudbright gun is a simple culverin, a barrel without a mount, and one suspects that this was the original form of the Dumfries gun. The guns were intended to be worn in the victor's hat, and a wheeled gun carriage would have made it rather large.

There were shoots for the siller gun on 20 occasions between 1723 and 1831, but the next one did not take place until 1901. The first account in verse concerns the shoot of 1777, and the earliest prose account dates from two years later.

In 1779 the *Dumfries Journal* recorded:

Friday last, being the anniversary of his majesty's birth day (who entered into the 42d year of his age) the same was observed here with particular demonstrations of loyalty and joy, but particularly by the incorporated trades of this place. The morning was ushered in by ringing of bells, which continued at proper intervals through the whole day. The seven Incorporated Trades, viz. hammermen, squaremen, weavers, taylors, skinners, shoemakers and butchers, headed by their conveneer and re-spective deacons, and accompanied by their journeymen and apprentices, amounting in whole to upwards of one thousand, with drums beating, colours flying, and fiddles playing, marched out of the town to a place called the Craigs, in order to shoot for the Silver Gun, which was given to them by one of our Scots monarchs, for the purpose of training them in the use of arms. Being arrived at the place, the masters proceeded to shoot for the Gun, which was won by the incorporation of Squaremen. The journeymen and apprentices at the same time began to shoot for their prize (a new hat) which was likewise won by the Squaremen. The number of spectators assembled on this occasion, was amazing: the field was almost covered with booths for the entertainment of the populace. The above procession went out at nine o'clock in the morning, and returned a little after six in the evening, when the several incorporations separated, and went to different houses, where entertainments were provided for them, and so concluded the day with joy. – At six in the evening the magistrates and town-council, with several other gentlemen, assembled in the Court-house, where they drank his majesty's health, and many other local toasts.[9]

The fullest account of shooting at Dumfries was written by John Mayne (1759–1836) in *The Siller Gun*. It deals with the shoot of 1777. In its first version, published not long after the event, it consisted of 12 verses. By 1836 Mayne, though living in Gloucester, had expanded it to five cantos, 275 verses, 1650 lines. Mayne knew and loved his subject, and he drew it in detail with the aid of his large Scots vocabulary. The events he described had survived the moral constraints of the kirk in one of its more severe periods, and had not yet been affected by the evangelicalism, prudishness and desire for social control which limited behaviour. His rumbustious verses are in the same spirit. Mayne's weakness is that he has no sense of structure or drama. Between the 1808 and 1836 editions he completely altered the order of the verses, moving blocks backwards and forwards, cutting a little, adding much. It makes no difference, except that there is more to enjoy.

The actual shoot for the siller gun is not the centre of gravity of Mayne's poem, or even the centre of levity. The various processions were equally important, and the fight between the soutars and the tailors is the most vigorous and memorable section.

The Siller Gun begins slowly, acclaiming the event and the admirable qualities of King George III. With the fourth and fifth stanzas we discover that Mayne's talent is for description:

> For weeks before this Féte sae clever
> The fowk were in a perfect fever
> Scouring gun-barrels in the river –

> At marks practising –
> Marching wi' drums and fifes for ever –
> A' sodgerizing!
>
> And turning coats, and mending breeks
> New-seating where the sark-tail keeks; [shirt-tail peeps out]
> (Nae matter though the clout that eeks
> Be black or blue;)
> And darning, with a thousand steeks,   [stitches]
> The hose anew!.[10]

He emphasises how special the day is going to be, how much it is anticipated: in effect, the festival begins weeks before the day of the shoot. Its elements are rehearsed piecemeal over and over again. After all, it is a long time since the last performance:

> Between the last and this occasion
> Lang, unco lang, seem'd the vacation
> To him wha wooes sweet recreation
> In Nature's prime;
> And him wha likes a day's potation
> At ony time![11]

This is the sixth stanza of the first canto, and Mayne has made the first of many references to drink. When it comes to drink, Mayne is the most direct writer on traditional festivals, repeatedly mentioning the alcoholic miasma which enveloped the proceedings. Fergusson, a far more skilful poet, manages to suggest this by the feeling he gives for the tone of Leith Races and Hallow Fair; his direct references to drink are few, for he is more concerned with the behaviour of the mildly drunk. Most other writers allow themselves a single reference, perhaps because it did not seem important, or because they believed in judicious concealment.

Mayne next brings the focus onto the part played by the social institutions of the burgh, for the first round of drinking is supplied by the deacons of the several trades:

> At first, fornent ilk Deacon's hallan
> His ain brigade was made to fall in;

> And, while the muster-roll was calling
> > And joybells jowing
> Het pints, weel spic'd, to keep the saul in
> > Around were flowing.
>
> Broil'd kipper, cheese and bread, and ham
> Laid the foundation for a dram
> O' whisky, gin frae Amsterdam
> > Or cherry brandy;
> Whilk after, a' was fish that cam
> > To Jock or Sandy.[12]

There is an implication of smuggled goods here: the Hollands and brandy had probably been landed quietly somewhere on the Solway coast.

Not merely the dancing later in the day, but the whole proceedings are enlivened by music. Mayne names the musicians. There is auld Sandy Brown of Lochmaben, a renowned player on the hauteboy, but 'whozzling sair, and cruppen down'. Among the fiddlers was Jock Willison (*c.* 1746–1821), once a soutar. His new trade allowed room for his weakness:

> For, oh! poor Jock
> Cou'd ne'er gang soberly to bed
> > Like ither fo'k.[13]

The procession makes its way to the Maiden-Craigs, at the northern end of the ridge which runs south from Dumfries towards Caerlaverock, where the shooting is to take place. The people and the competitors march together, accompanied by musicians, and when they arrive they find that:

> Craems, ginge-bread-stawns, legerdemain
> > And raree-shows
> Entic'd young sparks to entertain
> > And treat their joes.[14]

The shoot for the siller gun is the first great comic section of the poem. Drink, nervousness, and unfamiliarity with firearms all contribute to the fun: there is an element of unrule, for it is the established members of the community who are making fools of themselves. They, too, are drunk:

> 'Tak a gude waught – I'm sure ye're weary,'
> Says Anny Kaillie to her deary:
> John, fain to see his wife sae cheary
>   Indulg'd the fun
> Gat fu', and dander'd lang and eerie
>   And tint his gun –[15]

> Steeking his een, big John M'Maff
> Held out his musquet like a staff;
> Turn'd, tho' the chiel was ha'f-and-ha'f
>   His head away
> And, panting, cried, 'Sirs! is she aff?'
>   In wild dismay![16]

Mayne also describes an event which has some basis in history, when one individual becomes so confused that he charges his gun not with one shot but with six, including the gunpowder with each one: when he pulls the trigger, the gun bursts:

> When his gun snappit, James M'Kee
> Charge after charge, charg'd to the ee:
> At length she bounc'd out owre a tree
>   In mony a flinner –
> 'For GUDE's sake, bairns! keep back!' cries he:
>   'There's sax shot in her!'[17]

A winner eventually appears:

> WILLIAM M'NISH, a Taylor slee
> Rouz'd at the thought, charg'd his fuzee;
> Took but ae vizzy wi' his ee –
>   The bullet flies
> Clean through the target to a tee
>   And wons the Prize![18]

The third Canto begins with the senior inhabitants of the burgh at a loyal dinner, whilst some younger people roam the countryside and others dance or talk. Mayne has already mentioned 'The sappy kiss, and squeeze, between / Ilk blithsome reel'. He now imagines a mother anxiously watching her daughter dancing while men admire her sexuality. A young couple, drunk on 'cauld whisky-punch, and ale, nut-brown' disappear:

> Aft to the whins, frae 'mang the thrang
> Some laddie and his lassy gang;
> But, O! the sports sae sweet and lang
>   Within that shade
> Beguile to mony a future pang
>   The yielding maid!
>
> 'Twas then, in ecstasy, he saw
> Her weel-turn'd ancle straught and sma'!
> Her neck, her heaving breast, and a'!
>   O! strange delight!
> Wow! what is man or maid ava
>   In sic a plight? [19]

There has been drinking, there has been sex: it is now time for wholesale violence. Some fighting has already taken place, for during the shoot:

> Wull Shanklin brought his firelock hither
> And cock'd it in an unco swither:
> Ae drucken Souter jeer'd anither
>   To come and learn –
> Fuff play'd the priming – heels owr ither
>   They fell in shairn! [20]

The large-scale fighting has a specific beginning, for word is brought to William Greer, Deacon of the Taylors, that the journeymen shoemakers are holding a procession of St Crispin. He is angry because it had been agreed that St Crispin would not be involved on this day. The shoemaker chosen to represent the saint appears in scarlet robes, with sash, star and garter, and a tailor fights him. Soon the tailor is:

> Besprent wi' blood, besprent wi' glar
> His ein japann'd, his chafts a-jar. [21]

A free fight finally ensues:

> Rushing like droves o' madden'd nowt
> Rob's party caus'd a gen'ral rout:
> Foul play or fair; kick, cuff, and clout
> > Right side, or wrang
> Friends feghting friends, rampag'd about
> > A drucken thrang!
>
> To furnish weapons for th' affray
> Craems, tents, and stawns, were swept away:
> Puist fowk, unus'd to cudgel-play
> > And doose spectators
> Were a' involv'd in this deray
> > Like gladiators![22]

From this scene, Mayne takes us to dinner in the Town Hall where coffee is being drunk, claret circulates, loyal and patriotic toasts are drunk, and the company sings 'God Save the King' and 'Rule, Britannia'. The poem ends with Convener Thomson telling his family of the day's events.

Mayne's poem was popular and no-one said that he exaggerated. How, then, are we to interpret his picture of alcoholic consumption on a massive, even heroic scale? *Heroic* is perhaps an appropriate word, for ordinary folk normally consumed only small ale: spirit-drinking was confined to special days. The shoot was an opportunity to do something memorable in honour of king and country.

The atmosphere of the Siller Gun festivities is echoed in a song about another fair, 'The Sports o' Glasgow Green'.[23] Significantly, it was sung to the tune of 'The Blythsome Wedding', another folk carnival. It begins with Jocky and Jenny walking to the fair together in their best clothes: when they come within sight of Glasgow Jenny goes into a *slap* – a gap in a wall or hedge – and puts on her stockings and shoes. There were no sports associated with Glasgow Fair, but the song describes the shows and stalls: dwarves, giants, Punch and Judy, prick the loop, dicing, and sellers of *black jock*, a mixture of sugar or treacle and spices. After seeing all of this on the Green, the pair go to Clyde Street where they enter Lucky M'Nee's howff. Some time later:

> Forfauchen wi' drinking and dancing
> The twa they cam' toddling hame;
> Wi' rugging and riving and drawing
> They baith were wearied and lame.[24]

The shoot for the Dumfries siller gun was thus a sporting event which was part of a holiday typical of festivals in large burghs. Sweeties and dram-drinking were as important as the shoot itself. Mayne did not exaggerate this aspect of the day, for after the shoot of 1796:

> the procession returned to the town in the same order as they marched out, only not quite so steady, and I believe a few required some help home.[25]

The siller gun was the true successor of the pre-Reformation May-day play, when the world was turned upside down. It had no place in the controlled world of Victorian Scotland. In 1885 it was said that:

> this festival has of late become unpopular, from the number of accidents by which it is characterized. The drinking is never postponed to the termination of sport. The consequence is riot and outrage. A case is recorded of a man having fired when so overcome by liquor that the gun was held for him by his friends, and yet he hit the mark and was declared victor, though he was not aware of his good fortune till next morning.[26]

The parallel shoot at Kirkcudbright, however, was smaller, more sober and more civic.

THE KIRKCUDBRIGHT SILLER GUN

The Kirkcudbright Siller Gun, now preserved there in the Stewartry Museum, is the prize for a shooting competition which was first held in 1587.[27] Tradition has it that the gun was given to the burgh by James VI: there is no reason to doubt it. Nothing is known about early competitions.

The first recorded shoot took place in 1781, to celebrate the coming of age of the Prince of Wales, later George IV. The demonstration of loyalty which this implies is a parallel to the shooting on the king's birthday at Dumfries. As at Dumfries, the competitors were the members of the Incorporated Trades. Their minute book records the arrangements. Each Trade was to assemble at their Deacon's house at nine o'clock, and the Trades came together an hour later at the Moat Wall, 'each Deacon to have a spantoun and sash if it can be got'. The articles list four citizens who were not members of the Incorporated Trades because of their profession, including an exciseman and a 'Notor Publick', two of whom were to superintend the shooting. The target was a door and these two individuals:

> shall mark every man's name that goes through the door [hits the target] with the two initial letters of his name on the door in each side of the ball hole. And at last when the members of each Trade hath fired their gun the man's ball hole that is nearest to the mark to receive the Silver Gun from them and have the honour to carry her home.[28]

Thus each competitor had one shot, and rifles were not allowed: as at Dumfries there was a large element of chance.

The next shoot took place in 1830 in honour of the Earl of Selkirk's 21st birthday. The rituals were similar to those of 1781, and the order of procession was detailed:

> Groat Gun – Officer – Advance Guard – Band – Town Officers with Halberts – Standard Bearer – General Boxmaster – Convener – Old Convener – General Clerk with Minute Book – Essay Masters – Squaremen, two and two – *Clothers* – Standard Bearer – Deacon with two Supporters – Essay masters two and two – Members two and two – *Weavers* in the same order – *Shoemakers* in the same order – *Tailors* in the same order – *Hammermen* in the same order

The order in which the trades marched was drawn by lot.

The Deacon Convener of the Incorporated Trades, Peter Ferguson, wrote a memoir of the shoot for the Kirkcudbright siller gun in 1830 in the minute book of the Incorporated Trades. It celebrated the coronation of George IV:

At four o'clock in the morning the bells commenced ringing a merry peal, flags were displayed from the Castle, Jail, and Vessels in the harbour and a drum and fife belonging to the Journeymen and Apprentices of different Trades – commonly called 'the boys' – beat through the town, roused the lieges and announced the approach of the intended ceremony. At six o'-clock two pieces of artillery placed upon the Quay were discharged. At seven, the different trades met at the houses of their respective Deacons; and at half past seven they all assembled on the school green, the Convener and Deacons with Swords and Sashes and each member with a musket, where they were joined by the Steward Substitute and several other respectable inhabitants.

At eight o'clock precisely the whole Cavalcade (about 200 in number) under the command of Convener Ferguson with the Siller Gun displayed from a Ribbon round his neck marched off ... The Masters were followed by the boys of each trade with their respective flags marshalled in the same order and preceded by drum and fife. The whole body then proceeded from the school green up St. Mary's Wynd and along High Street round the Castle where it passed under a grand suspension arch erected by Mr. Rankine, Timber Merchant, and Mr. Law, Watchmaker, extending from the Church to the Castle and richly decorated with evergreens; then along Castle Street where it passed under a triumphal arch similarly decorated erected by Mr. McKeachie, Builder, and Mr. Noble, Flesher ... and thereafter down the road to the Shore Park being that field lying on the West side of the road between Mutehill and Blackmurray plantation, where a target was erected for the occasion. Here the boys left the Masters and proceeded to a field further down the shore, to shoot for a hat and medal, where a target was also erected by them for the occasion.

Shortly after arriving on the field a discharge from the artillery gave the signal for the commencement of the competition for the royal prize. The Trades then commenced firing, each member one shot; when after an anxious struggle Mr. Robert Gaylor a member of the Shoemaker Trade gained the honours of the day. The trades were then formed into a hollow square by the Convener who after an appropriate speech placed the Siller Gun round the neck of the successful candidate amid long, loud and reiterated cheering; and the successful candidate thereafter took his place in the procession upon the right hand side of the deacon of his trade.

The Masters were then rejoined by the apprentices and three rounds from the cannon concluded the shooting. The procession returned to the town:

> Passing under [another] grand triumphal arch ... towards the Cross where they were received by the Magistrates and invited after the fatigues of the day to partake of a bumper of rum punch out of the bowl presented to the town by Hamilton of Bargeny in the year 1707 ... On this occasion the health of the Earl of Selkirk, the Steward Substitute, the Magistrates and the Minister of the town and parish was drunk with rapturous applause and the Magistrates pledged in a bumper the healths of the Convener and Incorporated Trades.

After which the procession moved to the Convener's house. On leaving them he expressed his warmest thanks to the Trades for the manner in which they had conducted themselves during the day and thereafter each Trade marched to the house of their respective Deacon where they deposited their insignia; and thus the ceremony finished.[29]

The overall picture is of a festival which drew in many aspects of town life and must have involved the whole population. All would have been wakened by the fife and drum, all would have heard the cannon. The Trades were central to the shape of the day, and there is no evidence of the large numbers of country people who swelled the crowd at Dumfries.

In 1781 and 1830 there was a separate shooting competition for the apprentices. In 1838, on the occasion of Queen Victoria's coronation, William Johnston, a merchant in the burgh, gave a silver arrow as their prize. It was made by William Law, the Kirkcudbright clockmaker, out of three half-crowns. It indicates an awareness of the tradition of shooting for burgh arrows.[30] After a gap of twenty-one years the next shoot celebrated the centenary of the birth of Burns. In the second half of the nineteenth century competitions were more frequent and were linked with local events including the opening of the first bridge over the Dee at Kirkcudbright.[31] No other Scottish sport was as closely integrated with the life of its burgh as the Kirkcudbright siller gun.

The argument has been advanced that carters' plays grew up in the area around Edinburgh in imitation of Leith races. In Dumfriesshire the copying of the shooting for the siller guns took place. There is a record of the Trades of Kirkpatrick Durham shooting for a silver medal in 1793, before dining together in the Old Assembly Room.[32] At Kirkmahoe the squaremen met on New Year's Day to shoot for a silver medal and a silk napkin.[33] The first of these may be a short-lived or even unique event, but the second probably continued for decades.

ARCHERY [34]

> How can I choose but mourne? When I think on
> Our games Olympic-like in times agone.
> Chiefly wherein our cunning we did try
> And matchless skill in noble archerie.
> Henry Adamson, *The Muses Threnodie* (1638)

In the Middle Ages archery was not as important in Scotland as in England – as the English archers demonstrated at Falkirk, Homildon Hill, and elsewhere. James I was in captivity in England at the time of the Battle of Agincourt, and campaigned with the English in France in 1420–22. After he returned to Scotland he required all men to practise archery on Sundays (1424). Men were required to practise after mass, and burghs to set up butts. Subsequent monarchs repeated the instruction, accompanying it with the well-known prohibitions of other sports, particularly football and golf. Whilst the ultimate purpose of archery was to increase military strength, many of those who practised would never have fired a bow in anger, and war would have seemed a distant prospect to men on the bow butts. Almost as soon as practice began, archery was a leisure pursuit.

In 1528 six Scots defeated six Englishmen in an archery wager at St Andrews, so Scotland did have skilled archers, though a far smaller number than England. In his *Toxophilus* (1545) Roger Ascham was critical of the Scots' proficiency with the bow: he was, however, writing at the time of Henry VIII's invasion of the south of Scotland, the 'Rough Wooing', so we cannot regard him as unbiased.[35]

Archery was encouraged in the burghs, and continued as a sport after it had ceased to be relevant in war. At Lanark in 1603, John Hastie leased land from the Burgh of Lanark for 13s 4d plus the responsibility of building and maintaining butts: the ground was on the flats beside the river at Clydesholm.[36] In 1605 there was still a bower in Glasgow, and in 1625 the Town Council told their Master of Works 'to repair the buttis in the Gallowmuir for exerceis of schutting quha pleissis'.[37] In places where archery had taken place in the churchyard it was moved elsewhere. This happened at Selkirk where the presbytery gave instructions for the removal of the butts in the second decade of the seventeenth century on the ground that archery was associated with gaming.[38] Much of the evidence for seventeenth-century archery, including the surviving prizes, concerns archery in the larger burghs, but it is known at other locations such as Markinch in Fife.[39]

Archery remained a source of vivid imagery. In a vicious pasquil against episcopacy written about 1640 by a Dundee schoolmaster, just one bishop escaped censure – George Graham, Bishop of Orkney:

> Good Orkney onlie liueth [liveth] right: is skilled in
>   archery craft
> His string is Loue, his marke is Christ, a steadfast faith
>   hes shaft.[40]

Within burgh archery grew the practice of competing for prizes. The earliest survivals are medals attached to the Musselburgh arrow. They date from 1603. Thus they are part of the pattern of the establishing of burgh sports during the reign of James VI.

The Royal Company of Archers was founded in 1676, the first

sporting society of any kind in Scotland. Its roots lie both in the Scots burgh competitions and in the continental shooting guilds. These guilds have existed on the Continent since at least the fourteenth century. The largest concentrations were and are in Germany and the Low Countries. They sometimes used longbows, but more often crossbows or guns. They were not craft organisations, as guilds in Scotland were, but rather existed for sociable reasons, and to provide hospitals and burials for their members.

Most of the seventeenth- and early eighteenth-century archery prizes were silver arrows. They were the property of the various burghs:

Musselburgh	1603	(first medal)
Miekelour or Rattray	1612	
St Andrews University	1618	(first medal)
Peebles	1628	(first medal)
Linlithgow or Hopetoun	1629	(first medal)
Selkirk	1660	(first medal)
Aberdeen Grammar School	1664	(first medal)
St Andrews University	1675	(first medal)
Stirling	1678	(first record of the competition: the arrow does not survive)
St Andrews University	1704	(first medal)
Edinburgh	1709	
Musselburgh	1713	
Kilwinning	1724	
Dalkeith	1727	(first medal)

It is noteworthy that there are ten competitions which are known to have been in existence before the Edinburgh Arrow. This is evidence for a sport which had become deeply embedded in burgh life, for the burghs were not following the lead of the capital. All of the early silver arrows come from the east of Scotland or the Borders: the first in the west is the Kilwinning Arrow whose origin lies in archers from Edinburgh moving to Ayrshire.

The most important arrow extant is the Musselburgh Arrow, which bears a sequence of medals which runs from 1603 to the present day. Most of the medals are decorated with heraldic devices. One early one bears only a rose: it was added by Alexander Hay, the king's bowmaker, in 1667. Hay also won the Peebles Arrow in 1663. Hay's rose has something of a swagger, the pleasure in his status and his joy at the restoration of the Monarchy. The medals are not symbols of triumphs but of small victories. That for 1702 shows the winner, the advocate Robert Dundas, speaking to two other archers. His words are 'Hodie mihi', emphasising that he has been victor on the day, indicating the transitory nature of his success.

To win a prize three times was taken to be a great feat, and this happened to the Edinburgh Arrow. R. Dobie of Stoneyhill achieved it in 1649, and thus won the arrow. He returned it to the burgh. The next was George Drummond who commemorated himself with three enormous medals, the final one bearing the words:

> GEORGE DRUMMOND Merchant in Edinr Haveing won this Silver Arrow three times successively, And thereby according to Antient custome, Proprietor thereof. Doeth of his free good will, with advyce of the Royall company of Archers, gift the same to the Town of Musselburgh to remaine with them as a perpetuall testimonie of his Respect to the said town, And for the encourageing of Archers in all time comeing, conforme to ane agreement past betwixt the Magistrats of the said town and the said George Drummond recorded in their books, and publicke Records, of ye date 18 day of July 1711.

A similar text appears in the minutes of the Royal Company.[41] The appearance of legal phrases on a sporting medal is unusual: so was the man. George Drummond was a merchant and manipulator, six times Lord Provost of Edinburgh, one of the godfathers of the Edinburgh medical school. His string-pulling activities went far beyond archery. There was probably a social expectation that he would return the Arrow to the Burgh of Musselburgh; one is not surprised to learn that he was paid 56 pounds Scots for his 'civility' in doing so.

The winner in 1735 was John Murray of Broughton (1718–77). The reverse of his medal is engraved with the figure of a Roman soldier: from a cloud above emerges a hand which holds a sword which is striking the soldier. The motto is 'Dulce et decorum est pro patria mori' – it is sweet and fitting to die for one's country.[42] Murray was Secretary to Prince Charles Edward Stuart in 1745–46 but because of illness was not present at Culloden. Murray gave himself up to government troops and turned King's Evidence: thus he emerged with his life but not his reputation. A further text has been added to the medal: 'Quantum mutatus ab illo [How much changed from what went before] – March 11th, 1747'. Murray was expelled from the Royal Company in 1748.

There are three early archery prizes which are not arrows: the Stirling Burgh Prize for Archery, 1698, a silver box; the Silver Bowl of the Royal Company of Archers, 1720; and the Kilwinning Coconut Cup, 1746. Each of these represents a development in the idea of the prize. Like the arrows, the silver bowl was the property of an incorporation, and winners add medals to it: the novelty was that it was not an arrow. It emphasised the sociable nature of sport, for it is a punch bowl. The Stirling prize was to be owned by its winner, and not returned to the burgh at the end of a year. It is the first prize of this kind in Scotland, the first sign of the shift from winning as an honour which the winner was allowed to commemorate publicly by purchasing a medal, to winning as an achievement which society should honour, in part a shift in the nineteenth century from giving to taking.

The Stirling prize, however, is still an obvious part of the equipment of archery. It bears an engraving of an archery scene and could have been used as a grease box. The Kilwinning cup is like the Stirling box a prize to be won, but it is otherwise unrelated to sport. It was for the butts competition which was held before the papingo shoot. It shows another step in the separation of the idea of winning from the idea of play.

Archery remained a sport for a small number of enthusiasts throughout the eighteenth century. From the 1780s its popularity grew and new competitions appeared: the Royal Company, in particular, was given several new prizes. The most important was the King's Prize of a piece of plate of £20 value, which was first shot for in 1788. As with the King's Prize at Leith Races, the winner chose and purchased a prize of at least the stated value, and then was paid £20. The prize for 1800 is preserved in the National Museums of Scotland, a plain silver tray won by Thomas Charles Hope (1766–1844), Professor of Chemistry.[43]

At the end of the eighteenth century archery was used as a focus for demonstrations of loyalty, as with the Dumfriesshire Royal Archers who first met on the Kingholm at Dumfries.[44] This may also have been the reason for the founding of a Company of Archers at Paisley in 1806. They acquired a silver arrow which is hallmarked 1809–10. The word *Company* indicates that they were following the Edinburgh model with its military flavour.

By the 1840s archery had become a more widespread recreation, and there were a dozen clubs in Scotland. Apart from the two Ayrshire clubs already mentioned there were others at Dalry and Saltcoats; in and around Glasgow were the Glasgow, St Mungo, Burnbank, Kinning Park, Paisley and Partick Archers; and in Edinburgh the Albyn Archers, Caledonian Bowmen, and the Edinburgh Salisbury Archers. Further south were the Bowmen of the Border. There had been a club at Ayr in the 1820s,[45] and one at Denny in Stirlingshire had an unusual trophy – a group of poisoned arrows from Africa.

One reason for the sport's popularity was that men and women could compete together, and it was not an unusual pastime among the gentry. Susan Ferrier mentioned it several times in her novel *The Inheritance* (1824) when she was describing life in a country house. The Ballochmyle Archeresses, as well as the Irvine Toxophilites, were present at the Eglinton Tournament.[46] Subsequently there were archery meetings at Ballochmyle House, the home of Claude Alexander. From the beginning, there was an equal number of competitions for men and women. The women's prizes were usually brooches – one suspects of medieval design – but sometimes there were golden arrows or the Sundrum Challenge Cup.[47]

The clubs of the 1840s were soon dwarfed by the Grand National Archery Meetings, first held at York in 1844. The aim of the Grand Nationals was to improve standards by offering national competitions. Scotland was included in their itinerant meetings, and the seventh Grand National was held in Edinburgh in 1850. Archery was growing rapidly in the 1850s: in 1859 an enthusiast said that two or three clubs were being formed in Scotland every month.[48] This was the zenith of archery.

Under the threat of a French invasion, the Volunteer movement was created the following year. Regiments were set up all over Scotland, England and Wales in a few months. The middle classes and gentry who had made up much of the membership of the archery clubs took up part-time soldiering and learned musketry. Competitive archery clubs continued, though fewer in number, but the traditional competitions, with archers whose practise is unlikely to have been assiduous, were left behind.

THE KILWINNING PAPINGO

The *papingo* or *popinjay* is a target for an archery competition. It is a wooden effigy of a parrot which is set up on a high place and shot from below. The aim is to dislodge the bird. Its supposed origin was an incident in Virgil's *Aeneid*. In Sicily Aeneas finds archers shooting at a tethered dove. One misses, but breaks the bindings holding the bird, then, to quote Gavin Douglas's translation:

> With arow reddy nokkyt than Ewricion
> Plukkis vp inhy hys bow ...
> Hys arow he threw vnder the clowdis blak
> And persyt hir quyte owtthrou the bak;
> Hyr lyfe sche lost heich vp in the ayr.[49]

Popinjay competitions are found from the late Middle Ages to the present day in the Low Countries, northern France, and sometimes elsewhere. How they reached Scotland, and Kilwinning in particular, is not clear, but it is likely that the practice was brought to Scotland from the Netherlands. Henry VIII was promoting them in London in the 1540s, there was a papingo at St Andrews in 1572, at Ayr in 1595, and at Irvine in 1665.[50]

The Kilwinning papingo was started in 1688: though it has often been said that it dates back to the fifteenth century, there is no evidence for this.[51] It was founded by William Baillie (1656–1740), an Edinburgh merchant and member of the Royal Company of Archers. In 1688 he married and – apparently with the dowry – bought the estate of Monkton, north of Prestwick. He then lived in a house belonging to 'his uncle' – this could mean his wife's uncle – on the south side of the Green at Kilwinning.[52] It is the accident of this uncle having property in Kilwinning which led to the revival of archery there, with the Irvine papingo, still within living memory, as a model. The Kilwinning papingo was a competition for burgesses, professional men and local lairds. In 1724 they acquired a silver

26. Kilwinning Abbey, where the shoot for the papingo still takes place.

27.   Medal of Robert, Lord Dalkeith (Earl of Morton), 1622.

arrow, following the model of several Scots burghs, and they added medals to record their victories.

The earliest medals attached to the arrow are small, weighing no more than 10g. Like most of the eighteenth-century medals they do no more than commemorate the victor: there is no accompanying text or image. The name is stated, the year, and either his [denomination] or the profession, 'surgeon in Beith', 'schoolmaster in Kilwinning'. There is something of the headstone in the lapidary phrases. The first medal to be significantly larger is that of the Earl of Eglinton (35g), who won by proxy in 1731. The first with armorial bearings was added in 1756 by Gavin Ralston of Ralston, and it is unusual in having thistles worked into the rim. The other medals do not carry explicitly Scottish symbols. In 1764 a brief fashion was set of embellishing the reverse of the medal with the image of a flying bird being stuck by an arrow, and of complementing it with a motto. This reveals how flexible an image the papingo was by the middle of the eighteenth century: *Spero meliora* (1764), *Res antiquae laudis et artis aggredior* (1766), *Par hazard* (1768) and *Sine sanguine victor* (1770).

The 1785 medal, added by Captain Crookshanks of Bogside, is one of the two remarkable medals on the Kilwinning Arrow. The

28. The medal added to the St Andrews Arrow in 1697 by James Bethune of
Balfour, illustrating the passage from the *Aeneid* which may have been the literary
inspiration for the Kilwinning papingo.

image is of Cupid in a grove of trees, firing upwards at a disembodied
heart. There is a poem on the reverse:

> Cupid beyond my wish hath favoured me
> Your Captain ladies, this night I am to be
> Your hearts the prize, all Archers aim at
> Twang goes the Bow, Dear girls have at it
> Good ladies, pray put on your best attire
> I am in your Bosoms, the Celestial Fire
> Come not, in maiden beauties, coyest mood
> But, smiling look, as ye wou'd be Wooed.

This is far from the established graveyard or commemorative spirit.
There is an echo of the *fête galante*. A painting by Nicholas Lancret
of *le tir à l'arc* was engraved with a verse below it, which asked, is
this not a frivolous occupation? and answered no, it will allow the
winner to impress *sa maîtraisse*.[53]

In the nineteenth century the medals slowly increased in size until

29.   The medal added to the St Andrews Arrow in 1754 by Lord Doune, later the
Earl of Moray, with a view of St Andrews.

many of them weighed 50g. Then in 1833, a second outstanding
medal was presented. It was 80mm in diameter weighing 120g –
quarter of a pound of silver – more like a pennystane than the record
of a local archery competition. It says 'The Captainship of the
Kilwinning Pipings was obtained by Charles Lamb the Youngr ...'
This is Lord Eglinton's friend, who was later to figure prominently
in the Tournament. It was made in London: thus the error of *pipings*
for *papingo*.

   Archery was particularly popular between 1830 and 1860: old
competitions were revived, as at St Andrews, and new clubs sprang
up, most of them in Edinburgh and Glasgow. By the 1840s the
Kilwinning papingo was widely known and with the increasing
popularity of archery in the cities, and the opening of the railway to
Glasgow in 1840, it became a well-attended event. Most of the leading
competitors came from the city, such as J. G. Tennant of St Rollox
bleach works and John Findlay, 'gingham and pullicate manufacturer.' After 1860 the Volunteer movement encouraged rifle shooting
and its many competitions at local, county and national levels completely swamped the activities of occasional archers: the sport
survived in the hands of highly competitive target archers who had
their own competitions which were distinct from traditional events
such as the papingo. The papingo itself continued as long as its

enthusiastic patrons lived: the deaths of the 13th Earl of Eglinton in 1861 and of his distant kinsman Hugh Montgomerie of Bourtreehill in 1866, left it without support, and it was last held in 1870.

FASTERN'S E'EN AT KILMARNOCK

The distinctive event on Fastern's E'en at Kilmarnock was a foot

30.. The 13th Earl of Eglinton at the time of the Burns Festival of 1844.

race. It was a major holiday in Kilmarnock until 1840. The events
of Fastern's E'en were described in verse by John Ramsay, who wrote
of the event as it was in the late 1830s. One distinctive feature of
the day was the demonstration that the burgh's fire engine was able
to pump water over the highest buildings, particularly the church.
This showed the equipment was in good order. It was also an
opportunity to clean the streets, as at the Kipper Fair at
Newton-on-Ayr, and echoes the scouring of gun-barrels and the
mending of clothes before the siller gun at Dumfries.

By the time Ramsay as narrator arrives in the middle of the burgh
it has already been shown that the fire engine is effective, and Jock
Stewart is now picking out individuals for a drenching. Some are
willing to join in:

> And aye the callans were as keen
> To stand and get a blatter
> As they had Roman Cath'lics been
> And it a' holy water.[54]

Others, less so:

> Neist fluttered by a stranger Miss
> In fashion's finest glare
> Come in to town to taste the bliss
> And show and sell her ware.
> But what can a' this din excite
> This universal keckle?
> We turned about, and Jock, for spite
> Had spoiled her fishin' tackle.[55]

Evidently, a Glasgow prostitute has arrived by coach, and attracted
attention and opprobrium. The fire engine has quenched her ardour
and perhaps that of potential customers; though her clothes,
drenched and clinging, may have made her look like a contestant in
a wet T-shirt contest, so her commercial availability may have been
the more obvious.

Once this stage in the proceedings was over the Town's Officer
appeared with the drummer:

> The ane a halbert shouthered high
> And purse, breeks, shoon, and bonnet
> The laurels for the victory
> Hung gaudily upon it.[56]

On the halbert were the prizes, a cloth pouch given by the tailor guild, leather breeches given by the glovers, a pair of shoes and a blue Kilmarnock bonnet.[57] Just before three o'clock the Town Council emerges from the Town Hall and marches to the race course. The varied crowd watches them, then follows. There are gingerbread sellers and *blackman wives* – vendors of confections made of boiled treacle – and Johny Mickie is calling out his wares: 'Almanacs for the present day, and if ye canna read them, ye may eat them'. There is a whisky stall; there are pickpockets.

Visitors have arrived from all the neighbouring towns and villages, and Ramsay derides most of them – presumably because they are not from Kilmarnock. For example:

> Newmill's dog-fechters hae come down
> Some squintin' through their glasses.

There are 'Galston wabsters lazy', Crookedholm 'woollen-spinners greazy', and also:

> The waggon drivers rough and rude
> Hae wauchled frae the Troon.[58]

These were the men who worked on the Kilmarnock & Troon railway, opened in 1808 and still at this date powered by horse. Ramsay then adds several verses of gossip about local individuals, when suddenly:

> 'Stand back! stand back!' is bawled about –
> Sic ruggin' and sic rivin' –
> The big folks threaten, thump, and shout
> As brutes they were a' drivin.[59]

Two foot races take place, and Ramsay describes them briefly, rather in the way that Robert Fergusson ignores the races themselves in 'Leith Races'. What strikes Ramsay is the emotional state of the gathering:

> But ance wi' a crowd we're blent
> It's spirit's a contagion
> We catch, whatever be the bent
> Mirth, mischief or religion.[60]

To the last line he adds a note: '*Vide* those pitiful and pernicious excitements termed "Revivals".' The reports of Paisley races at the same period show a fear of the crowd, seen from the outside; but Ramsay is on the inside. He is afraid that people, including himself, will lose their individual minds to the single mind of the mass, and that this mind is emotional and volatile:

> A wee thing lifts them up the brae
> A wee thing makes them sad.[61]

This is not the spirit of the rational human being who has free control over his own actions, a creation of the Enlightenment in the eighteenth century. It is, rather, an accurate identification of the nature of the crowd which had attended traditional festivals for hundreds of years. It draws our attention to another reason for the demise of traditional sports days, namely that they were understood to produce an emotional state which was not suitable for the modern cog in the economic machine.

ANNUAL SPORTS AND FAIRS

Having seen something of the character and variety of burgh sports and horse races in the last two chapters, we can now make some general remarks about them.

Sports performed several social functions. They drew people together, as at Fastern's E'en at Kilmarnock:

> But ilka toun, and parish roun'
>   Their willing tributes gie.[62]

Or at the Dumfries siller gun:

> Frae far and near, the country lads
> (Their joes ahint them on their yads,)
> Flock'd in to see the show in squads;
>   And, what was dafter

> Their pawky mithers and their dads
> Cam trotting after![63]

At one level the holiday was part of social existence, broadening human contact. Many people in the eighteenth century lived from day to day in small villages and fermtouns, and the circumstance of simply seeing unfamiliar men and women, and talking to them, was an important human experience. It was also a way of understanding what was happening in the county and in the country by hearing others' experiences. The play day thus had much in common with the hiring fair, but men and women at the play did not have the pressure of having to find a place for the next six months. The point of the play was its pointlessness: there was more freedom for social interaction. Some sports emphasised this by their place in the calendar, such as the Kipper Fair which came at the end of the salmon-fishing season.

Having a horse race, or better still an ancient trophy, gave status to a burgh, just as a boy from Fetteresso mocked another Angus lad, 'Ye haena a cock fecht at your skweel, man'.[64] The flood of visitors showed that the place was worth visiting, and everyone took trouble to dress well. Before Leith races the instruction was given 'Come, bonny lasses, busk ye braw',[65] and according to Fergusson's poem the town guard marked the occasion by shaving. Even if some of the visitors' money was spent on the wares of itinerant blackman wives and gingerbread sellers, much also went to the keeper of the dram shop and to other shopkeepers. Where the sport was the province of the burgh's Incorporated Trades, both it and the surrounding rituals emphasised their important roles in civic life. Whilst one could explain the demise of the Dumfries Siller Gun after 1831 as impatience with a sport that was not a real competition, or say that in the nineteenth century many aspects of the irrational began to be considered pointless, the lack of interest in the old festival is more likely to have stemmed from the declining economic importance of bodies like trades and guilds which encouraged restrictive practices.

One of the most distinctive features of traditional sports days was heavy drinking, particularly by senior members of the community.

Pillars of local society made fools of themselves, and rational thinking was dissolved in ardent spirits.

Play days were the Scots equivalent of Carnival, the festival which on the Continent precedes the self-denial of Lent. As in England, but to a greater extent, in Scotland Carnival was displaced from Fastern's E'en to a summer festival, partly because of the short daylight in February. One of the features of Carnival in Europe is social violence: this remained on Shrove Tuesday in Britain in the form of football games.[66] Fighting at the end of the summer play day was common, reaching its peak in the rammy at the end of Leith Races. On the Saturday nights the booths and crames (stalls) which had done service all week were demolished in a free fight.

Both Carnival and the Scottish play day involved a procession. In Catholic countries the idea of the local pilgrimage, when the whole population walked behind a crucifix or relic to a local shrine, was alive and full of religious significance in the nineteenth century. In Scotland the head of the procession was taken by the secular symbol of the day – the siller gun or the town's prize for the horse race. As with a pilgrimage or carnival procession, everyone could join in: the first horse race in Scotland at which admission was restricted to those who paid at the gate was held in Glasgow in 1869.[67] At Kirkcudbright the importance of the Siller Gun procession was emphasised by triumphal arches built for the occasion. The goal, as with a pilgrimage, was a point some distance from the town, often of some charm, in other words a place where people were particularly conscious of nature, the open beach or the steep hill round the Maiden Craigs.

Another aspect of the Continental Carnival was the inversion of society for a limited period. The same phenomenon is found in the election of boy bishops at Christmas, both on the Continent and in England. Of course, the temporary inversion of society does not threaten its structure, but validates it. It is a deeply conservative practice. Inversion is difficult to detect in post-Reformation festivals in Scotland because so much of the symbolism of acting and dress was stopped by the Kirk. There was, however, something more frightening to those in power – equality for the day. This was partly induced by drink, but neither did the play itself respect persons. In

'The Christmas Bawing of Monymusk' the schoolteacher is knocked 'heels o'er gowdie', head over heels, and when the meek parish clerk appears, the next act is inevitable:

> Dafy Davy Don wi' a derf dawrd [violent push]
> Beft [knocked] o'er the grave divine
>   On's bum that day.[68]

There were, of course, limits: to land the parish clerk in the *glaur* – the mud – was one thing, but to do the same to the minister would have been quite another.

Both at Carnival and on St John's Eve, a common midsummer festival in Europe, there was an underlying meaning, renewal or regeneration.[69] This may be the significance of the destruction at Leith. It may also lie beneath the public baptism of the crowd at Kilmarnock, and the presence of three unexpected figures at the Dumfries Siller Gun, arranged by the gardeners:

> Amang the flow'ry forms they weave
> There's Adam, to the life, and Eve:
> She, wi' the apple in her neeve
>   Enticing Adam;
> While Satan's laughing in his sleeve
>   At him and madam![70]

At St James's Fair at Paisley purification by both fire and water was symbolised by the lighting of bonfires or *tandles* – from the Gaelic *teannáil* – on islands in the River Cart. Tandles were also lit at Marymass at Irvine. These traditions were by no means dependent on the sporting content of the festivals at which they were performed, but sport, particularly in its emotional and irrational aspects, created a psychological space in which symbolic activities could survive. The symbolism of regeneration also related to the sexuality of the play. Carnival and sex are closely linked: in France the number of conceptions peaked twice in the year, the first time in February, the time of Carnival, and the second in May.[71]

Traditional annual sports were, to modern eyes, irrational. The competitors for the siller guns, intoxicated and using inaccurate firearms, had each one shot only. They were little more than a lottery. The horses at carters' plays were not trained to race and there were complaints at Newton-on-Ayr when fair competition was promoted at the expense of fun.[72] Élite horse-racing may in itself have been truly competitive, but the crowd were not particularly interested in it: they were more interested in one another.

The irrational and playful content of a play day gave scope for sexual activity. Even in the assembling of the Incorporated Trades at Dumfries, John Mayne found a sense of regeneration:

> Brisk as a bridegroom gawn to wed
> Ilk Deacon his battalion led.[73]

In the march to the Maiden Craigs, the siller gun itself was carried at the head of the procession:

> Suspended frae a painted pole
> A glimpse o't sae inspir'd the whole
> That auld and young, wi' heart and soul
>   Their heads were cocking
> Keen as ye've seen, at bridals droll
>   Maids catch the stocking![74]

This is a reference to a wedding custom. After the marriage the bride threw her left stocking to guests, and the person who caught it was believed to be the next to be married. The pole is an obvious symbol of fertility, a portable maypole. In an atmosphere in which emotions could be given more freedom than at other times of the year, sexual activity flourished. In England, meeting for sports and games was an important part of courtship,[75] and the same was true north of the Border.

The disorder of a race or play day was not chaos, for there were patterns in it, some general and some specific to that particular holiday. There was a collective understanding of what was allowed, though the unwritten rules might be different from those is existence at other times of the year. There is a European proverb, 'In carnival, all things are permitted'.[76] In Scotland, 'A's fair at the ba' Scone' – within certain limits. In the nineteenth century the growth of written law, which was much less flexible, was both a symptom and a cause of the decline of freedom on play days.

REFERENCES

John Mayne, *The Siller Gun*, is abbreviated as *SG*, and references are to the edition of 1836.

1. Anon (1871), 152.
2. Murray (1899), 77.
3. Adam (1899), 239.
4. Anon. (1890–91), 132.
5. Pretsell (1908), 38.
6. Truckell (1986), 31, correcting McDowall (1986), 325–9; Marwick (1890), 44.
7. McDowall (1986), 327.
8. McDowall (1986), 327–8.
9. *DWJ*, 8 June 1779.
10. *SG*, 5.
11. *SG*, 6.
12. *SG*, 9–10.
13. *SG*, 43.
14. *SG*, 37.
15. *SG*, 35.
16. *SG*, 89.
17. *SG*, 120.
18. *SG*, 122.
19. *SG*, 102–3.
20. *SG*, 121.
21. *SG*, 112.
22. *SG*, 115–16.
23. Ord (1930), 397–9.
24. Ibid., 399.
25. Grierson (1981), 202.
26. Guthrie (1885), 102.
27. This section is based on Clark (1961).
28. Clark (1961), 2.
29. Clark (1961), 8.
30. Clark (1961), 9.
31. Clark (1961), 9–14.
32. *DWJ*, 15 January 1793.
33. *DWJ*, 11 January 1825.
34. For a short survey of archery in Scotland, see Buchanan (1979).
35. Ascham (1788), 98–101.
36. Anon (1893), 113.
37. Quoted by Murray (1899), 76.
38. Craig-Brown (1886), 54.
39. Simpkins (1914), 175–6.
40. Maidment (1868), 23.

41. Balfour Paul (1875), 306–7.
42. Horace, *Odes*, iii, 2, 13.
43. National Museums of Scotland H. MEQ 1625.
44. *DWJ*, 17 June 1794.
45. Strawhorn (1985), 139–40.
46. Anstruther (1963), 195.
47. *AA*, 20 October 1842.
48. *AA*, 4 August 1859.
49. Douglas (1957–64), ii, 221.
50. Burnett & Urquhart (1998).
51. Ker (1900), 292–4.
52. Patterson (1857), 138–9.
53. Reproduced by Carpentier-Bogaert (1996), 43.
54. Ramsay (1855), 27.
55. *Ibid.*, 28.
56. *Ibid.*, 30.
57. M'Kay (1880), 125–8.
58. Ramsay (1855), 34–5.
59. *Ibid.*, 40.
60. *Ibid.*, 41.
61. *Ibid.*, 42.
62. Ramsay (1855), 36.
63. *SG*, 7.
64. Banks (1937–41), i, 14.
65. Geikie (1847), 42.
66. Burke (1978), 187–8.
67. *NBDM*, 28 May 1869.
68. Crawford (1987), ii, 111–12.
69. Burke (1978), 180–1.
70. *SG*, 24.
71. Burke (1978), 186.
72. Burnett (1995–96).
73. *SG*, 19.
74. *SG*, 23.
75. Malcolmson (1973), 54.
76. Quoted by Burke (1978), 202.

CHAPTER EIGHT

The Medieval Revival and
the Earl of Eglinton

The medieval revival was a cultural movement which began in the eighteenth century and reached its peak in the second quarter of the nineteenth. It affected many aspects of intellectual activity and taste, particularly literature and architecture, from Macpherson's *Ossian* (1760) and Bishop Percy's *Reliques of Ancient English Poetry* (1765) to the Adam Brothers' 'Castle Style' and the rebuilding of the walls of Hume Castle (Berwickshire) in the 1780s to create a dramatically gothic skyline. Its most visible secular memorial in Britain is the Palace of Westminster. At its literary centre is Walter Scott, both the poet of the nostalgic *Lay of the Last Minstrel* (1805) and the novelist of the fabulously popular *Ivanhoe* (1820) which was set in the twelfth-century England of Richard the Lionheart.[1]

There was also a medieval revival in sport which began earlier than Scott but drew some of its fervour from him, and at its peak the most conspicuous individual was the 13th Earl of Eglinton, often remembered as the spendthrift who held the Eglinton Tournament in 1839 – but also a socially active and responsible man.

It would be difficult to argue that the medieval revival brought an increased enthusiasm for sport in general, but it did encourage a taste for archery and tilting, and it gave colour to other sports. The revival of archery began in England about 1780. The most famous English archery association, the [Royal] Toxophilite Society, was founded in 1781. Archery at this point was for the comparatively affluent and those with literary tastes: another sign of new enthusiasm was the reprinting in 1788 of *Toxophilus* (1545) by Roger Ascham, once tutor to the young woman who would become Queen Elizabeth of England. The development of archery and other medieval sports was slowed, however, by the Napoleonic Wars.

Although the competition for the Paisley Arrow began in 1806, sport in Scotland did not begin to show medieval characteristics until the 1820s, when it was swept forward by Walter Scott's romanticism. The medieval reached its peak with the Eglinton Tournament, and was over by 1860.

The interest in the Middle Ages can be seen partly as a quest for certainty – for stability, or well-anchored roots – in the face of, first, the Industrial Revolution, and by the 1820s of radical agitation. One expression of this was a renewed interest in popular culture, in the rituals, festivals and pastimes of the people, on the assumption that in their simplicity they preserved worthwhile social practices which had been lost by the more sophisticated and more literate. It was as though Rousseau's Noble Savage was alive in every village. Henry Bourne's *Antiquitates Vulgares* (1725) remained an isolated work until half a century later John Brand used it as the core of his *Observations on Popular Antiquities* (1777): then followed expanded editions and a variety of derivative works, one might say popularisations. This concern to record and expound popular traditions was British rather than merely Scots. The antiquarian Joseph Strutt (1749–1802), author of *Sports and Pastimes of the People of England* (1801), had broad enthusiasms and wrote on church history and the history of costume, as well as on his own trade of engraving. His last work, left incomplete on his death, was an unusual novel, *Queenhoo Hall* – unusual because Strutt's purpose was to give a description of life in the fifteenth century. The plot hardly mattered and scarcely existed. *Queenhoo Hall* contained sport: one of the events in the novel was an archery competition at games held on May Day.[2] Its particular relevance here is that the publisher asked another author to provide the ending to *Queenhoo Hall* – Walter Scott.

Scott's propaganda for the medieval encompassed the whole of its culture, including recreation. In *Ivanhoe* (1820) he included an archery competition for the prize of a silver bugle (Chapter 13), and it was won by Locksley, otherwise Robin Hood. Scott's Robin Hood was a near-ideal character, very different from the one who had appeared in real medieval plays. His rival had appeared to be unbeatable when he hit the very centre of the target: Locksley split the arrow in two with his own. In this, there is an echo of the episode in the *Aeneid* in which one archer loosed a tied dove from its perch by cutting its tether, but another transfixed the moving target. *Ivanhoe* was hugely popular, and was in the Earl of Eglinton's mind when he conceived his Tournament.[3] *Ivanhoe* emphasised one image of archery: it was historical and heroic. An account of the competition for the Marchmont Arrow in 1831 said, 'its principal charm lies in the associations we connect with it,- Robin Hood, and the cool green recesses of Sherwood – the cloth-yard shafts of Cressy and Agincourt'.[4] Scott's medievalism can be clearly seen at Abbotsford, which he built in 1816–23, both in the architecture and in the contents. There are crenellated bookcases, the fireplace in the hall is modelled on the Abbot's stall at Melrose Abbey, and there are several suits of armour. Scott's collection of antiquities also expressed his enthusiasm for field sports, including sixteenth- and seventeenth-century matchlocks, James VI's hunting bottle and hunting knives once owned by Prince Charles Edward.

Scott was familiar with the history of archery in Scotland. In 1818 he wrote a letter to James Boswell, son of the biographer, in which he said:

> The Burghs had most of them silver arrows or similar prizes frequently shot for by the neighbouring gentlemen. There is one preserved at Selkirk, another, I believe, at Peebles, and others in other places; but the exercise is now out of fashion.[5]

Scott had himself found the lost Selkirk Arrow – just as he had rediscovered the Regalia of Scotland – and the Royal Company of Archers came to Selkirk to compete for it in 1818.[6]

In the same period there was a revival of enthusiasm in the Royal Company. They built Archers' Hall in 1776. The medieval content appears in the second decade of the nineteenth century, when gothic lettering appears on their prizes: on a medal on the Musselburgh Arrow in 1812, the Edinburgh Arrow in 1814, and the Peebles Arrow in 1816.

Archery grew rapidly all over Britain in the 1820s. The revival of the Kilwinning papingo began in 1828, when it was resolved that 'The uniform dress to be worn by members of the society when

31.   The medieval magnificence of the Eglinton Trophy, presented to the Earl of
Eglinton in 1843. *National Museums of Scotland.*

shooting for the silver arrow ... to consist of a double-breasted long green coat with silver buttons, the coat to be lined with white silk, the buttons to be made with cross arrows with points downwards, white cashmere vest with uniform buttons'.[7] Present, too, was the young Earl of Eglinton, but it is important to see that the Middle Ages had become a controlling image before he was able to exercise an influence on the day's events. The *Glasgow Herald* said, 'we could easily have imaged that not a few of [the archers] might have worthily drawn a bow with Robin Hood, or shot a bolt with Little John!' This was to become a stock observation in descriptions of archery competitions. The Earl had won the captaincy two years before by using a proxy – he was then only thirteen years old – but in 1828 he shot and himself won, and was duly compared with the hero of Sherwood Forest. The archers marched from the Abbey to Kilwinning Cross, being offered drinks by 'every gaucy publican':

> Here the military band struck up a merry strain, and amid a wondering circle of matrons, maids and children the archers laid their bows aside and instantly prepared to minister to Terpsichore; not ... to dance with the fairest rosy cheeked maidens of the village ... – here as your archer mated only with archer – bowman with bowman! or, in other words, there was a rare set to at the bull reels, to the infinite amusement of the million.[8]

The false note is the name of Terpsichore: dancing had been part of popular festivals in Scotland for a millennium and more. The watching crowd of women and children is the key to a continuity which included far more than shooting for the papingo: they had been there when the men came back from a wapenschaw in the fifteenth century.

The distinctive sport of the chapmen of Scotland was tilting at the ring. They met at Dunkeld and later also at Stirling. The charter of the chapmen who met at Dunkeld was said to have been originally given by James V, and they met there annually until 1776, when they gathered in alternate years at Coupar Angus. Having held their court, they dined and finally, according to the *Statistical Account*:

> they spend the evening in some public competition of dexterity

and skill. Of these 'riding at the ring' (an amusement of ancient and warlike origin), is the chief. Two perpendicular posts are erected on this occasion, with a cross beam, from which is suspended a small ring: the competitors are on horseback, each having a pointed rod in his hand; and he who, at full gallop, passing betwixt the posts, carries away the ring upon his rod gains the prize.[9]

In 1707 the burgh of Stirling gave a gold ring as a prize for tilting. It is probable that tilting had a continuous history through the eighteenth century into the nineteenth, though evidence is lacking. The advertisement for the Chapmen Sports at Stirling in 1845 said that 'The Lord Principal and Baillie Court of the Ancient Fraternity of Chapmen, of the Shires of Stirling and Clackmannan, hereby intimate, that the brethern will engage in the ancient game of the ring ..'.[10] This could be taken to be another medieval revival, but revivals were the province of the aristocracy and middle classes. As Alexander Geddes said of the Scots language, traditions survive best among the 'uncurruptit poor',[11] and in addition the chapmen had an independent place in society. Assuming their sports continued through the eighteenth century, there is no reason why tilting could not have been part of them: traditions tend to survive when there is a protective institution, whether it is an annual games day or a Lowland school at which shinty was still played in the nineteenth century.

It is certain, however, that at the time of the revival of medieval sports tilting became more widespread and was taken up by men who were not chapmen. For example, it appeared at Lanark in 1849. At first the riders aimed to catch on a lance a 2½-inch ring suspended 10 feet from the ground, but in 1851 they made it more difficult by introducing a hurdle before and after the catching of the ring. The prizes were hunting saddles, bridles, and 'a superior silver-mounted switch' – the horses and riders were presumably all hunters.[12] Tilting was carried out at an archery meeting at Linlithgow in 1849.[13]

The Scone ba' game was revived as football rather than handball. On Hansel Monday 1836 the Lord Provost of Perth led the young men of the town against the youth of Scone under Lord Stormont.

The presence of leaders from the upper ranks of society gives the impression of feudalism: this was another exercise in medievalism. The play was controlled by two judges and an umpire, and drew a crowd of 14,000. It lasted for half an hour only, because the crowd did not understand the one modern feature of the game: that they were not supposed to be part of the play.[14]

The medieval spirit reached sports which did not have a medieval origin, such as curling and cricket. One example is Dr Archibald Crawford's pamphlet *The Crune of the Warlock of the Peil – Pryce, a Bawbee* (1838) in which the poem was preceded by an introduction in consciously archaic language:

> The followand Historie, or Legend of auld Ringan Sempill was gatherit fra the auldwarld carlins, the suthfast believars of the Lochuinyoch Mythologie. This Ringan wonnit in the Peil, as Keipar of that Fort, till its dinging doun. He was a lamitar, and the quierest auld and wee bodie. He was a camsheuch and capernoytit carl, and seildin made his compeirance afore frem fock.

And so on. The poem is a warning from the warlock, or ghost, to curlers, to leave off their sport in the thaw at the end of the bitterly cold February of 1838.

> Curlers, gae hame to your spedds, or your plews
> To your bouks, to your planes, or your thrummils;
> Curlers, gae hame or the ice ye'se faw throu
> Hame, swith! to your elshins [shoemakers' awl],
>   or wummills. [wimble, i.e. awl or gimlet]
>
> A long fareweil to greins and beif
> To yill to whisky and baiks:
> Fu of cracks is the ice; but we'se smuir our dule
> Be gorbling up parritch and caiks.
>
> We'se nae mair think of the slitherie rink
> Nor the merrie soun *Tee high*
> Nor *inwick heir*, nor *brek an egg thair*
> Nor *he's far owr stark, soup him bye*.[15]

This is medieval, but artificial; the cynic will suspect that the Scots language has been deployed partly to divert attention from the author's inadequacy as a poet. These verses are written in the shadow of *Tam o' Shanter*: there is the same transition between momentary excitement and day-to-day reality – the dancing will stop, the pursuit will fail, the ice will melt – and there is a similar supernatural element. Despite its attempts to seem medieval, 'The Crune of the Warlock' is a modern poem because it emphasises the difference between play on the ice and the mundane world of work: there is no economic benefit in curling.

Mention of the supernatural brings us to a particularly Scots problem in the creation of a historical context for modern activity. The Presbyterian church was not seen as having evolved from the Roman Catholic, but as a new foundation on the sound rock of the Bible. Any appeal to a world which contained priests, mass, ritual or saints could only be made with an acknowledgment of the errors of our ancestors: it was not a starting point for explaining nineteenth-century curling. The supernatural offered an alternative, and it is significant that two of the leading proponents of a medieval vision of society, and of sport as a part of that vision, also wrote of other worlds with conviction – Walter Scott and James Hogg.

Another pastiche of a medieval document was printed at Glasgow in 1835: the British Library copy is endorsed 'only 23 copies printed'.[16] The title was 'The Pump: ane richt lamentable dirge, composit be Bailzie Peakodde, Poet Laureate to ye Cricket Club.' It ended with a 'Note by Franciscus Cardownie, Esq. Magister de Spectaculum. The remainder of this invaluable MS. is unfortunately lost ..'.[17] It was in black letter, and the title page included a woodcut which bore Dürer's monogram.

At Fingask in Perthshire, curlers and patroness indulged in a feudal charade. They played on that recent innovation, the artificial pond, 'the most beautiful field of ice that was ever seen, being so pure and keen, like one vast sheet of glass'. The ladies from Fingask Castle were cheered on their arrival: they lunched beside the rink. The points match was won by Charles Robertson of Buttergask, and 'the members of the Club, and the spectators [about 130 all together] ... formed into a large circle (in the centre of which was Miss

Thriepland), and the victor then advanced, and kneeling down on
one knee before that lady – Miss Thriepland, with the most
consummate grace and dignity, crowned the victor with a chaplet
laurel wreath, at the same time adorning his manly breast with the
massive and brilliant medal'. She dubbed him on the shoulder with
a curling broom, in a mock-knighting gesture. Luncheon, toddy, and
more curling followed.[18] This series of events contains much that is
medieval, and it is significant that it involves a highly literate part
of society: the words of Scott would have been part of the *lingua
franca* at Fingask, particularly for a family like the Thrieplands who
had a Jacobite background. The act of knighting the winner is
significant for it implies that the lasting status that he gained from
the day's events came not from his achievements but from the
Thrieplands. That it was an unmarried woman who conferred the
honour takes us straight back – via the Queen of Beauty at the
Eglinton Tournament – to the medieval tournament. And the laurel
wreath, like the motto on the New Abbey curling medal of 1830
which mentions bearing the palm, refers to the Olympic Games.

ST RONAN'S GAMES AND THE MARCHMONT ARROW[19]

The archery contest at the Ronan's Border Games is one of the
clearest examples of a competition which was invented and given a
medieval flavour without having a clear basis in local history. In the
nineteenth century the Kilwinning papingo was believed to have a
continuous tradition dating back to the reign of James III and James
IV, and so to have a genuine medieval origin: perhaps the desire for
this to be the case led to a credulous attitude to its early history.
There was no such tradition at Innerleithen: archery had not been
practised there since the days of Sunday shooting in every parish.

The St Ronan's Games at Innerleithen and the associated St
Ronan's Border Club were created by James Hogg, 'the Ettrick
Shepherd' (1770–1835) in 1827. Hogg's accomplices were Professor
John Wilson (1785–1854), otherwise Christopher North, and Henry
Glassford Bell (1803–74). At the dinner on the evening of the first
Games, Wilson took the chair and Hogg sang to the company. The
following year three major literary figures, Sir Walter Scott
(1771–1832), his son-in-law and biographer John Gibson Lockhart

(1794–1854) and William Blackwood (1776–1834), joined the Club. The idea of a general sporting club was modelled on Edinburgh clubs such as the Gymnastic Club and the Six-Feet Club: Bell was a member of the latter and Scott its 'Umpire of the Games, who has been elected for life'.[20]

Here we can see an alignment which was important for the development of sport in the second quarter of the nineteenth century – the enthusiasts were all Tories. Most were associated with *Blackwood's Magazine* – Blackwood as publisher and editor, Wilson and Lockhart as the chief contributors. Wilson was the main author of 'Noctes Ambrosianae', which appeared in *Blackwood*, and Hogg was the model for their central character. Bell edited the *Edinburgh Literary Journal* between 1828 and 1831, and counted among his authors Lockhart, Wilson and David Macbeth Moir (1798–1851). Moir was a Tory and physician, who wrote for Blackwood and attended him in his last illness, and he shared Hogg's interest in the traditional life of ordinary people: his novel *Mansie Waugh* (1827) includes the already-quoted description of a race for cart-horses near Dalkeith. Politically, *Blackwood* was matched by the Whig *Edinburgh Review* – and none of the leading figures associated with it, such as Francis Jeffrey and Henry Brougham, were sportsmen.

Hogg and his Tory friends were keen athletes. For example, Hogg was an expert at fishing, curling, running, jumping and wrestling, and he came second in the competition for the Marchmont Arrow in 1831.[21] His grandfather, Will o' Phaup, had been a famous runner. Christopher North was an all-round athlete, whose feats of walking, running, rowing and boxing were well-known. He had been a member of the Royal Company of Archers since 1823.[22] Bell was a skilled quoiter and enjoyed a range of other sports.

The founding of the Border Games was an attempt by Hogg to establish an event which would increase the sense of local community.[23] He believed that rural Scotland was becoming demoralised as agriculture became more commercial; emigration also was biting deeply. In the Borders, people were being forced off the land and drawn into working in textile mills and living in overcrowded towns. The woollen industry had started to work on an industrial scale in the 1790s, and since then standards of living had fallen. By the 1820s

Britain was in the depths of the depression which followed the Napoleonic Wars. Many were afraid of the 'combination' of the working classes, and the Peterloo Massacre was a recent and frightening memory. Those who remained on the land found that their status had changed. Once farmers had lived with their family of servants, providing friendship and moral leadership, but the fabulous profits made during the Napoleonic Wars had turned them into gentlemen who would not dine with their servants and who managed their farms thorough grieves.[24] Hogg wanted ordinary people to have more fun, whether it came from sport or penny weddings.[25] One can see the St Ronan's Games as a Tory reaction to the uncertainty produced by industrial unrest, seeking safety in the past – a paternalistic form of Toryism in contrast to the severe authority with which the government had conducted the 'Radical War' in 1820.

Hogg boasted that it was by his 'own single exertions' that 'manly exercises' were continued in the Borders: otherwise they would have died out in the rapid changes of the early nineteenth century. There is much truth in this, for it was he who gave money for prizes and extracted more from farmers and his wealthy Edinburgh friends, and he infused the Games themselves with all of his own vigorous character. Though he was proud of having played a large part in saving Border sports he was realist enough to recognise that it was a disadvantage that women did not compete. In a description of the changes in rural life which he had observed he said that 'since the extermination of penny-weddings, kirns, and family dinners, the peasantry have not an amusement in which the sexes join', and that this made men 'rude and repulsive'.[26] Again we see the strength of his nostalgia. Hogg, Scott and politics were linked through a ba' game which was held in 1815 on the Carterhaugh, at the meeting of the Ettrick and the Yarrow. Both wrote poems about it, linking the football match with the presence at it of the banner of the Scotts of Buccleuch, and so with Border warfare and their own patriarchal view of society.

Innerleithen owed much of its prominence to a Scott novel, *St Ronan's Well* (1824). Although it is not one his more famous books, it was highly popular in the 1820s. Scott did not model the village of St Ronan's on Innerleithen – the connection was made by his readers. He did, however, recognise the Games in a note added to the Magnum edition of *St Ronan's Well*. Having ended the novel by saying 'The little watering-place has returned to its primitive obscurity', he commented:

> *Non omnis moriar*. Saint Ronan's, since this veracious history was given to the public, has revived as a sort of *alias* ... to the very pleasant village of Innerleithen on Tweed ... prizes for some of the manly and athletic sports, common in the pastoral districts around, are competed for under the title of Saint Ronan's Games.[27]

Albeit inadvertently, Scott thus shares with Hogg the responsibility for locating the Games at Innerleithen.

The best summary of activity on the day of the Games is given by Lockhart in his life of Scott. Lockhart was present in 1830 and 1831,[28] and wrote:

> a yearly festival was instituted for the celebration of *The St. Ronan's Border Games*. A club of *Bowmen of the Border*, arrayed in doublets of Lincoln green, with broad blue bonnets, and having the Ettrick Shepherd as Captain, assumed the principal management of this exhibition; and Scott was well pleased to be enrolled among them, and during several years was a regular attendant, both on the Meadow, where (besides archery) leaping, racing, wrestling, stone-heaving and hammer-throwing, went on opposite to the noble old castle of Traquair, and at the subsequent banquet, where Hogg, in full costume always, presided as master of the ceremonies. The Shepherd, even when on the verge of threescore, exerted himself lustily in the field, and seldom failed to carry off some of the prizes, to the astonishment of his vanquished juniors; and the *bon-vivants* of Edinburgh mustered strong among the gentry and yeomanry of Tweeddale to see him afterwards in his glory, filling the president's chair with eminent success, and commonly supported on this – which was, in fact, the grandest evening of his year – by Sir Walter Scott, Professor Wilson, Sir Adam Fergusson, and *Peter* Robertson.[29]

The judge Patrick Robertson (1794–1855), familiarly Peter, was another staunch Tory.

The Marchmont Arrow was presented to the Bowmen of the Scottish Border by Sir William Purves Hume Campbell (1767–1833) of Marchmont in Berwickshire. There is no evidence of Campbell being an active archer, though his son Hugh (1812–75) was admitted a member of the Royal Company of Archers on 24 May 1833.[30] After the 1829 games a report – perhaps it was written by Hogg himself – said that Campbell had presented a silver arrow and a yew bow for competition, but no contest had been held since it was advertised too late.[31] The first competition was therefore held in 1830. From then until about 1845 the Games were held in a haugh called the Batty, perhaps the former site of the bow butts.

The names of the competitors for one year, 1834, have been discovered.[32] There were eleven, and those who can be identified fall into one of two categories. There were literary men from Edinburgh such as Henry Glassford Bell, one of the sons of William Blackwood, and 'Clapperton' – probably William Clapperton, author of *The Poetical Scrap Book* (1824). Secondly there were archers, often with Border connections: John Haldane, the winner in 1834; Walter Lothian, winner in 1830 and 1843; Francis Harper of Housebyres, near Melrose; and Lord James Andrew Ramsay (1812–60), later 10th Earl and Marquess of Dalhousie, and President of the Council of the Royal Company of Archers in 1848–60.[33] Hogg, of course, was a member of both groups. He was present as usual in 1835, and after dinner 'delighted the meeting with many of his best songs'.[34] He died two months later.

Why did the competition for the Marchmont Arrow cease in the mid-1840s, only fifteen years after its beginning? Archery societies in Ayrshire were thriving, and archery in Glasgow reached its zenith at exactly this time. The answer is twofold. First, key individuals who took a particular enjoyment in archery had departed: Hogg and Scott were dead and Henry Glassford Bell moved to Glasgow in 1839. Second, partly as a consequence, the St Ronan's Games ceased to be of interest to professional men from Edinburgh, and became merely a local festival.

In contrast, the competitions arranged by the Royal Company of

Archers continued throughout the nineteenth century because the Company was a large body in the capital city, and had a function as the Royal bodyguard in Scotland which did not depend on archery. The shooting of the papingo at Kilwinning lasted until 1870 because it enjoyed popular support and was linked to the whole of local society: for example, the final act every year was a reel danced at Kilwinning Cross in which the Captain – usually a local laird – partnered an old woman of the town. The irony of the St Ronan's competition was that although it copied a medieval sport, it transformed it into a game for a social élite, and kept at a distance the people of the Borders whose ancestors had heard James I's injunction 'that all men busk thaim to be archaris fra they be xij yeres of eilde'.

THE MIDDLE AGES, THE TOURNAMENT, AND THE EARL OF EGLINTON

In October 1861 the Kilwinning correspondent of the *Ayr Advertiser* wrote a eulogy on the lately-deceased Earl of Eglinton:

> How often had we seen him on the shaven sward of the bowling green, at the archery meetings so suggestive of the merry greens-ward of long-gone summers, at the chase with pack in cry across the stubble rigs, at the curling bonspiels in the red December days, and, on any of these occasions, mingling with a freedom in which there was no thought of condescension among men of every condition, speaking to the farmer, or the shoemaker, as though he had been his familiar, and him an Earl!' [35]

At the end of this rich piece of prose we have a fine example of obsequiousness, and the existence of much of the evidence for the Earl's sporting activities depends on the social idea that what an aristocrat does is more worthy of record than the actions of anyone else. This quotation also shows that the Earl of Eglinton loved sport. Another obituary said 'It is not easy to connect him with the gloom of the burial vault: he lived in the sunshine and the free winds of heaven'.[36]

Archibald William Montgomerie was born at Palermo in 1812 and succeeded his grandfather at the age of 7, becoming 13th Earl of

Eglinton. He said of himself, 'He had dwelt in youth through the pages of the Talisman and Ivanhoe,'[37] and his genealogy and environment encouraged this enthusiasm for the Middle Ages. He was descended from a kinsman of William the Conqueror, one ancestor captured Henry Hotspur, and another killed Henri II of France, father-in-law of Mary Queen of Scots, in a tournament. His ancestral home – completed shortly before his birth – was the machicolated and crenellated Eglinton Castle (1798–1803).

He was educated at Eton. From his boyhood we have one tangible relic of his athletic inclinations, a very early hobby-horse, probably made between 1818 and 1823.[38] The glimpses we have of him as a young adult suggest that he was a typically dissipated young aristocrat of the period. On his own account he drank very heavily form the age of 16 to 21: 'the headaches in the morning were dreadful to think of'.[39] On one occasion he was involved in a drinking contest which was excessive even by the standards of the Jockey Club.[40] He became heavily involved in aristocratic sports, especially the turf, and he spent thousands of pounds on a string of racehorses. He played cricket in Switzerland and went stag hunting in France with the duc d'Orléans, soon to become King Louis-Philippe.[41]

In time, he changed his habits. Later in life he was a member of two Tory governments: Lord Derby's first (February-December 1852) and second ministries (February 1858-June 1859). Disraeli, who took his politics seriously, complained that Derby was 'always at Newmarket or Doncaster', and another Conservative wrote 'as a leader of a party he is more hopeless than ever – devoted to whist, billiards, racing, betting ... nothing but odds and tricks'.[42] Eglinton fitted comfortably into Derby's social circle. His public reputation, however, was as the man who held the Eglinton Tournament in 1839, a mock-medieval reaction to his disappointment at the abandonment of much of the traditional ritual at the coronation of Queen Victoria.

As a young man, Eglinton was fascinated by the Middle Ages. After the Tournament a banquet in his honour was held in Irvine, and Eglinton told the gathering:

I have pored, when a boy, over the exploits of King Arthur, till

I could have given up my bright hopes of future years for the grave that held the glories of a Sir Tristram or a Sir Launcelot. I have pored over the pages of Froissart, till I fancied I heard the clang of armour and the shrill blast of the trumpet calling me to the tented field – and I have awoke from chivalry to find my self in a more refined, but a most unromantic age, when all save dull reality is scoffed at, and imagination must confine herself to the everyday occurrences of modern life.[43]

His disappointment was that of many of the aristocrats who had been dismayed by the passing of the Reform Bill in 1832 and the ensuing decade of whig domination: they referred to the Queen's 'half-coronation' and feared that the lack of pomp and ceremony (and expenditure) was a sign of a break with the past. Eglinton stood out because he decided to do something. He planned jousting and other armed feats in the policies at Eglinton Castle, the press 'rolled the snowball', and something in the region of 100,000 people arrived. After a fine morning there was sudden and torrential rain which continued for the rest of the day – the *Paisley Advertiser* shrewdly observed that 'this cast a damp on the proceedings', and the result was a memorable farce, ankle deep in mud.[44]

One of the most striking things about the Eglinton Tournament was the size of the crowd. We can compare it with regular events, such as the annual races on Leith sands which drew quite large numbers: 20,000 people in 1791, for example. Other crowds arose for unusual if not unique reasons. When Vincenzo Lunardi took off in his balloon from St Andrew's Square, Glasgow, in 1785, 100,000 were said to be present. Six weeks before his starting point had been in Edinburgh, at Heriot's Hospital, and John Kay, the caricaturist, said that the crowd on that occasion numbered 80,000.

The Tournament attracted a significant quantity of criticism. The following quotation comes from a *Gazetteer of Scotland* which was published in parts – in other words it was part of the Whig-tinged March of the Mind. It praised the 12th Earl for having contributed to economic advancement by building Ardrossan harbour:

Happy it would be for themselves, their posterity, and the population of the territories in which their estates are situated, if

persons of rank and fortune copied the example of this muni-
ficent and patriotic gentleman. But something different must be
said respecting the enormous expenditure ... upon a gorgeous
pageant, in imitation of the Tournament of the Middle Ages,
– a 'passage of arms,' as a tilt with wooden poles smoothly
rounded at the end, over lists strewn with saw dust five inches
deep, yielding soft repose to unhorsed knights, was somewhat
facetiously termed.[45]

The apotheosis of this phase of Eglinton's life was the presentation
to him in 1843 of the Eglinton Trophy.[46] It was made by the Queen's
Jewellers, R. & S. Garrard of Panton Street, London, and its
metropolitan manufacture confirmed his British status as a
sportsman. It was a Gothic fantasy, half-architectural, half-sculptural
and a little poetic. From a heavy wooden base soared silver pinnacles
in which there were figures standing in niches, and in the middle
was a scene in which armed knights attended a nobleman. It had
much in common with the Scott monument, and with a wedding
cake. One might even speculate that the Eglinton Trophy had a
political significance. Public monuments to the plebeian Burns, both
at Edinburgh (1820) and Alloway (1830) were in the Greek manner:
the ancient Greeks were democrats. Abbotsford, the Scott
Monument, and the Eglinton Tournament were Gothic, and have a
hierarchical shape. The trophies of the major English horse races of
the 1840s were often medieval in style, illustrating events such as the
death of the blind King of Bohemia at the Battle of Crécy or the
capture of Henry III at the Battle of Lewes, with the inscription
'Hold your hand I am Harry of Winchester' (the words 'Haud yer
haun' do not appear on any Scots trophy).[47] These prizes were won
by the primarily Tory horse-racing fraternity.

Eglinton's medievalism continued to affect his support for archery.
At the Eglinton Tournament, Lady Jane Seymour, Queen of Beauty,
was led to her throne by a bodyguard of 50 Irvine archers, 'dressed
à la Robin Hood'.[48] Eglinton took over the Irvine Toxophilites and
encouraged them to adopt medieval costume and pseudo-medieval
ritual. The reports of their meetings of 1840 and 1841 are inadequate,
but the 1842 event was called the third meeting 'commemorative of

32.   The Irvine Toxophiles in procession at the Eglinton Tournament, 1839,
from the *Illustrated London News*.

the Eglinton Tournament', the 19 bowmen were again 'dressed a la
Robin Hood'.[49] At the 1846 race meeting at Eglinton Park he was
titled 'Lord of the Tournament and Master of the Sports'.[50] The
meeting of the Irvine Toxophilites in the same year illustrates the
ritual and pageantry which Eglinton encouraged. The Glasgow and
Ayr Railway brought competitors from Kilwinning and Glasgow.
Wearing club uniforms, they assembled at the Eglinton Arms. The
Glasgow club wore dark green, 'profusely braided on the breast';
the Partick, light green with gold facings; and the Irvine Toxophilites
themselves were also dressed in light green. As leader of the County
club, the Earl wore their new uniform of a dark green frock with
matching facings (the medieval imitation is clear), a broad belt with
a silver clasp and long white gloves, plus the president's white silk
sash and a white feather in his bonnet.[51]

The archers marched in procession to the butts, preceded by the
Kilwinning Instrumental Band. The butts were in the playground of

Irvine Academy, where there was a marquee in which refreshments were served. There was a new banner displaying Latin mottoes. Competition was for a medal,[52] and the winner held the Eglinton Gold Belt, 'of elaborate workmanship, richly set with studs, and carved in the most beautiful manner' for a year. The medal and belt were won by William Ferguson of the Partick Club: in a ceremony Captain White, the victor in the previous year, in a feudal gesture returned the Gold Belt to Eglinton, who then presented it to Ferguson. Later, the archers shot at the 'Elevated Target', an obvious derivation from the Kilwinning papingo.[53]

The Irvine archery competitions and the Kilwinning papingo were similar to the shoot for the Marchmont Arrow, for they were solely for lairds, larger tenants and figures of some substance in the burghs and cities. Eglinton did not try to open them to a wider social range of archers: the very fact that the archers wore an elaborate uniform indicates that it was a costly business. Instead, for working men he promoted sports which were already accessible to them, such as bowling and curling.

EGLINTON AND ONE NATION TORYISM

The Eglinton Tournament was, as we have recognised, a reaction to the Reform Bill of 1832, and an individual's whim. Benjamin Disraeli mordantly described the effects of the same Act of Parliament in one of his novels, reflecting on the changes to the House of Lords and the House of Commons:

> one House of Parliament has been irremediably degraded into the decaying position of a mere court of registry, possessing great privileges provided it never exercises them, while the other chamber ... assumes ... somewhat of the character of a select vestry, fulfilling municipal rather than imperial offices ...[54]

This indicates the double difficulty of an aristocrat like Eglinton. On one hand, his role in ruling the nation as a member of the House of Lords had almost been removed, but at the same time his local status had also been reduced as parliament became involved in more and more aspects of life. In the early 1840s Disraeli was leader of the loose group of 'young England' conservatives, who included

Alexander Baillie-Cochrane, whose estate was at Lamington in the Clyde Valley, and ABC was a friend of Eglinton. Eglinton was part of their circle if not at this time a sufficiently active politician to have been labelled as a 'young Englander' himself. They took an interest not in economics or the politics of power, but in social and cultural issues. Disraeli praised one of them because 'he delighted in the household humour and homely pathos of Wilkie', and another begins the statement of his family's role in English history: 'The finest trees in England were planted by my family; they raised several of your most beautiful churches .. '.[55] Baillie-Cochrane was praised for his support of popular festivals.[56] The Young Englanders sought to bring the country together, to combat the idea of 'Two Nations' which Disraeli described in his novel *Sybil* (1845). Eglinton was at one with them.

Eglinton's achievement was to recover from his Tournament, and to accept that he lived in 'a most unromantic age', as he had himself described it. He modified the way in which he took ideas from the Middle Ages, and instead of adopting certain sporting practices which he believed were medieval, he adopted the more general vision of a people who behaved as a people, a set of classes which lived amicably together. After the Tournament he sent out a circular:

> when I hear evil disposed persons endeavouring to sow conten-tion between the richer and the poorer classes, I will point to the occasion which has just passed, for a refutation, and deny that contention can exist where all seem actuated by one com-mon feeling of kindness and confidence.[57]

Thus it was said that the Tournament:

> inaugurated, if it did not indeed suggest, LORD EGLINTON'S life-long confidence in the masses; and his long cherished opinions, that if the State or the aristocracy wish to elevate the working-classes, out-door amusements, recreation in public parks, &c., free mingling of classes in innocent pastime, will do more to raise the self-respect of the humble, and to fortify them against intemperance and vicious courses, than the most eloquent sermons or the severest statutes.[58]

The same train of thought was illustrated again when Eglinton took a leading part in the Burns Festival of 1844. It celebrated the eighty-fifth anniversary of the poet's birth, and his sister and two of his sons were present. It was a huge event: the procession from Ayr to Alloway was said to have numbered 50,000. At the dinner Christopher North gave a long dull speech and used up more than his allotted time. When Eglinton's turn came he discarded his prepared text and made a short contribution which delighted his audience by its simplicity and sincerity. He said of his own passion for the Middle Ages: 'That dream is over – the days of chivalry, when knights sallied forth with lances in hand ... have now passed away, never to return.' Instead, he envisaged cheap sports for the poor, whole parishes playing together. Ayr, he pointed out, was a sporting county: with two race meetings, two coursing clubs, and 'quoiters almost invincible, clubs of curlers innumerable,'[59] thus linking in a single vision the sports of the gentry and of the people. He also emphasised Burns' appeal to all classes.

Part of his motivation concerning sport was to enable people to enjoy themselves. He relished his own sporting activity, and the logic of 'One Nation' implied that what a nobleman enjoyed would give pleasure to others too. Whilst one can suggest socio-political reasons for his encouragement of sport it would be perverse to ignore the simplest interpretation, that he was an open-hearted man who wanted others to be happy. Yet at the same time Eglinton's aim was not only sporting, but also political, to show the continuing relevance of the aristocracy. Eglinton accepted that aristocrats had no place in practical politics, and instead sought to exercise a more limited form of social leadership. He showed that landowners could still have a public role. He can be contrasted with the central figure in Lampedusa's great novel, *The Leopard*: the Sicilian duke sees and understands Garibaldi's revolution but chooses for himself the private consolations of hunting and religion. Eglinton saw that change was inevitable and participated in it.

Yet he remained a Tory, for he said:

> The encouragement of such games as curling and bowling, especially among the poorer classes of our countrymen, will do

more to promote their comfort and welfare and tend to their good conduct than all the beer halls and Sunday-trading bills the legislature has ever passed.[60]

Not Blue Books and Acts of Parliament; not the new police force or explicit social control – but competition and laughter in the open air. Like Hogg, Eglinton did not find a way of including women in his vision of sport, though the female members of his own family were curlers and archers.

EGLINTON'S SCOTS PATRIOTISM

Eglinton, as we have seen, had political reasons for encouraging sport. He was also a strong Scottish patriot as well as a convinced Unionist. Thus his patriotism was chiefly cultural, and affected the choice of sports which he patronised, though it included the belief that the Scots should have an equal standing with the English.

The clearest manifestation of Eglinton's patriotism was his support for the National Association for the Vindication of the Rights of Scotland: it was he who presented their petition to the House of Lords in 1854; the only other speaker in its favour was the Duke of Montrose. The Association's concern was that the Union had given Scotland and England equal rights but that since 1707 Scotland's rights had been eroded. Some of the Association's arguments are still echoing 150 years later. For example, Scotland's *per capita* representation in parliament was lower, for there were only 53 Scots M.Ps. rather that 72 on the same basis as England – yet Scotland made its full contribution to the Exchequer. Government expenditure per capita was lower in Scotland than in England. English medical qualifications were valid in Scotland, but not Scots ones in England, though Scots medical schools – said the Association – were the best in Europe. The 16th Article of the Act of Union had said that the Scots mint would be continued, and the 19th its Court of Admiralty – neither had been carried out. The Ordnance Survey in England and Ireland had cost two million pounds, but only £130,000 had been spent in Scotland. One and a half million had been spent on Royal Parks in England, but just £16,000 on those in Scotland. The British Museum was supported and given money to build on a large scale, but there was no government-supported museum in Scotland. And so on.

Despite the support of thirty-nine town councils, and despite the Unionism which the supporters of the Petition, the burghs and Eglinton himself professed and emphasised, the Petition was voted down.[61] 'There is not another imperial interest unrepresented in the Cabinet', said the Petitioners. Finally, thirty-two years later, the office of the Secretary for Scotland was restored, and after another seven it became a Cabinet post.

Eglinton also led the opposition to the Bank Act (1845), which would have removed the power of the Scots banks to issue notes, and it was he who engineered a last minute compromise. There is an obvious parallel here with Scott and *The Letters of Malachai Malagrowther*, for in 1826 Scott too had successfully challenged an attempt to restrict the issue of banknotes to the Bank of England.[62] After the crash of the Western Bank in 1857, Eglinton helped to stabilise the situation by declaring his confidence in Scots banknotes.

There are other examples of his cultural patriotism. Eglinton's racing colours were tartan and yellow, and the painting of his *Flying Dutchman* beating *Voltigeur* at York in 1851 shows a thistle on the collar of his jockey's silks, and another on the front.[63] At the Burns Festival in 1844 some speakers praised English writers, Wordsworth particularly, but Eglinton was the only one who spoke about contemporary Scots authors, Christopher North and James Hogg.[64] At another dinner in 1844, in the George Inn at Kilmarnock, Eglinton was honoured as 'Patron and Promoter of our national sports and games'.[65]

EGLINTON AS A PATRON OF SPORT

The Tournament was a turning point in Eglinton's promotion of sport. Before 1839, his main interest was in horse-racing, but afterwards his enthusiasm was more various. The three sports which he patronised most actively were curling, bowls and golf. All three were distinctively Scots: Eglinton was a sporting patriot.

Eglinton adopted five tactics for encouraging sport. First, he was a keen player of several sports, especially curling, golf and bowls. He led by example: his activities were reported both in the local *Ayr*

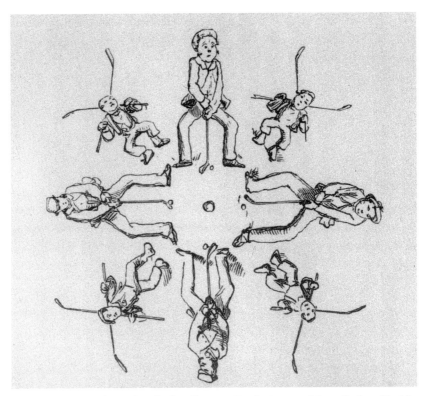

33. Golfers: a tailpiece by Charles Altamont Doyle (1832–93) from Robert Clark's
Golf: the Royal and Ancient Game (1875).

Advertiser and in the Glasgow papers. Next, he played with men from many backgrounds, not only his own landed class. Third, he provided sports grounds, such as the greens for the bowlers on his estate, and he gave turf to many more clubs. Fourth, he was a prolific donor of prizes. Finally, as an extension of prize giving, he created competitions and had his staff organise them and sometimes provided meals for players.

In bowling and curling Eglinton 'mixed genially on a common ground with the city merchant, the rural tenant, the country tradesman, and the cottar'. Not, it should be noted, with the miner, not with the Irish immigrant. 'Cricket, golf, curling &c., own him as their patron; and while he is an animated participant among his compeers, he loves to have a tussle with the sturdy yeoman and the brawny mechanic'.[66] In the 1850s he played in a Glasgow *v.* Ayrshire match at Kingston Green in Glasgow, against a rink 'composing decent shopkeepers from Tradeston, some with cutty pipes'[67] – the smoking of a cutty pipe indicating their closeness to the working class. Thus far went Eglinton, but no further. When W. W. Mitchell, author of the first laws of bowls, wrote of Eglinton -

> He greatly loved his fellow-men
> But saw a gap between
> An' closed it up, an' ilk class
> Became ilk other's frien'.[68]

– he was using poetic licence to allow him to make a more sweeping statement than was justified. Nevertheless, Eglinton was recognised as having tried to limit the damage which the Industrial Revolution was perceived to have done:

> In 'merrie England' athletic games have long been popular, and their beneficial results have had no small effect on the national character. There, rich and poor meet on common ground, all difference of rank being sunk in their enthusiastic pursuit ... Many are the noble examples of the aristocracy, both here and in England, who promote and encourage these pursuits, as a counteracting influence against the inroads of immorality and intemperance. Chief among these patriots ... stands ... the noble Earl of Eglinton and Winton.[69]

This is social leadership rather than social control. A different emphasis can be seen in a paragraph in the *Ayr Advertiser* in 1841 in which a 'National Games of Scotland' was suggested. It would be held on New Year's Day, 'to substitute innocent sports for the unmeaning dissipation which but too often takes place'.[70] Here, the possibility of social control is much nearer the surface; but there is no evidence that Eglinton attempted to use sport in this way.

One of the most striking aspects of popular leisure in nineteenth-century Scotland was the consumption of large quantities of whisky by working-class men – and to an extent women – which only declined slowly. In 1861 the *Glasgow Herald* argued that Eglinton's encouragement of sport had been effective in countering this threat to the stability of society:

Curling bowling and other kindred games have had a most sanitary [sic] effect in withdrawing from the demoralising influence of the dram shop; and we have no hesitation in saying that one-tenth of the ardent spirit is now consumed than was taken two or three years ago, prior to the establishment of more wholesome amusements.[71]

Curling, as we have seen, was the leading winter sport in the Lowlands before the sudden rise of football. Eglinton took to curling wholeheartedly, having artificial ponds laid out at Eglinton Castle and allowing himself to be seen as a curler by accepting the Presidency of the Royal Caledonian Curling Club. Curling had a different character in city and country: in the former it was socially exclusive, in the latter, inclusive. Thus it appealed to Eglinton, for as he put it 'curling was the medium for bringing together all classes of the community in a friendly spirit of Competition, from which all religious, & political differences, & all social asperities are banished'.[72] He also relished the Scottish nature of curling, emphasising its Scots language in saying to a curlers' dinner at Kilmarnock in 1844, 'You have placed me on the very tee of sportsmen. I am, as it were, surrounded on every side by friendly guards, open to no port or inwick, accessible only to the Kilmarnock twist, but that I know will never be erected against me'.[73]

Eglinton's lasting contribution to curling was the Eglinton Jug and the competition for it. This giant piece of highly-chased silver was first played for in 1851. The competition was between the curling clubs of Ayrshire, and was held on two days. On the first, winners emerged from the three divisions of the county, Cunningham, Kyle and Carrick. On the second, the three winners played to identify the winners of the Jug. The limited number of days on which curling was possible lent an urgency to proceedings. In 1860, for example, the first round was held on Boxing Day, when rinks from Cunningham met at Crawfurdland Loch, from Kyle at Tarbolton Loch, and from Carrick at Mochrum Loch. The overall result was decided the following day.[74] The whole event was made possible by the train services of the Glasgow & South Western Railway, by farmers who lent their carts to transport men and stones to the lochs, none of which were close to a station, by the electric telegraph to tell club secretaries that the lochs were bearing well enough for the competition, and by Eglinton's staff who administered the whole thing. His patronage went beyond merely commissioning the prize.

In curling, Eglinton took up a sport which was already successful and promoted it. In the 1850s, however, the modernised sport of bowls was still largely confined to Glasgow and north Ayrshire, and his interest contributed significantly to its development. Seven years after presenting the Jug for curling, Eglinton awarded a Cup for competition between the bowlers of Glasgow and those of Ayrshire. The organisation of the match was complex. It was held on the greens of Glasgow or Ayrshire in alternate years. One club visited each of the home clubs, and the names of the victors and the margin of victory were telegraphed to Eglinton Castle. There, the overall result was calculated and telegraphed back to the players. The man who was responsible for this was Robert Gardiner, 'General Secretary of the Bowlers of Ayrshire', who was in the employment of the Earl. Eglinton presented a variety of other bowling prizes, including one for clubs on his land.

William Mitchell, the Glasgow solicitor who was the other individual who contributed significantly to the growth of bowls in this period, paid tribute to Eglinton in the poem quoted above, and described him in action on one of the Glasgow greens in the first Glasgow-Ayrshire match:

> The Earl himself, at the head of five rinks from Ayrshire, played on the Willowbank Green, acted as driver of the middle rink and was supported by Mr C——, a somewhat demonstrative admirer of his lordship. In the course of the game, his lordship having played a bowl as directed by Mr C——, the latter began to flatter it as it coursed up the green by exclaiming and re-peating, with greater and still greater emphasis, 'I like you, my lord! I like you my lord!! I like you my lord!!! ... but suddenly and involuntarily changing the phrase as he saw the bowl approach and pass without effecting the object intended into, 'O Lord! you're too strong!' This ejaculation not only moved the risibility of his lordship but sent a general titter through the

players on the green and even communicated itself to the gay and fashionable assembly of ladies and gentlemen who crowded its banks.[75]

Mr C—— is Hugh Conn, curler, bowler, auctioneer and innkeeper in Kilwinning. Apart from a *frisson* of blasphemy, this quotation illustrates the fascination exercised by an aristocrat in 1857: Eglinton must have been aware of the power that it conferred. Mitchell dedicated to him the first book on bowls, his *Manual of Bowl Playing* (1864). When Eglinton died, the bowling community went into mourning, and the greens of Glasgow, Ayr and elsewhere were closed on the day of his funeral.[76]

He died after playing four rounds of the golf course at St Andrews in one day. An obituary said: 'To his munificence the golfers, the bowlers and the archers of Ayrshire are lastingly indebted for many a memorable tourney – the best of bonspiels in all three games having been for prizes out of a purse that was ever open'.[77] In the 1850s golf was a far less widespread sport than curling and bowls, so his patronage was more limited. He gave gold medals to Prestwick and Prestwick Mechanics (now St Nicholas) Golf Clubs. It was because of his interest, and that of his friend J. O. Fairlie of Coodham, that the event which in retrospect can be seen to be the first Open Championship was played not at St Andrews but at Prestwick. Eglinton presented the original prize, the Championship belt, which was won outright by young Tom Morris in 1870 and so superseded by the present claret jug. The choice of a belt as prize is connected with the Middle Ages. The common form of trophy of the medieval shooting guilds was a collar – and collars were common symbols of status showing membership of, say, an order of chivalry. The belt is merely a variant on the collar. It was also part of the tradition of the trophy or prize being something to be worn, which again stems from the Middle Ages. The Open Championship belt was not the first belt which Eglinton had presented, for we have already noted the Eglinton Gold Belt for the butts competition at Irvine, which like the Open Belt was held for a year while the winner retained a medal.

Eglinton thus supported Scottish sports with enthusiasm, and he also patronised sports which were imported from England. In 1860 he inaugurated the first racquet club in Glasgow.[78] He was commodore of the Royal Northern Yacht Club.[79] Cricket, most English of sports, grew rapidly in mid-nineteenth-century Scotland, and when he took the chair at a dinner in Glasgow to honour the All-England Eleven's visit in 1849, it was as the most sporting nobleman in Scotland rather than as a cricketer. Thereafter, he supported clubs such as Irvine Eglinton, but his son was a more active patron of the game. In one instance he is known to have encouraged a general sports day. His grandfather had founded the town of Ardrossan as the harbour which was to be at one end of the never-completed canal to Glasgow, and there games were held on Eglinton's birthday, including boat, sack, horse and foot races and quoiting.[80] In this, there is another hint of the feudal.

Having recognised the sports which Eglinton patronised, we can now list those with which he had no connection. He did not support folk football, which Hogg and Scott had loved; indeed, Eglinton did not enjoy the eighteenth century 'riot, revelry and rout' which had captivated the more traditionally-minded Scott. Nor did he follow prizefighting. His friends at Eton and in the London of the 1820s and 1830s would have been followers of the Fancy. The 1820s were by no means the worst decade in the history of the prize ring: Tom Spring, Jem Ward, Bill Neat and Tom Hickman 'The Gas Man' were all active. This, after all, is the decade when Hazlitt wrote his essay on 'The Fight', and his even more memorable lines on the death of Cavenaugh, the Irish fives player, whom he turned into a hero. Eglinton had no interest in handball, though it was popular in central Ayrshire. Quoiting, too, was popular in the county, and other landowners encouraged it. The *Ayr Advertiser* said in 1830: 'We should like to see our gentry taking an interest in this sport. The game has nothing of the brutality of the English prize-ring, while it possesses all that is necessary to prevent the people from sinking into that state of enervation and effeminacy which is the certain precursor of the decline and fall of all empires'.[81] Eglinton ignored it. During his lifetime, cock-fighting and other animal sports were being suppressed all over Britain. Nevertheless, one Ayrshire landowner was conspicuous for supporting them – the 4th Marquis of Hastings (1842–68). At his coming-of-age celebrations he appeared as Charles II. Eglinton may have been an improvident young man, but Hastings was wild, discarding his fortune on horses before dying at the age of twenty-six. He was an avid supporter of cock-fighting and ratting, sports which in his lifetime were both low and illegal.[82] His sporting activities, however, seem to have been confined to the south of England.

Eglinton avoided cock-fighting, athletics, prizefighting and quoiting because of their links with gambling; folk football, cock-fighting, and prizefighting because of their violence and cruelty. He gave up racing at Bogside in 1853 when he became Lord Lieutenant of Ireland, and he sold all his horses. Racing meant gambling, and was associated in England with the prize ring and cock-fighting. Rounders and handball seem to have failed to attract his attention because they were the sports of farm labourers and miners, and handball had strong Irish associations. He regarded all sports which required access to the land as being for the owners of that land, and he did not promote them beyond that limited circle. He similarly regarded all sports which involved the use of weapons, even obsolete weapons such as the bow and arrow, as being confined to a limited social group.

Who was Archibald William Montgomerie, 13th Earl of Eglinton? Toasted at dozens of dinners and memorialised profusely in obituaries, one aspect of him emerges, one set of related characteristics – he was cheerful, active, good-natured, well-meaning, and most vividly, everybody liked him. 'The Earl of Eglinton was without question the most popular nobleman in the kingdom', said one obituary.[83] The *Dictionary of National Biography* closed the case: he was 'a high-minded nobleman and a thorough sportsman, with frank and genial manners and no particular ability'. It was important to Eglinton to be liked by everybody. He was unusual in one way, for he wanted to be liked by the people as well as by his own class. He achieved this goal, not by being daring, unusual, or eccentric, but by being what people wanted him to be, and giving them what they wanted to be given. It is for this reason that I think we can trust him to reflect the true spirit of sporting activity. Yet at the same time he did not change the way in which sport developed, but rather accelerated its growth and, as we will see below, helped to foster the development of the idea of competition.

REFERENCES

1. For the background, see Girouard (1981).
2. Strutt (1808), i, 20–4.
3. Anstruther (1963), 119.
4. Anon (1831), 77.
5. Grierson (1933), 128.
6. Craig-Brown (1886), ii, 64–6.
7. Kerr (1900), 298.
8. *GH*, 8 September 1828.
9. *OSA*, xx, 433.
10. Reproduced by Sloan (1986), 7–8.
11. Geddes (1792), 444.
12. *FH*, 2 January 1851.
13. *GC*, 24 July 1849.
14. *AA*, 12 January 1836; Baxter (1898), 25–6.
15. Crawford (1838), 4.
16. Peakodde (1835).
17. Ibid., viii.
18. *PC*, 16 and 23 January 1850.
19. The account presented here is a revision of Burnett & Dalgleish (1995), which contains more detail on the arrow itself, the medals attached to it, and the craftsmen who made them.
20. Anon. (1829), 5.
21. Groves (1987), 5.
22. Balfour Paul (1875), 378.
23. Groves (1987), 5.
24. Hogg (1985), 44.
25. Groves (1987), 5.
26. Hogg (1985), 49.
27. Scott (1832), ii, 358.
28. Anon (1830), Anon (1831), 76.
29. Lockhart (1902–3), vii, 192–4.
30. Balfour Paul (1875), 380.
31. Groves (1987), 18.
32. *GH*, 18 August 1834.
33. Balfour Paul (1875), 222, 243.
34. *DT*, 19 August 1835.
35. *AA*, 10 October 1861. For a general account of Eglinton's sporting activities, see Dixon (1865), 288–95.
36. *GC*, 12 October 1861.
37. *AA*, 10 October 1861.
38. Dodds (1992).
39. Anstruther (1963), 49.
40. Fairfax-Blakeborough (1973), 205.

41. Anstruther (1963), 59.

42. Woodward (1962), 169. The Derby had been founded by his grandfather.

43. *PA*, 2 November 1839, quoting the *Glasgow Courier*.

44. Anstruther (1963) gives a good account of the events.

45. Anon (1840), i, 490.

46. On display in the council chamber of North Ayrshire District Council.

47. The Stewards' Cup, Goodwood, 1853, and the Ascot Gold Vase, 1860, both in the National Horse Racing Museum, Newmarket.

48. Strawhorn (1989), 139.

49. Aikman (1839), 10.

50. *AA*, 14 May 1846.

51. *GA*, 31 August 1846.

52. The 1846 medal is in the National Museums of Scotland, H. 1955.321.

53. *AA*, 3 September 1846.

54. Disraeli (1845), book I, chapter V.

55. Disraeli (1845), book IV, chapter V.

56. *EEC*, 11 September 1858.

57. Aikman (1839), 17.

58. *AA*, 10 October 1861.

59. *AA*, 21 March 1844.

60. *GH*, 12 September 1857.

61. *AA*, 1 December 1853, quoting the *Glasgow Constitutional*; *AA*, 13 April and 12 October 1854.

62. Johnson (1970), 973–6.

63. In the National Horse Racing Museum, Newmarket.

64. *Illustrated London News*, 10 August 1844, 94.

65. *AA*, 21 March 1844.

66. *AA*, 8 July 1858.

67. Hedderwick (1891), 203–5.

68. Quoted by Pilley (1987), 96.

69. *AA*, 8 July 1858.

70. *AA*, 4 January 1841.

71. *GH*, 16 October 1861.

72. Letter of 2 June 1851, quoted by Smith (1985), 32.

73. *AA*, 21 March 1844.

74. *AA*, 3 January 1861.

75. Quoted by Pilley (1987), 95.

76. *AA*, 10 October 1861.

77. *GMJ*, 7 October 1861, from the *Ayrshire Express*.

78. *GH*, 5 October 1861.

79. *AA*, 7 September 1854.

80. *AA*, 3 October 1844, 6 October 1853.

81. *AA*, 24 July 1834.

82. Blyth (1966), 67–72.

83. *GMJ*, 7 October 1861.

CHAPTER NINE

The End of Tradition

In previous chapters we have described a range of traditional Scottish sports. By the early nineteenth century a number of general trends become clear, trends which affected the place of all sports in society. The more violent sports were, as in England, in decline. Wagering was a characteristic of certain sporting circles, and games days, with several events being performed in succession, appeared for the first time in Lowland Scotland. Both of these developments can be seen emerging in an unusual Edinburgh sporting club, the Gymnastic, which existed between about 1770 and 1820. The increasing quantity of evidence available, particularly in newspapers, makes it possible to say a little about the place of women in sport, and to notice the odd absence of sport from Aberdeenshire at the beginning of the nineteenth century. Finally, the distribution of sports through the year altered so that in the early Victorian era it was significantly different from the pattern which had been largely unchanged since the Reformation.

THE DECLINE OF TRADITIONAL SPORT

Dangerous and cruel sports were in decline at the beginning of the nineteenth century.[1] By 1860 some, such as cock-fighting, had gone underground. The new police forces put down hainching and other vigorous ball games which were played in the streets, including shinty, handball (the descendent of caich), heuch-and-yanky, whose nature is unknown, and cat-and-bat, a form of cricket.[2]

Bare-knuckle boxing was always rare in Scotland. This was stated explicitly in a report of a fight held at the time of the Dumfries Races in 1816. The bruisers, Carter and Oliver, were well known in the English prize ring, and one of the seconds was the current champion of England, Tom Cribb (1781–1848). As was the English practice, the fight took place close to an administrative boundary, at Springfield Farm near Gretna. The boundary was that between the two counties: prizefighting at the highest level penetrated no more than a few hundred yards into Scotland. The fight:

> created a stir singularly rich and ludicrous in our northern hemisphere, coaches, tax-carts and donkeys, fleshless horses, beggars and blacklegs, the White and the Black [the innocent and the villain], the swindler and the gentleman, *chumming* and betting, advising and instructing. Springfield beheld a multitude, so multifarious and heterogeneous as completely laughed to scorn a Gretna marriage.[3]

Newspaper reporters are notoriously knowing, but this account is written from the outside: bare-knuckle fighting must have been unfamiliar to the writer. There was no patronage of the kind which had supported boxing in England – from the aristocracy in the eighteenth and early nineteenth centuries, and from the Duke of Clarence, later King William IV, particularly. The appearance of 'the Bath Butcher', Daniel Mendoza (1764–1836), recruiting for the Fifeshire Fencibles in 1796, is a rare example of a leading English prizefighter appearing in Scotland, if in an odd rôle.

Sandy M'Kay, called the Scottish champion, died in 1830 after a fight in England: his opponent was tried for murder. 'Another of these blackguard and degrading exhibitions', said the *Scotsman*. Ironically, it is in the following thirty years that prizefighting appears sufficiently frequently in Scots newspapers for one to conclude that this was the undistinguished zenith of the sport in Scotland. One popular venue was the area round Castlecary, which was roughly equidistant from Glasgow and Edinburgh, and on the boundary of Stirlingshire and Dunbarton. Nevertheless, the Sheriff-Substitute from Falkirk successfully stopped a fight there in 1846.[4]

In Scotland, the prize ring was rarely mentioned without criticism. In 1833 a fight between a weaver and a bottle blower at Partick was watched by 'as select a parcel of vagabonds as we have ever before seen congregated in so small a space'.[5] When in 1850 a boxer appeared in the Trades' Hall at Montrose, the local paper said he had 'a very thin, but, for the occasion, far too numerous an audience'.[6] Bare-knuckle fighting continued in a minor way until towards the end of the nineteenth century it was replaced by organised glove fights which included the boxing booths which were to be a distinctive part of working-class leisure, particularly in the cities.

Shinty had been played all over Scotland in the seventeenth century, and it was still common at the beginning of the nineteenth. A recollection of Hamilton about 1810 said that:

> The boys, instead of being confined, like those of the larger manufacturing towns, in unhealthy cotton mills, are permitted ... to play at the ba' and shinty, or at bows and arrows ...[7]

The game, however, was in decline. A few miles from Hamilton, shinty was played on Hogmuir Common at East Kilbride until about 1840.[8] Govan-born James Nicholson, in his poem 'A laddie's exaltation o'er the finding o' his whittle', published in 1870, imagined what he and the knife would do together: 'crummie sticks we'll cut galore' –

> An when the frosty winds blaw keen
> Shinties to fung the fleeing bool.[9]

As the century advanced, there were fewer references to Lowland shinty. It was still being played at Moffat Grammar School and Forfar Academy in 1876 – or rather it had 'not quite fallen into desuetude', and in Edinburgh at the High School and at Edinburgh Academy where it survives to this day as *hailes*.[10]

There were three reasons for complaints about shinty: the game itself was dangerous to passers by, as was bulleting, and also matches in some places, such as the Mearns, were likely to end in a fight.[11] It was also opposed because boys made their shinties from hawthorn hedges, and the best clubs were made with the root forming the striking part: farmers resented the damage.[12]

If some sports were in decline, others were being reshaped. Several long-established horse-race meetings came to an end around the mid-century. The last races were held at Cupar in 1841, Aberdeen in 1847 (though there was a brief revival in 1875–76), and Dumfries in the same year. There, it was an emotional occasion for after the last race 102 ploughs were assembled to destroy the turf in a single day.[13] This is reminiscent of the treatment of a healing well near Aberfeldy. It was a depression on top of a boulder where dew collected. When a new road was built the boulder was blown to pieces and used to surface the road. One wonders about the underlying emotions, the guilt which might have arisen from being responsible for ending a centuries-old tradition.

The continuation of some events was dependent on individuals. In the 1830s and 1840s the leading figure in Scottish horse-racing was William Ramsay of Barnton: he organised, bred, financed, and officiated.[14] Stirling Races were in abeyance between 1813 and 1837: with Lord Dalmeny, it was Ramsay who set them going again. He supported the attempt to set up Glasgow Races at Pollok in 1838. For nine years out of ten from 1835, his horses gained the most famous prize in Scotland, the Ayr Gold Cup. At a hunt dinner at Forfar in 1840 his health was drunk with 'rapturous view hollo's'.[15] The famous racing journalist, the 'Druid', said that when Ramsay died in 1850 the Scottish turf, hunting and road racing all 'drooped'.[16]

Following Ramsay's demise, Stirling races, run since the sixteenth century, lasted only four more years. The Free Church broke away from the Church of Scotland in 1843, and took with it most of the extreme evangelicals, among them Peter Drummond, who became an elder of the Free Kirk. His language was lurid:

> Ah! there will be no racing there [in hell], but everlasting chains; no Italian music, but weeping and wailing, and gnashing of teeth.[17]

Drummond's chief objections were to gambling, which he believed ruined poor people, and to the thieves and beggars who followed the races. In 1854 he added that at a time when soldiers were dying in the Crimea 'Three successive days of humiliation and prayer' would be more appropriate than horse-racing.[18] The opposition of some members of the public is not likely to have been directly responsible for the demise of the races. However, smaller meetings like Stirling were dependent on a handful of patrons and if Free Kirk pressure made one or two of them hesitate to be seen to support racing, then the future of one meeting could easily come into question in the absence of a strong-minded enthusiast like Ramsay.

THE WAGER AND THE CHALLENGE

In 1838, on the afternoon of Hansel Monday, the 68-year old David Proudfoot of Craigend, south of Perth, wagered 7s 6d that he could wheel a wheelbarrow from Bridge of Earn to Edinburgh and back. He reached Edinburgh the following day, rested a day, and returned with a certificate from the owner of Gibb's hotel to prove his feat.[19]

Wagering was a characteristic feature of sporting activity between the middle of the eighteenth and the middle of the nineteenth century. We can distinguish it from betting on an event such as a horse race or a game of cards. The latter was common in certain circles, as Burns wrote of Robert Fergusson:

> My curse upon your whinstane hearts
> Ye Edinburgh gentry –
> The tythe o what ye waste at cartes
> Wad stow'd his pantry.[20]

To bet on cards was to accept a set of rules. The wager involved the creation of rules, a playful testing of the boundaries of sport, judgement, and achievement. It was thus an inventive activity, and often the feat which was suggested had an element of fun in it. The serious undertone between the two (or more) men who discussed and then made the wager was that one understood the world better than the other, or like David Proudfoot, that he had a better estimate of his own capabilities, his own physical power.

There was an element of the absurd in many eighteenth-century wagers. About 1795 the Laird of Usan, a decorous and careful man, attended Montrose races, and at dinner drank extensively – to the point where he backed himself to smash all the *pigs* – all the crockery that could be got – in Montrose without using a stick or other weapon. The wager was with 'The Hon. Mr. M——' – almost certainly Maule of Panmure, hard drinker and hard liver. Maule had a stage set up in the marketplace. Usan threw teapots to the ground, and, wearing fisherman's boots, trampled on the rest. 'He's dancing – send for the fiddlers', cried the crowd. Usan seems to have won his bet, but he felt that he had lost his reputation and never again appeared at the races.[21] Two points arise from this wager. First, it required public performance: the spectator, even if present only retrospectively was part of the wager. Indeed, one aim of these wagers was to create an anecdote. This leads to the second point, that the framing of the wager was improved by ingenuity, for the more improbable it was on the surface, the better the banter before and after.

Captain Barclay of Urie, properly Robert Barclay Allardyce (1779–1854), who was known throughout Britain as a sportsman, in 1809 walked 1,000 miles in each of 1,000 consecutive hours for a wager of 1,000 guineas. Though he was an Angus landlord, he performed this feat at Newmarket – significantly, the centre of horse-racing, where betting was at the core of life. It was the beginning of half a century of heavy gambling on athletics.[22] Barclay was a member of the *fancy*, a trainer of prizefighters including the unfortunate Sandy M'Kay. Like other wealthy sportsmen of the period he drove stage coaches, particularly the Edinburgh-Aberdeen *Defiance* of which he was part-owner. He was a leading cattle breeder, walking large distances over the Highlands to look for animals with which to deploy his ideas: both in agriculture and in sport he was an agent of change.

Increasingly the clock and the watch played a part in wagers. In 1829 David Ritchie of Challoch laid 100 sovereigns with two other Wigtownshire lairds, Sir James Hay and M'Taggart of Ardwall, that he would walk the 52 miles from the King's Inn at Stranraer to Ayr in 15 hours. He left at 3.07 a.m. – there is a clear implication of a wager made over drinks after dinner – took breakfast at Ballantrae, lunch at Kirkoswald, and arrived at Ayr more than half an hour within his time.[23] In 1845 a man backed a horse which was one of the team on the Glasgow to Balfron coach to ride 19 miles from Glasgow to Balfron in an hour and a quarter, and he won with 9½ minutes to spare.[24] Mechanical timekeeping was the first technology to affect sport, several decades before the railway.

The wager had a broader form, the challenge. Whereas the wager concerned a single event, the challenge was an assertion of superiority over any competitor in the nominated sport. Challengers were invited to try to take the championship from the holder. The idea of the champion is taken from medieval chivalry. Challenges were already familiar in the English prize ring, and at the present day it is still the method for producing winners at the highest level of boxing.

The challenge was important because of the absence of organisations to manage other forms of competition. In athletics, this was to change with forming of the Scottish Amateur Athletics Association in 1883. Before then, athletics outside the schools and universities was largely professional, and the challenge was its commonest form: it was dramatic and attracted the large crowds which the promoters sought. It was a British phenomenon: here is a Scots example. In 1840 an Englishman who called himself Merrylegs issued a challenge through the sporting papers: he would race any man in Scotland over three miles, giving him a quarter mile start for £100 a side. With the aid of the railway, a 'huge' crowd assembled at Paisley where the race took place in thick fog and only those on the finishing line could see that Merrylegs lost to a farmer's son from Strathaven.[25] Athletics was at this stage part of the world of the *fancy*, the world of prizefighting, horse-racing, gambling and hard drinking. Merrylegs took his pseudonym from a successful race horse.

THE AESCULAPIAN AND GYMNASTIC CLUBS

The Gymnastic Club was an association of Edinburgh medical men and their friends. Founded about 1770, it was like many other small Edinburgh clubs who dined and drank and talked and talked. It differed from other clubs because the members also met for physical exercise. They must have been well known because the individual members were conspicuous Edinburgh figures.

The Gymnastic Club had its intellectual roots in the eighteenth-century belief that exercise was good for health. This was set out in *Domestic Medicine* (1769) by the Edinburgh physician William Buchan. The point was argued at even greater length by Sir John Sinclair in his *Code of Longevity* (1807): longevity was a requirement for reading its four tedious volumes. The originality of the Gymnastic Club was to link the maintenance of health with the promotion of sociability, and use the well-developed idea of a Club to create a structure for sports. The Gymnastic Club meetings were the first in Lowland Scotland to incorporate several different sports, and so they form a prologue to the growth of general games days in the second quarter of the nineteenth century.

Andrew Duncan (1744–1828) was an Edinburgh physician and Professor of the Institutes of Medicine – which we may translate as physiology – from 1790. His family had been minor lairds in Fife but his uncle sold the estate at Pinkerton which Andrew would have inherited. In later life, nevertheless, he retained an interest in the East Neuk. A typical story about Duncan concerns his involvement in the repair of the tomb of Dr Archibald Pitcairne in Greyfriars churchyard. Pitcairne, a relentless Jacobite, had in his will left a Jeroboam of wine with the instruction that it was only to be opened 'at the restoration' – the restoration of the Stuart monarchy being assumed. Duncan decided that the restoration of the tomb was a sufficient reason, and the bottle was drunk.[26] This anecdote is typical of a man who had a weakness for claret and weak puns, and was an admirable organiser.

Duncan was a highly sociable man in a city full of clubs: he founded several for his friends. It is not clear whether he was the founder of the Gymnastic Club for two surgeons, William Inglis and 'Lang Sandy' Wood, may have had larger parts than Duncan in its inception, but from near the beginning he took a leading part. The Aesculapian Club, which Duncan instigated in 1773, was a medical dining club and it still exists.[27] The two clubs were closely linked in membership and sporting enthusiasms.

The Gymnastic Club's early years are shadowy. Some glimpses of later activity can be seen in the Aesculapian minute books. Wagers were frequently made over dinner, as to whether one of the members would be married in the next year, or whether the government was about to fall. These bets were in magnums of claret or of punch, or of fresh melons. One of the golfing wagers recorded was this, in 1797:

Dr Duncan offers to bet a Magnum of punch against Mr Alex Wood that in the Match at golf to be played to-morrow – Mr Alexr Wood aet 70 & Master Alexr Wood aet 7 against Dr Duncan aet 50 & Master H. Duncan aet 5 The Duncans shall be victorious. Mr Wood accepts.

So the two medical sportsmen played in partnership with their grandsons: the result was a draw.[28]

In an invitation to a Gymnastic Convention about 1820, Duncan wrote:

> There will be gowfing and bowling
> There will be laughing and Fun
> There will be sensible nonsense
> And sometimes a very bad pun.[29]

This is based on the song 'The Blythsome Wedding' which was probably written in the seventeenth century. It must have been a favourite of Duncan's, for he used it as the basis for a number of other occasional pieces. It points out that Duncan and his friends were aware of the tradition of festivals which ended with dining and drinking. It also draws our attention to Duncan's activities as a preserver and continuer of Scottish traditions.

Duncan and his friends were consciously Scots. When he wrote an obituary of Professor Alexander Munro *secundus* (1733–1817) in the form of a pamphlet, he printed an appendix containing songs which Duncan and Munro had sung together. Munro's family protested that the publication of songs along with the obituary was in poor taste. Duncan removed the songs from the pamphlet, and inserted them into a new one with an additional 36 pages of similar Scots material. Duncan wrote a new version of the song 'Was you e'er at Crail Town', referring to the Gymnastics. It began:

> Was you e'er on Leith Links?
> Play'd you e'er at High Jinks?
> Was you e'er at Hadden's Hole;
> Saw you e'er the Games of Pol?

– *the Games of Pol* being the *Ludi Apollinares*, for Apollo was supposedly a victor in the first Olympic Games, and gymnastic contests were a feature of feasts of Apollo. The significance of *Hadden's Hole* is not clear: it refers either to one of the subdivisions of St Giles's Kirk, or to the prison within the kirk building where Sir John Gordon of Haddo was held before his execution in 1644;[30] or perhaps the name had been transferred to a familiar howff.

High Jinks was a drinking game in which one of the company threw a pair of dice calling as he did so 'High Jinks'. The number indicated who should next drink, or pay a forfeit. The song continued:

> There an assembled band of Doctors
> Drink, laugh, and sing, like Good Health Proctors;
> To drive dull care from plodding Brains
> And cure the Bones of aching Pains.[31]

As well as being consciously Scots, Duncan was consciously classical, though he was aware of Buchanan and Ruddiman and would have seen himself as being Scots in this too. Thus the adoption of the name *Ludi Apollinares*; Duncan himself was *scriba praetorius*. The Gymnastic Club had three cups to which winners added medals. In form, they were simple Greek urns rather than the baroque two-handled cups which were then the fashion in horse-racing.

At the Gymnastic meetings there was an atmosphere of frivolity, not competition, and the sociable behaviour of Duncan and his friends and colleagues extended through a series of dining clubs at which there were songs and recitations: there was every encouragement to original composition. The most fluent and witty of the writers was Sir Alexander Boswell (1775–1822), eldest son of the biographer:

> If of Murder and Death
> Chill the Blood, in Macbeath
> Talk of *Duncan*, we hear ravens croaking
> But Duncan that's here
> Is th' assassin, I fear
> Who kills us, remorseless, with joking.[32]

In time, enthusiasm for Gymnastic events waned. A minute book recorded the distribution of prizes after one of their meetings, probably about 1815:

1. To Dr Hamilton, victor in golfing, because, although absent, he had intended to have golfed, and none came to oppose.
2. To Dr Barclay, victor in bowling, for his decided superiority.
3. To Dr Cheyne, victor in swimming, because, had he gone into the sea, he would have beat Dr Duncan, who did not swim that day.[33]

Looking beyond sport and socialising, we can see that Duncan was aware of the power of an institution to effect change. Shocked by the death of Robert Fergusson in Edinburgh's inadequate madhouse he worked until a humane asylum was finally set up in 1819: it has evolved into the Royal Edinburgh Hospital. He was the central figure behind the Royal Public Dispensary (1776), which gave cheap medical treatment to the poor. He ensured that the Royal Medical Society, a student body, received a royal charter in 1786: his immediate aim was to enable it to own property and so secure its future, but his real goal was to promote discussion as part of medical training – again we see Duncan's awareness of the virtues of sociability. This extended beyond death. From time to time his students died far from their foreign homes and he paid for their burial: their small headstones are grouped round his in Buccleuch burying ground.

The significance of the Gymnastic games is that they were both forward- and backward-looking. They were traditional in that they were for a limited group – perhaps twenty at the most – and had no thought of spectators. Sport to the Gymnastics was not an isolated activity, but part of a sociable day. In as far as there was a sense of competition, it stemmed either from wagering, or from seeking the honour of adding a medal to a cup. But the Gymnastic games were also forward-looking: they had a purpose, the maintenance of health, and they had a written structure; and thus they were a model for the holding of general games days.

ABERDEENSHIRE

On the basis of the limited evidence available to us, there is no reason to suppose that sport in Aberdeenshire and Moray in the seventeenth and early eighteenth centuries was much different from that in other areas of Lowland Scotland. There were horse races at Aberdeen and Huntly, and the tradition of football matches on Christmas Day was as strong as anywhere in the country. Alexander Johnson (1746–1813), minister of Monquhitter in Aberdeenshire said that in the middle of the eighteenth century:

[Farm servants] frequently met to exert their strength in

wrestling, in casting the hammer, and in throwing the stones; their agility at football, and their dexterity at coits and penny-stane.[34]

Yet an examination of Aberdeen and Aberdeenshire newspapers in the first half of the nineteenth century shows that there was surprisingly little sport there, far less than in the Midland Valley or the Borders. As early as 1791 Johnson said that 'athletic games' were only for schoolboys. What had happened?

Part of the answer lies in changing patterns of work. Johnson described the alterations brought by agricultural improvement over the previous half century:

> It deserves notice, that before rational farming dawned, servants had in summer little to do, but to drive peat, cut grass, and pull thistles. They slept through the greater part of the day, and executed the little work incumbent upon them during the night.[35]

The author of the *General View of the Agriculture of Aberdeenshire* (1811) agreed. Around 1770, he said, the labourer had less work than thirty years later, when there was frequent ploughing, and the hoeing of turnips and potatoes, resulting in a 12-hour day in summer.[36] By the 1790s the minister of Drainy in Morayshire said that his parishoners 'seldom indulge in relaxation or diversion'.[37]

Johnson saw the vanishing of adult sport as part of the spread of purely rational behaviour in Scotland: he implies that it was one of the beneficial results of the Enlightenment. He linked the decline of sport with the disappearance of bonfire-lighting at midsummer and Hallowmas, and the decline of the penny wedding which he condemned as a drunken riot. This is to see sport as necessarily violent, or at least as depending on strength – the opposite of rational thought. By mentioning sport along with hallowfire Johnson associated it with pagan, and therefore irrational, belief. Underlying his view is the idea that the Enlightenment had done away with a strenuous and pointless form of physical activity.

Johnson also makes the broader point that men were working far harder, and in this sense scientific agriculture was inimical to sport: it destroyed the time available for it. William Alexander's stories of

Buchan life in the middle of the nineteenth century contain individuals who begin as penniless farm loons with only a little ability, who rise through solid hard work. The interminable darg dominated North-East farming life to a greater extent than other parts of Scotland. There was a 'ferocious work ethic', someone has said.

Yet sport, as we have seen, did not need to take up many hours in the year. Two other factors contributed to its limited presence in this period: the pattern of settlement, and the nature of the sporting tradition in the north-east.

Traditional sport was played primarily by young men: in Aberdeenshire and Banff many of them were distributed in the fermtouns, a few in each one. North-east farms were typically medium-sized, worked by one family with the minimum of hired help. Before about 1840 land reclamation, which could potentially fill every hour of the day, was being carried out intensively. Most farm folk had neither time nor money to spend on leisure. After 1840 came the boom years, when the demands of the growing industrial population brought burgeoning profits and scope for sport and other forms of enjoyment. At the same time the improvement of road transport and the advent of railways lessened the isolation of many fermtouns.

There were only a few larger towns, and most of those that did exist were on the coast – Banff, Macduff, Fraserburgh, Peterhead – and had their economic base in fishing. Sport was not a component of the life of fishing communities. Aberdeen, the dominant city, did not itself have a strong sporting tradition. The annual horse race, common in the larger burghs further south, was held only sporadically at Aberdeen: in the 1660s, 1790s, 1816–29, and finally in 1843–47.[38] The attempt to set up 'the Ascot of Buchan' a few years later was a total failure. We have already seen that the example of Leith Races contributed to the shaping of the Carter's Plays: there was no similar example in Aberdeenshire. Bowling has a continuous history in Glasgow and Edinburgh, but after attaining some popularity in mid-eighteenth century Aberdeen it died out by 1820 and was not revived until the middle of the nineteenth century. Curling, already highly popular further south before the end of the eighteenth century, did not appear in Aberdeenshire until the 1840s.

When sport was revived in Aberdeenshire it spread rapidly. Curling first appeared there in the late 1840s: within thirty years it had been taken up enthusiastically everywhere. Summer games with a more or less Highland flavour were begun. In 1830 the only games were in upper Deeside and Donside. By 1855 local games were held in the following places in Aberdeenshire and Banffshire: Auchterless, Banchory, Cruden, Cullen, Fiddichside (near Balvenie), Glenbuchat, Insch, Logie Coldstone, Lossiemouth, Lumphanan, Midmar, Oldmeldrum, Peterhead, Strathdon – and finally, in the middle of September, at Braemar. There 'the scene became very grand, the greatest sovereign on the face of the earth condescending in such a gracious manner to countenance the amusements of her Highland subjects ...'.[39] Royal patronage gave an impetus to these games, but they were increasing in number before Queen Victoria first went to Braemar Highland Gathering in 1848. Some games were developed under the patronage of a laird such as the Farquharsons of Corrachree who gave prizes (in both senses) at the Cromar gathering at Logie Coldstone.[40] Others were organised by Friendly Societies: the Lonach Gathering, for example. Finally, some were administered by societies which had been formed purely to hold games like the Peterhead Athletic Club and the Banffshire Lower Association for the Promotion of the National Games of Scotland, or at Oldmeldrum by young men who simply wanted 'to try their agility at athletic games'.[41]

By the 1860s the amount of sport in Aberdeenshire was not signifcantly different from any other part of rural Scotland, though there was a higher concentration of games days and less of other sports.

WOMEN AND SPORT

Before the second half of the twentieth century, the chief role of women in sport was as spectators. Sport was also an opportunity for men to show their strength and virility to women as well as to one another. In the medieval tournament, knights fought for the esteem of their lady, and in the nineteenth century women watched cricket matches. Sports which were closely linked with the administration of the burgh such as the siller guns, excluded women:

neither could they become apprentices, journeymen, masters or members of the town council. The psychological relationship between sport and war made sporting women seem incongruous, for they were trespassing on a male activity.

There was far less sport for women in Scotland than in England, particularly because of the southern tradition of smock races, for which the prize was a smock or shift. These were usually coupled with a foot race for men with the prize of a hat. They were held all over England at Whitsun or Midsummer, and it has been reasonably conjectured that they embody a pagan fertility rite. They certainly contained a sexual element. The competitors rarely wore more than their shifts, and on occasion they wore nothing at all: a race for a Holland smock on Walworth Common (Surrey) in 1748 was held between 'two women stark naked'. As soon as moral questions were raised by Evangelicals around 1830, smock-racing came to an abrupt end.

There is a record of the deliberate introduction of a smock race in Scotland, at Tarbrax near Forfar in 1798, where three races were held for a shift, a red petticoat, and a pair of stockings. The innovator was Col. Fothringham: as a military officer he would have had the opportunity to become familiar with English popular culture.[42] At Aberdeen in 1766 it was advertised:

> that there are two races to be run for men; the first for a piece of English cloth for a coat, a bonnet, and a pair of shoes; the second for 10/-. And two races for women, the first for a piece of check for a gown, some yards of linen, and a silk napkin; the second for 10/-. The above prizes are given by the Honourable Company for Water Drinkers at Peterhead.[43]

Peterhead was then a spa: thus the Water Drinkers had gone there for their health, and are likely to have included English people who were aware of the tradition of smock racing.

In the period before nineteenth-century evangelical seriousness limited the behaviour of women there is a range of references to women enjoying sport. It was not common for them to do so, but it was probably widely known. For example, the following notice appeared in the *Belfast News Letter* in 1739:

Edinburgh, Feb. 11. A famous curling match was lately play'd
on the water of Skarr in Nithsdale, between the married wives
and the young girls of the parish of Tinron; the maids shew'd
a good deal of dexterity in handling the STONES, and will, no
doubt, be very expert in time; but they were defeated by the
more experienc'd wives, after a tryal of a great many hours.[44]

Almost a hundred years later the *Dumfries Journal* reported:

FEMALE CURLING! – To such a height has the manly game of
curling arrived of late in Keir, that on Tuesday last two rinks
of blooming maids, the one from the estate of Capenoch, the
other from that of Waterside, met on the *Ged* Loch, to contest
the palm of victory. A more interesting spectacle could not well
be witnessed. Hundreds of spectators met at an early hour, some
purely from amusement – others to gaze with delight on the
fair forms of their sweethearts, removed altogether to a different
appearance [than] that in which they had so long been accus-
tomed to contemplate them ... The *curling* broom they
managed with as much dexterity as the *household* one, and the
channel-stone as the distaff ... The evening was spent with as
much hilarity as the day – the rattling sound of the stone having
given place to the spirit-stirring sound of the fiddle, and a
footing on the cold ice being exchanged for the 'tripping on the
light fantastic toe' in the evolutions of the mazy dance.[45]

It is remarkable that they refer to almost exactly the same place.
The Scaur Water is a tributary of the Nith which rises in the round,
remote hills north-west of Thornhill; the parishes of Tynron and
Keir are adjacent and the lands of Capenoch and Waterside are
side-by-side on the south bank of the Scaur. Other examples of
women curling are recorded from nearby Sanquhar in 1820 and 1826,
and from Lamington, on the other side of the Lowther Hills.[46] A
sport does not need to be practised often to have a continuous
tradition, and one is inclined to think that in long cold spells the
women of Nithsdale were allowed to play. This might be only once
in ten or twenty years, sufficiently rarely to make it memorable, but
sufficiently frequent to constitute a living tradition.

The curling match on the Scaur between the married and single women contains the same idea of contention for fertility which is in the much more common matches at football, curling and other sports, between bachelors and married men. This distant echo of a fertility rite is also heard in the women's football match at Musselburgh, also on Fastern's E'en.[47]

Middle-class women had some opportunities for sport. For example, they had their own archery competitions, and after the mid-century croquet. Just beyond the period of this book small numbers took up golf, bowling and curling, and in the 1880s tennis.[48] The number of women who had access to these sports was small; though not as small as the number of women who boxed, as two did on Glasgow Green in 1828.[49]

The main involvement of women in sport in the nineteenth century was as patrons or spectators rather than players. Wealthy women presented sporting prizes, such as the miniature silver curling stone which Mrs Houison-Crawfurd of Craufurdland gave for competition between the curlers of Fenwick and Kilmarnock. Whilst many sports were watched only by men, one or two attracted women. The clearest case is horse-racing, particularly when as at Marymass at Irvine it was part of a general holiday. Families were often noted at Paisley races, where they picnicked in the middle of the course.

THE EARLY VICTORIAN YEAR

During the nineteenth century the relationship between social life in Scotland and the calendar was completely reconstructed. Local fairs declined and events with a specific purpose became much more common. The pattern of livestock markets, both in time and geography, was rebuilt round new forms of transport. Fairs had had a wide range of commercial and social purposes but they became increasingly focused on pleasure. Marymass at Irvine, for example, was before about 1850 a horse fair and a hiring market for hands for the harvest. Later, the main activities were eating, drinking and watching the horse races. Agricultural shows were a new element for country life, and horticultural shows were held both in town and country. Chapmen, who had taken their stand at fairs, selling all kinds of goods, were replaced by static tradesmen in the towns and villages, and these trades took up holidays which were specific to the place.

The macadamised road, the steamboat and particularly the railway enabled more people to travel to places and events – sportsmen and spectators could travel further and more often. The Eglinton Tournament and its vast crowd was at the beginning of this change. Many of the crowd came by rail from Ardrossan: trains had been running for only a few weeks. After the opening of the Edinburgh and Glasgow Railway in 1842 east and west were drawn together. Spectators could travel from Edinburgh to Irvine races, and home in a day. The railway network spread rapidly. It was possible for curlers to hold Grand Matches between the north and south of Scotland. The first to attract a large attendance was held at Lochwinnoch in 1850. The rink from Penicuik left at 4 a.m. to catch the first train at Edinburgh, and reached the Renfrewshire venue at noon. They were home at midnight, exhausted – but the journey would have been impossible ten years before. Quoiters, too, started to range more widely: almost as soon as the Edinburgh and Northern Railway was opened across Fife, men from Markinch and Burntisland played together for the first time.

There were thus increased opportunities for sport: it was becoming less tied to named holidays. At the same time holidays were changing in their individual importance and character. Some, like Christmas, were slowly taking on the features of the English festival; others, like Fastern's E'en, were simply fading away.

In the first half of the nineteenth century the winter holidays were less important for sport and other rituals than they had been earlier. Auld Hansel Monday was still being celebrated in East Lothian at the time of Waterloo: at Aberlady there was quoiting and shooting in the morning, and in the afternoon foot races and putting the weight. Finally, there was a shinty match.[50] By this time, the holiday was in decline. Writing of Yule, meaning the holiday which lasted a week or more, the *Aberdeen Journal* in 1839 talked of:

> the decay of ancient hospitality which is so much lamented over, and the desuetude into which many of the excellent old sports and pastimes of Yule have fallen.[51]

The cause of the decline was said in the same report to be 'the great enlightenment of the Age': this is not an explanation but sarcasm. Christmas, New Year and Hansel Monday became days for eating well and particularly for drinking: newspapers compared the amount of public drunkenness with earlier years.

Rational recreation was slowly increasing. On New Year's Day in 1850 in Edinburgh the working classes enjoyed sedate leisure, visiting the Scott Monument, the Corn Exchange, Heriot's Hospital, the Botanic Gardens and the Museum of Antiquities.[52] In the country, ploughing matches were held from December to March, but especially over the holiday period when the dinner afterwards could be relished. In one instance, at Fordoun in Angus, a laird started a games day on Auld Hansel Monday to try to distract the people from drinking: more is said about this event in the next chapter. New Year's Day did not achieve its present prominent place in the sporting calendar until the rise of football as a spectator sport in the 1870s.

By Victoria's time the sports of the first three months of the year were few: curling when the weather was suitable, and for the wealthy fox-hunting and hare-coursing. Fastern's E'en declined in importance in the first half of the nineteenth century as cock-fighting disappeared and folk football became rare. The new sport of steeplechasing was becoming more common and it attracted crowds of a few thousand. At this date it was held over a farmer's fields along an *ad hoc* course chosen to present a few awkward moments. The riders were all amateurs, and most meetings were organised by army officers. St Patrick's Day was celebrated with football by immigrant Irishmen at Edinburgh for several years before 1840 when a fight with the police seems to have ended the fixture.[53] Similarly, there was little sporting activity in the early winter. Football and rugby were to fill this gap in the last third of the century.

Summer sports began, albeit infrequently, in April. Archery, golf and cricket appear. They were soon joined by horse-racing on the flat. In comparison with the modern practice of using each race course several times a year, most were visited only once. For example, in 1840 the season began at Kelso at the end of April: this was probably the least important meeting, where one event was a sweepstake of five bolls of oats, rather than cash. At all other meetings stakes were in cash. Kelso was followed by races at Musselburgh in July, Monifieth and Stirling in early August and Paisley and Dunbar at the end of the month. The Western Meeting was held at Ayr at the beginning of September. Perth a month later and Dumfries at the end of October closed the season. This was a typical pattern on which there were annual variations; it was quite common for races to miss one or more years because of distractions to the owner of the course or the enthusiast who found time to organise them.

The most active period for sport was late July and early August. General games which included a dozen or more events were by this period quite common, and cricket was increasingly popular: these new developments are described in the next chapter.

REFERENCES

1. For a summary of the evidence, see Malcolmson (1973), 45–51.
2. Anon. (1873), 34.
3. *DWJ*, 8 October 1816.
4. *FH*, 12 February 1846.
5. *GH*, 26 August 1833.
6. *MS*, 27 September 1850.
7. *HA*, 6 December 1856.
8. Niven (1965), 305.
9. Nicholson (1870), 36.
10. Grant (1876), 180.
11. Inglis (1894), 95.
12. Murray (1927), 426.
13. Fairfax-Blakeborough (1973), 322.
14. Fairfax-Blakeborough (1973), 272–7.
15. *EA*, 7 April 1840.
16. Quoted by Fairfax-Blakeborough (1973), 274.
17. Quoted by Sloan (1986), 22.
18. Sloan (1986), 20–3.
19. *PC*, 16 January 1850.
20. Burns (1993), 107.
21. Gilles (1840), 662.
22. For the English background, see Birley (1993), 239–42.
23. *GH*, 30 October 1829.
24. *EEC*, 24 July 1845.
25. *EA*, 3 November and 1 December 1840.
26. Comrie (1932), i, 277.

27. Stuart (1949).
28. Minutes of the Aesculapian Club, 4 August and 1 September 1797.
29. Andrew Duncan, *Invitation for a Gymnastic Meeting (c.* 1820). National Library of Scotland L. C. 1021 (35).
30. Harris (1996), 632.
31. *A New Edition of an Old Song* (Edinburgh, 1816), 4. NLS ABS 2.94.55(7).
32. Alexander Boswell, *Song for the Harveian Anniversary of the Circulation Club at Edinburgh* [1816], pp. 2–3. NLS ABS. 2.84.55(6).
33. Quoted by Omand (1875), 100.
34. *OSA*, xx, 145.
35. *OSA*, xxi, 140.
36. Keith (1811), 513.
37. Tranter (1987a).
38. Fairfax-Blakeborough (1973), 265–7.
39. *AJ*, 19 September 1855.
40. *AJ*, 1 August 1855.
41. *AJ*, 29 August 1855.
42. Goulstone (1982), 29–42.
43. Quoted by Fairfax-Blakeborough (1949), 13.
44. *Belfast News Letter*, February 1739.
45. *DWJ*, 16 February 1830.
46. Kerr (1890), [women curling]; Guthrie (1885), 124.
47. Guthrie (1885), 36–7.
48. Tranter (1989), 36–7.
49. *GH*, 10 October 1828.
50. Reid (1910), 35–8.
51. *AJ*, 2 Januaray 1839.
52. *EEC*, 3 January 1850.
53. *EA*, 29 March 1840.

CHAPTER TEN

The Modernisation of Sport

Sport in Scotland, as in most parts of the Western World, changed enormously in the nineteenth century. It grew, its character altered, and it developed many new social roles.

The first sign of increasing scale was that there were more events. For example, the Royal Company of Archers had a larger number of competitions from the 1820s. Cricket, which we will examine in detail later, was hardly played in Scotland in 1825 but was popular all over the Lowlands by 1860. Golf expanded slowly until the mid-century, and then was played much more widely. Bowling was a rarity in 1820 but common in Glasgow and Ayrshire by 1860, and still expanding. Curling was the most popular of all participation sports: when the third Grand Match between the North and the South was played at Lochwinnoch in 1850, there were 127 rinks – over 1000 curlers in a single match.

The size of crowds was increasing well before the railway network began to develop. Crowds were frequently said to have been 'immense' which we may interpret as meaning much larger than before. Before the Western [horse-racing] Meeting of 1834 the *Ayr Advertiser* observed that it was becoming increasingly popular with strangers and then recorded a crowd of 20,000 on one day.[1] In 1840 there were 13,000 – another account thought perhaps as many as 20,000 – at Monifieth Races, 7000 at Kelso in October, over 3000 at Roslin Games, and 'many thousands' at a steeple chase at Bangour in West Lothian.[2] The Monifieth figure is large because a few months earlier it had been connected to Dundee by railway. In golf, the size of crowds began to be an issue in the same period. In 1870 the final round of a match between Tom Morris and Willie Park was played at Musselburgh before – or rather among – a crowd of six or seven thousand who time and again encroached on the players until the referee, Robert Chambers, declared that the last six holes would be played another day.[3]

Many themes can be drawn out of the changes in sport in the nineteenth century. For example, by 1900 – and beyond the scope of this book – football was played weekly as a spectator sport by professionals. A team of English professional cricketers had visited Scotland in 1849. Dozens of sports had organised themselves by founding clubs, and league and cup competitions were played by these clubs. A particularly early example is the Grand Caledonian Curling Club, founded in 1838 (it achieved royal patronage in 1843), a national sporting association which set up competitions between clubs for 'Local' and 'Provincial' medals. Team sports were played far more than before. Sport had assumed a new cultural role, for Scottish independent schools followed English public schools, and Scottish universities copied English ones in adopting the 'athletic ideal': playing fields and gymnasia proliferated. A leading proponent of sport in education, H. H. Almond of Fettes, refereed the first rugby international in 1871.

Three topics which illustrate creation of modern sport in Scotland beginning in the 1820s: the growth of games days, the increase in the competitive spirit, and the import of cricket from England.

NEW GAMES

In England general sports days, at which many athletic events took place, have a continuous history from the Middle Ages to the nineteenth century, chiefly as part of church wakes and similar parish festivals. This continuity did not exist in Lowland Scotland, although the festival with sports must have existed in the Lowlands before the Reformation.

They took place, however, in the *Gàidhealtachd*. Our knowledge of early Highland Games is shadowy, but it is likely that they took place in the eighteenth century. They were gatherings of people from wide areas, and not comparatively local events like English wakes. In the nineteenth century they became a key source for the development of Lowland Games, most of which were Highland in character if not in name. Highland and Lowland Games, and their English equivalents, evolved into modern athletics.

By 1820, the events in Highland Games showed in various ways their sources in Celtic culture. At Braemar there was a medal for reading Gaelic. Competitions for the best-dressed man – implying the wearing of Highland dress – were common. Piping and dancing competitions appeared at almost all Games, even if the ideas about Highland dress were heavily influenced by Lowlanders, Walter Scott and the Wilsons of Bannockburn who wove the tartan. An event similar to a Highland Games was held by the Brigade of Guards at Aldershot. It had a Scots content in the organisation of heavy events and the Highland reel, but English folk traditions were also present in Cumberland and Cornish or Devon wrestling, and the English hornpipe.[4] This emphasises the importance of tradition in the invention of modern games days.

The core events at Highland Games were explained by a traveller who saw a *kirn* – harvest celebrations, here with games – about 1820:

> A party of Celts amused themselves, and me, among others, by their extraordinary feats in 'putting the stane', hopping [i.e. the hop, step and jump], leaping, and running [there was a hill race].[5]

After 1820 Highland Games grew rapidly and spread to the Lowlands.

An early example of a Highland Games outside the Highlands was held in 1828 on the island of Inchkeith, in the Firth of Forth, with the same events:

> although the day was exceedingly unfavourable, it did not appear to damp the spirits of the Highlanders present, or to have much effect in marring their sports, which consisted of rifle shooting, throwing the hammer, putting the stone, hop-step-and-jump, and steeple foot racing. The Chieftains were attended by their pipers, and dressed in full Highland costume. M'Donald of Clan Ranald wore the sword that Prince Charles used at the Battle of Culloden, which relic, of course, was an object of much attention during the day amongst the mountaineers.[6]

Engraved on the prize medal for these Games was THE HIGHLAND CLUB OF SCOTLAND/AMOR PATRIAE.[7] This we can interpret as an expression of the cultural nationalism which Scott encouraged. We have already seen him as the figure who fired sportsmen with enthusiasm for the medieval: now we meet him as the image-maker who chose Highland dress to represent the clothing of all Scots, the Scott of *The Lady of the Lake* (1810) and *Waverley* (1814).

The Highland Club had a charitable function. It was announced at their New Year dinner in the same year that it had sufficient funds to educate fifty children – and the children then marched round the tables behind a piper.[8] Several of the Highland Games were by the 1820s organised by friendly societies – the Lonach Gathering in Strathdon is an example. The Highland Club was thus taking up a similar social role. This is distinct from Lowland Games, which were purely for sports and other competitions.

Lowland Games, as well as having their roots in Highland Games, were also derived from the practice of having one or two additional events at horse races. Thus at Paisley in 1659 there were two horses races and a foot race for a pair of white hose, and at Aboyne there was 'a horse race, a man race and a woman race'.[9] At Largo in Fife in 1669 the horse race was accompanied by a foot race.[10] At Newton-on-Ayr in the middle of the nineteenth century there was a foot race, an old wives' race for a pound of tea, and climbing the greasy pole, as well as the horse race.[11]

The St Ronan's Games at Innerleithen have already been described as part of the medieval revival of sport. Begun in 1826, they were also the first athletic sports in the Lowlands to be widely known, and they form a model for subsequent Lowland and Border Games. In 1831, for example, they drew a crowd of nearly 4,000,[12] and the Glasgow, Edinburgh, Kelso, Dumfries and other newspapers contained notices of them and often very full descriptions.

Charles Doyne Sillery (1807–37), a minor poet and religious writer, gave a vivid description of events at the St Ronan's Games in the *Edinburgh Literary Journal*. There is space here to quote only one of his stanzas. Copying Christopher North's attempts to convey the ebullience of James Hogg in the *Noctes Ambrosianae*, Sillery showed the Ettrick Shepherd at the centre of the action in a description of a foot race:

> 'Stand back!' baw'ld Hogg; 'Once! – Constables, I say
> Keep the crowd back – Twice! – Odd! we canna see –

Clear the course – Brodie, gar your baton play –
That'll do fine – noo tak a breath awee –
Twice! – O! ye deevils, fast! rin! rin away!
They're oot o' sight already! back to me
My hearties! – glorious! round the pole! they leave it!
Well done, Rob Laidlaw! – in, in! – Lord, ye have it![13]

At Innerleithen foot races, particularly the longer ones, were usually won by shepherds. Football and wrestling were the roughest games, the former being a match between Innerleithen and Traquair, 50 or 60 a side, including the River Leithen within the playing area.[14]

One of the few nineteenth century sporting events which had a pre-Reformation origin was the Red Hose Race at Carnwath. The Somervilles of Carnwath held their land on the condition, said to have been laid down in 1387, that they gave a pair of red hose as a prize for a foot race.[15] Richard II of England had burned Edinburgh two years earlier, and the race is supposed to have been an encouragement to messengers who would be ready to warn of the next English invasion. Firm evidence for the race dates from 1456.[16] It was originally held at midsummer but migrated to the day after St Lawrence Fair, the great lamb fair which in the 1830s was still held on 22 August, St Lawrence's Day according to the Julian calendar. In 1832 a variety of running, leaping and quoiting events were added to the Red Hose Race, and the following year the *Glasgow Herald* commented that they might soon 'hold a place in public estimation little inferior to the far-famed Border Games'[17] – meaning St Ronan's Games.

The Redhall Games were unusual because, though similar in form to summer Games, they were held in January. They were started in the late 1840s by Carnegie of Redhall (near Fordoun in Kincardineshire) to provide an alternative to a full day of drinking at Auld Yule. The sports were those of summer games days, and all the prizes were awarded by Carnegie: usually clothes and sometimes a kebbock of cheese. The Games were not particularly large: the crowd was estimated to be 600 to 700 in 1850. There was a typical mixture of heavy events, jumping, wrestling and dancing, and the *sweir-tree*.[18] This last, also known as *sweir-draw* and *sweir-erse*, was a game in which, to quote *SND*, 'two people seated on the ground facing one another with feet pressed against feet, grasp a stick between them and tug so that one tries to pull the other to his feet.' In the North-East it was 'pullin e swingle-tree'.[19] In the Borders it was played without a stick and called *sweirdrauchts*. *Sweir* means lazy. It is an ancient pastime, for two men playing at the *sweir-tree* was carved on a misericord at Beauvais Cathedral about 1490.[20]

For a few weeks at the beginning of 1850 the *Montrose Standard* printed a description of a piece of local or national news in the form of a chapter from the Bible under the title 'Chronicles', and thus we have an eccentric description of the Redhall Games:

1.   And on the fifth day of the month, the people who dwell in the hill country of the province of Mearns, and whose occupations were the tending of cattle and the tilling of the ground, did rest from their labours.

2.   And it was proclaimed through the whole province, that as many as were willing should come to the plains of Redhall, there to make sport, and to delight themselves.

3.   And while the sun was yet high in the firmament, a very great multitude had assembled; even seven hundred two score and three persons.

4.   The lords also, and the great men of the country, with their wives and their little ones, did come.

5.   And many of the women were beautiful to look upon, and the children had ruddy countenances.

6.   And the strong men did show their powers, and their mighty strength: in wrestling, and in the throwing of great pieces of iron, and in tossing high in the air large trees from the forest, also in the throwing of very great stones taken from the brook.

7.   And the little boys and the little girls did run swiftly, and received good things.

8.   The young women also did run, and Kate, who was light of foot as a wild roe, was chief amongst the damsels.

9.   And many prizes were given unto the people, and they returned to their homes, well pleased and happy.[21]

Redhall Games lost their interest in the late 1860s when professionals started to compete: the small, local crowd preferred winners from among its own number.[22]

At Montrose there was an interesting example of tradition becoming the springboard for a modern games meeting. The Town Council in 1850 revived the practice of awarding a silver arrow for competition, as other burghs had done in the seventeenth and eighteenth centuries. It was not an open event, for the ceremonies began with the presentation of the Arrow to the Royal Company of Archers, who then marched in procession with the Council from the Town Hall to a natural amphitheatre on the racecourse. The shooting began on Thursday and continued on Friday morning, when there was a crowd of 8000. It was a sociable occasion, for archers 'occasionally wandered from the duties of the game to pay their *devoirs* to the ladies, and at the same time *devour* a little refreshment themselves.' The *Montrose Standard* continued, 'It almost reminded one of the lists of Ashby', making a reference to *Ivanhoe*. In the afternoon it grew to 15,000 when there were 'Scotch Games': throwing the hammer, putting the stone, and foot, wheelbarrow, donkey and pony races. There was also a 'greasy poll', perhaps the product of an unsatisfactory encounter between journalist and barber. Four thousand of the crowd had travelled to Montrose by train.[23]

In Dumfries, Games were first attached to the Rood Fair in 1858 under the name of 'Dumfries Border Games'.[24] Competition was an important part of them: the first thing that the newspaper report said was that large prizes had been offered with the aim of 'securing good competitors from a distance, as well as bringing out the best of the district'.

The competitors – as far as we can judge from the prize list – did not come from the Dumfries area only. If we exclude competitions which were open to Dumfries men alone, there are 28 names: 11 from Dumfriesshire, 10 from elsewhere in Lowland Scotland, one from Ross-shire and 8 from the north of England. Englishmen dominated the wrestling, winning five of the eight prizes, and the largest prize of the day went to James Pattison of Weardale, who won £6–10s. Most of the other prizes were £1 or less. The other event for which a large sum was awarded was piping, where

Alexander Glen, one of the family of Edinburgh bagpipe-makers, was given £2–10s.

The Games were organised for spectators. The venue was 'on the Dock' – an area on the right bank of the Nith below the town. There was a double row of seats round the ground, which was about 80 yards in diameter, and a grandstand seated another 500: places in the front row were reserved for the provost and other members of the Council. At mid-day, the people were standing ten deep round the ring and there were between 5000 and 6000 present, and others watched from a footpath on the hill to the west.

Part of the variety of the Games came from the piping and dancing competitions, all for men. Border Games were overtly Scottish, and they defined themselves as such by adopting piping and dancing from Highland Games. To the newspaper reporter at Dumfries 'the Highlanders ... were the most attractive objects, and their music and dancing the finest pastimes of the day'. The Highland flavour, though Scots, was also British, associating Dumfries with the Army, for some of those wearing the kilt 'in their martial bearing evincing in no small degree "the fire of old Rome" ... their flag, with its motto "We'll hae nane but Highland bonnets here," recalling our countrymen's recent heroism on the heights of Alma'.[25]

By the 1850s there were several dozen Games in Scotland. In that year Games have been traced in the Borders at Innerleithen, in the South-West at Dumfries, in the West of Scotland at Barrhead and Wishaw, in the East at Edinburgh, Leith, Dalkeith, Alva, Errol, and Montrose. Those proliferating in the North-East were discussed in an earlier chapter. There were minor variations in the events at different Games: at Kilbirnie piping was included, but there were only athletic events and quoiting at Auchinleck on the same day.[26] The Games at Dalry in Ayrshire were unusual in including the pole vault.[27] In Midlothian, quoiting was especially popular at Roslin Games, and as we have seen, the Border Games at Innerleithen finished with a football match.

In the nineteenth century we find for the first time sports being established to make money – not directly, through gate money, but in the confidence that a crowd will always be thirsty. An early example is Errol races. There was a hiring fair at Errol, and James

('Mickie') Watson, landlord of the Errol Arms, made large profits from refreshing those who attended it. Patrick Bell invented his famous reaping machine in 1826, and it was first used on his brother's farm in Perthshire. Watson feared that the new machine would decrease the number of hands who were needed in the fields, and so the number of people who were likely to come to the fair. He therefore started as an attraction the 'Carse Derby', a horse race, and soon foot races too. The winner of one of the foot events was chosen to wear the bell for the 'bell race'.[28] In this there were five competitors: the four blindfolded ones tried to catch the fifth, who had the bell tied to his back, within a stipulated time. The bell race was also recorded at Ceres in Fife.

THE REGATTA

The regatta was a species of Games Day in which there was a limited range of events. The earliest Scottish one which has been traced is the Loch Ryan Regatta which began about 1820 and stemmed partly from pride at British naval success in the Napoleonic Wars. Indeed, this was true of all Victorian regattas. The one at Loch Ryan was described in 1842 as a 'briny tournament' – this is three years after the Eglinton Tournament – but also as a battlefield: 'the very sun of Austerlitz shone upon the anxious combatants'.[29] It continued until 1893.

Regattas grew in number between 1820 and 1850 and were particularly popular in the second half of the nineteenth century. The regatta which was started at Grangemouth in 1851 had the unusual feature of events both on water and on land. There were sack races and a greasy pole, though rowing was the most important sport. The most spectacular was sailing: in a high wind one of six entrants was dismasted as the race started, a second soon sank and a third stopped to rescue its crew.[30] There were horse and boat races at the Lammas Fair at Inverkeithing; and at Dumbarton foot and horse races as well as events on the water.[31] At Loch Ryan hack races were held on the sands to amuse the crowd between aquatic events, and in 1842 a more sophisticated meeting was organised nearby at two days' notice.[32]

Other regattas were held on Loch Lomond, on rivers such as the

Tweed at Sprouston and Coldstream, the Forth at Stirling where there was a crowd of 8000 to 10,000 in 1859, and on the Forth at Granton.[33] There were also regattas on smaller stretches of water such as the Castle Loch at Lochmaben in Dumfriesshire, and on the Union Canal at Hermiston.[34]

After the opening of railways, the crowds at regattas grew. The Dundee Regatta of 1850 illustrates the way in which the creation of events and the assembling crowds had progressed more quickly than the organisation of the races. The regatta had been advertised as being open to all comers, but when a delegate from Perth attempted to enter a number of boats, he was told that only Dundonians were eligible. The Manager of the Tay ferries intervened and insisted that Perth crews should race, otherwise he would withdraw his subscription. The regatta took place before a crowd of 10,000: management of the events was in the hands of a Commodore. The rules were inadequate and not properly understood by the crews. Ad hoc judgements were made against the Perth men – said the Perth papers. The *Ariadne* of Perth won the first race and the Commodore disqualified her from the second on the grounds that she had already won, and despite the fact that an entry fee had been paid on her behalf.[35] The modern mind will see this as bizarre and unjust, but this extreme form of handicapping was practised in other sports such as archery. In 1850 the unpredictable nature of sports was still part of their appeal.

The first paddle-steamer on the Clyde was Henry Bell's *Comet* in 1812. In 1828 the Royal Northern Yacht Club augmented their regatta by starting an annual steamboat race. There was already commercial competition between skippers, and the race sharpened it. In 1835, however, winning became too important: someone on the *Earl Grey* screwed down the safety valves on her boiler, and whilst she waited at Greenock the boiler exploded:

> the most fearful spectacle of all was the vessel herself – the roof of the ponderous boiler poised in mid-air, over which the funnel lay crushed and broken – the uptorn decks exposing the cabin, into which the upper flues of the boiler had forced their way; while hats and portions of male and female attire were strewed around ...[36]

The root of this tragedy was a lack of understanding of the destructive power of steam under high pressure, and probably a failure to realise how quickly a boiler could corrode. However, it was also a metaphorical demonstration of the pressures produced by competition, and to competitiveness itself we will now turn.

SPORT AND COMPETITION

Competition is an integral part of most kinds of sport, but in different centuries and circumstances the importance of winning has varied. To the Ancient Greeks the point of sport was to be the victor: the records of the Olympics do not record who came second.[37] Another factor was equally important in sport between the Middle Ages and the nineteenth century: the sportsman wished to be seen to be skilful.

In *The Muses' Threnodie* (1638), Henry Adamson remembered a feat with the bow:

> I mourn, good *Gall*, when I think on that stead
> Where yee did hail your shaft unto the head;
> And with a strong and steadfast eye and hand
> So valiantly your bow yee did command;
> A slidderie shaft forth of its fork did sling
> Clank gave the bow, the whistling air did ring;
> The bowlt did cleave the clouds, and threat the skyes
> And thence down falling to the mark it flies.[38]

> Closely I hit the mark upon the head:
> Then on the plain we caprel'd wonder fast
> Whereat the people gazing were agast:
> With kind embracements did we thurst and thrimble
> (For in these days I was exceeding nimble;)
> We leap'd, we danc't, we loudly laugh't, we cry'd
> For in the earth such skill was never try'd
> In archerie.[39]

This quotation shows the spirit in which Gall and Adamson played: sport was primarily a matter of exercising their skill, and a fine shot was a matter of pleasure to all concerned. The idea of competition, of winning and losing, is only vaguely present. The same idea can be seen in another poem, 'The Last Dying Words of Bonny Heck, a Famous Grey-Hound in the Shire of Fife', by William Hamilton of Gilbertfield (*c.* 1665–1751), probably first published in 1706.[40] Bonny Heck boasts of her skill:

> What great Feats I have done my Sell [myself]
> Within Clink of *Kilrenny* Bell. (ll. 13–14)

She also describes another of her abilities, her wit:

> So well's I cou'd play Hocus Pocus
> And of the servants make Jodocus
> And this I did in every Locus
>   throw their Neglect.
> And was this not a Merry Jocus
>   quo' bonny Heck? (ll. 61–6)

At the same time, she talks of his overall superiority:

> They'll witness that I was the Vier [one who vies]
> Of all the Dogs within the Shire
> I'd run all Day, and never tyre (ll. 19–21).

And most decisively:

> At King's-Muir, and Kelly-law
> Where good stout Hairs gang fast awa
> So cliverly I did it Claw
>   with Pith and Speed:
> I bure the Bell before them
>   as clear's a Beid. (ll. 31–6)

– by both skill and speed Heck 'bure the Bell' – a phrase derived from horse-racing. Much of this poem is about skill and wit. The dog boasts of showing her superiority by making a fool of servants – *hocus* means a fool. As well as speed, she mentions her *pith*, her power, her inner essence: whisky was 'the pith o the maut'. A gentleman saw himself as being universally accomplished, a complete man, and Heck makes a similar claim – and her name labels her, additionally, as being both skilled and sexually attractive. *Heck*, as a noun, is given no less than eight meanings in the *Scottish National*

Dictionary: one of them is a carter's instruction to his horse to turn left, which relates to the greyhound's ability to make a good turn in pursuit of the hare, and another is an animal's rump.

Wit is important because of the practice of singing of songs after the dinner which followed the day's sport, particularly amusing songs written by the singer. We have already seen this at the Gymnastic Club, and it was a feature of nineteenth-century curling. Sir Alexander Boswell (1775–1822) was inventive and consistently effective in his use of the Scots language:

> Let rogues and let fools
> Rin to cards and to dice
> And gamblin, sit girnin and gurlin,   [complaining and
> growling]
>
> But honest men ken
> That tho' slipp'ry the ice
> Still fair-play an' fun gang wi' Curlin.[41]

Boswell is praising the fun of the play itself, as against playing with another motive such as making money, when the result matters more.

Competition had not been an outstanding feature of eighteenth-century sport. If we look at Burns' 'Tam Samson's Elegy', we see the wholehearted enjoyment of sport – 'up the rink like Jehu roar' – but when we compare this with the description of his spiritual grandson, Booler Jamie, written by Michaelson Porteous (1796–1872) of Maybole, we discover that:

> O' skips the vera pink was he
> At countin' shots aye dour to see
> A' bools but his ain side's aglee
>   Whilk he'd maintain:
> Though I'se no vrite that he would lee
>   Auld Jamie gane.[42]

Winning mattered to Booler Jamie and to the Earl of Eglinton, in the case of Jamie to the point where a little careful cheating is tolerable. This spirit brought another change, for others copied Eglinton by giving prizes themselves. In 1862, John Lyon, a baker in Galston in Ayrshire, presented a pair of bowls to the local bowling club 'which have tended greatly to cause a spirit of emulation amongst the members'.[43] Robert Smith, late of the Customs at Troon, gave a medal in 1844 to Troon Curling Club, on his leaving for Campbeltown.[44] The importance of this, and of dozens of similar gestures, is that it is not patronage, but rather a sign of the adoption of competition as a goal by the ordinary members of a club.

The giving of prizes also related to the public recognition of winners. At the beginning of the nineteenth century, exercise was also seen as something unpleasant but which 'inured [the soldier] to the hardships of the field'. Walter Thom, in his book on *Pedestrianism* (1813) quoted the Irishman Richard Lovell Edgworth:

> As to EXERCISE and AMUSEMENTS for the pupils in a military academy, they should all be calculated to promote and sustain manly dispositions ... A military school should have annual competitions and prizes for foot-races, leaping, wrestling, fencing, and firing at a target.[45]

Whilst Edgworth and Thom were both writing during the Napoleonic Wars, they were also aware of the Greek and Celtic traditions of preparing for war through games. To Thom the list of sports would seem like a modernised version of those at Scottish Highland Games; to Edgworth they must have harked back to the stories of early Irish heroes. Thom continued:

> Though the prizes need not be absolutely wreaths of oak or parsley, yet whatever they are, they should be more honourary than lucrative. The victors should be rewarded also with the applause of the public, the countenance of the great, and sometimes, perhaps, with the patronage of the government.[46]

This is a crucial moment in the development of sport, for Thom is emphasising the importance of public recognition of winners: the wreaths of oak and parsley are a direct reference to prizes at Greek games. Where Duncan and his friends had made modest wagers and commemorated their victories by adding medals to the Gymnastic Club Cups, Thom said that recognition should not come from the members of a small club, but from those in positions of power, perhaps even the state itself.

James Hogg, writing of St Ronan's Games, believed that the public status of being a winner would draw men into sports:

> by publishing annually all the victors' names in the newspapers, and the distance [in jumping or throwing], and the competitor next to him, a stimulus was given for excellence in all the manly exercises ...[47]

Thus he was encouraging competitiveness. Hogg's motives, as we might expect of such a complex man, were several: publication advertised Border culture, and he was probably less concerned to give a moment in the spotlight to a few individual men, than to ensure that through competition enjoyment of the Games, and therefore the Games themselves, continued. It is as though the Games themselves, and through them Border life, were competing for survival.

At Highland and Lowland Games there was a prize for every event, either cash or a medal, or both. Sufficient money was available by 1860 for it to be possible for an individual, such as William Tait of Castle Douglas or the North-East hero Donald Dinnie, to make a significant part of his living by going round the 'circuit' and dominating the prizes lists at each one.

The practice of giving prizes came from horse-racing. In the eighteenth and early nineteenth centuries it was the only sport organised on a national basis: the prizes at the major meetings, including the Town's Plate at Leith or the Ayr Gold Cup, were in effect national prizes. In addition, in the eighteenth century it was only in horse-racing that it was common for the winner to retain the prize. In other sports, the winner was allowed to keep the prize for a year, often having to give a bond for it, and was obliged to add to it a medal commemorating his own victory. The prize was owned by a society, and the winner presented a small token to it. Scottish examples include most archery prizes and the Silver Jack of the Edinburgh Society of Bowlers.

The rapid increase in the number and significance of prizes can be seen if we move forward in time. The West of Scotland Artillery and Rifle Association held their meetings at Irvine from 1864: they were part of the Volunteer movement.[48] In 1870 they held an 8-day meeting at Irvine in June: the first two days were for artillery competitions, the rest for rifle shooting. The *Ayr Advertiser* gave a report filling two and a half columns.[49] Most of the principal prizes were in cash. Others were awarded by noblemen or by trade associations: there was a match rifle presented by James Morrison, the Earl of Glasgow's Challenge Plate, the Ironbrokers' Cup, the Stock Exchange Cup, the Wine Merchants' Cup, the Counties' Cup (given by landowners), and the Glasgow Corporation Challenge Cup. There were also many cash prizes. Finally, there were 'Extra Prizes': a claymore, an Enfield rifle, a suit of tweed, a writing desk, a case of sherry, a cape, a camp blanket and pillow, and a guinea packet of embossed paper. These were given by tradesmen who were giving whatever was appropriate to their trade, even if it was inappropriate to shooting. The point was that the prize-winners made a material gain, something more solid than the mere honour of hanging a medal on an arrow.

In September 1860 the newly-formed Angus & Mearns Rifle Association held Games at Montrose. Lord Elcho explained that the idea of the Association was to supplement the Volunteer movement by providing a way of raising standards by holding competitions for, he said, rivalry and competition were characteristic of the British and of their sports. The prizes were cash or rifles, and Elcho announced that 'we wish to make the rifle now, in the days of Queen Victoria, what the bow was in the time of the Edwards'.[50] Even in 1860 some must have been surprised by his conflation of Scots and English history. He had also brought together the idea of re-creating the medieval wapenschaw with an emphasis on competition which had not been overt in the Middle Ages. We do not know the names of the winners of fifteenth-century archery competitions, and there is no evidence of even informal prizes, but in 1860 every prize and every winner was listed in local papers. Some of the cash prizes were handsome: £10 was not unusual for the winner of each of six or eight events in one day. A structure was created which covered the whole of Britain: the National Rifle Association, whose first meeting had been held at Wimbledon two months before Angus & Mearns Games. The first winner of the Queen's Prize – incidentally a Scot living in England – received £250.

Highland, Border and general athletic games produced winners.

The medieval idea of the champion was still current in some areas such as boxing, and it was used again from the late nineteenth century by the promoters as a way of focusing competition. The new idea, which started to appear in the middle of the century, was the sporting hero – the man who might not be the victor in every match or competition in which he played, but who stood out from his contemporaries because of his ability to win. He was a public figure. There is nothing in Scottish sporting prose before 1859 to match the obituary of Allan Robertson (1815–59), 'the greatest golf-player that ever lived', an extended eulogy of a man whose only social distinction was his skill on the links.[51]

Fletcher Norton Menzies (1819–1905) was the younger son of Sir Robert Menzies of Menzies.[52] He was raised in Perthshire, and when he went up to Oxford he became a rowing enthusiast. He developed a new style using a long stroke, but the Boat Club was indifferent to his ideas. Menzies therefore trained his own crew in his own methods and raced them against the University boat – successfully.

Menzies was now in control of the practical side of Oxford rowing. He designed and built his own boat, which beat Cambridge in 1842. There was no University Boat Race the following year, but Menzies continued to train the Oxford crew, and at Henley, in the final of the Grand Challenge Cup, they met 'Cambridge Subscription Rooms'. This was a crew made up of undergraduates and recent Blues, and was probably stronger than the typical University boat. It was the race of the year. Minutes before the start Menzies collapsed. Oxford proposed a substitute. Cambridge denied that one was eligible, hoping to force Oxford to withdraw. Oxford therefore raced with seven men against eight, and won. There was a sensation – in Oxford, at least – and the race became known as *Septem contra Camum*, a play on Aeschylus's *Seven against Thebes*. The seven successful oarsmen and cox presented Menzies with a handsome silver cup as a token of their admiration for him.[53]

Menzies was given a second piece of silver because of his leadership in another sport. After he returned to Perthshire and farmed in Glenlyon, Weem Curling Club in 1856 gave him a claret jug to recognise his work as their President, 'as an expression of ... respect and esteem, and a grateful sense of his good services to the club and

34.   The monument to Allan Robertson (1815–59) beside the Cathedral, St Andrews.

35.   The monument to 'Young Tom' Morris (1851–75) in St Andrews.

kindness to the members'.[54] Menzies was far more than merely a club official, for he was a larger than life character and a significant local figure as the younger brother of the laird. When he died one of the Perth newspapers said, 'And so the phenomenally tough old gentleman has reeled off his "pirn". What a fine compound he was of hickory, whalebone, tartan and – Menzies!'[55]

36.   The Weem Jug, 1856. *National Museums of Scotland.*

37.   The Weem Jug: the presumed miniature portrait of Fletcher Norton Menzies. The curling stone is missing from his right hand. *National Museums of Scotland.*

The practice of honouring a man by presenting him with silver had become common after 1750: it was a way of giving cash, since the silver could be melted down, but in a way which enabled the recipient to enjoy his glory in a semi-public way. Yet the Weem jug is not directly in this tradition. Much of its cost must have been for engraving it, and for the modelling of the miniature curler on the stopper. The idea of looking at the jug as scrap silver is shocking, because it expresses real affection for a distinctive individual. Yet the idea of competition is not wholly absent from it. In the middle of the nineteenth century the honours system, both military and civil, was being expanded rapidly, and the Victoria Cross was instituted in the year Menzies was given the jug. It was a method of rewarding public service which seemed more appropriate as British society became more competitive. The Weem jug can be seen as a local honour.

THE ENGLISH GAME OF CRICKET

Cricket is essentially an English game, but it is making rapid progress in Scotland.[56]

38.   The Weem Jug: a scene at a curling match, derived from the oil painting by Sir
George Harvey. *National Museums of Scotland*.

Thus the *Kilmarnock Weekly Post* in 1859. Cricket we view to-day
as the archetypal English sport, the major pastime of the village
green, which echoes to the sound of leather on willow and the shouts
of sturdy yeoman while their elders sup mild beer in front of a
timber-framed inn. It is something alien to Scotland, we suppose,
and feel proud but embarrassed when Freuchie wins the national

39.   The Weem Jug: the climax of a match on the carse lands below Stirling Castle.
National Museums of Scotland.

(British) championship for village clubs. Yet in the middle of the nineteenth century cricket was highly popular in central Scotland, and although it may to an extent have been seen as an English game this is not obvious from its limited Scottish literature. Certainly, the Scottish climate caused difficulties:

The fact of Caledonia being stern and wild has long been a

matter of congratulation to the poetic child, but it is a constant source of disgust to the cricketer.[57]

At the beginning of the eighteenth century the game was still quite localised in south-east England, and it spread all over England in the following decades. We should not overestimate the depth of the cricketing tradition in England. The real growth of the game there, which changed it from an occasional pastime over most of the country, with more frequent matches in Kent, Sussex and Hampshire, to being a national enthusiasm, belongs to the period after 1820.[58] In Scotland, the chief growth took place after 1840, and the sport was widespread when, two decades later, a journalist said that 'up to a recent period [cricket] was exclusively an English Sport, [it] has within the last few years become fashionable and is fast becoming a popular amusement in Scotland'.[59] In other words, it had been played by the middle classes for some time and was being taken up by artisans.

Cricket is the first clear example of a sport being imported from England, and it therefore deserves detailed examination. It was played to a very limited extent in Scotland in the eighteenth century. It is difficult to believe that the English soldiers who flooded into Scotland in 1745/6 did not bring cricket with them, but evidence has not yet emerged. The well-known 'first cricket match in Scotland' took place at Earl Cathcart's seat at Schaw Park, Alloa, in September 1785, when Hon. Colonel Talbot's XI played the Duke of Atholl's XI. The latter team included the Earl of Winchelsea (1752–1824), the leading figure in the founding of the Marylebone Cricket Club eight years earlier. Most of the players were English: no further matches in Scotland followed from it. However, a Scot, the Duke of Hamilton, had already joined the MCC, and a traveller hoping to inspect Hamilton Palace in 1785 found that 'as the Duke plays cricket every afternoon, strangers don't get admittance then'.[60]

The first cricket clubs in Scotland were founded at the beginning of the nineteenth century: at Perth in 1812, Glasgow (the University *c.* 1828, Albion *c.* 1832, Thistle *c.* 1838), Edinburgh (Brunswick 1830, Grange 1832), and at Barrhead in Renfrewshire (*c.* 1838).[61] In Glasgow, most of the early clubs met on the Green, and the printed rules of one of them survive. They suggest that in 1819 it did not feel securely established:

XXI. Any Member proposing to break up the Society, shall be expelled on the information of two witnesses.[62]

Such evidence as is available indicates that the game was taken up at first by the urban middle classes. The players dressed in uniform, as a poem of 1835 said:

The game was ready to begin, the Cricketers were seen
With yellow shoes and jackets white, upon the Glasgow
    Green.[63]

When, on this occasion, the match began late, the spectators were irritated:

The *Keelies*, cheated of their fun, began to show their ire
By launching at the hapless band a cloud of dogs and cats
While some did cry 'their castors "tile" [knock their hats
    off] – or brain them with their bats.[64]

The most important mechanism for the spread of cricket to Scotland was the arrival of Englishmen who were already familiar with the game. Textile workers from Yorkshire, Lancashire and Leicestershire introduced cricket to Hawick about 1844.[65] Two Yorkshiremen who had been brought in to install looms in the tweed mills started the club in Selkirk in 1851.[66] Penicuik's club was founded by men who had come to work in the paper mills.[67] When the Findhorn viaduct was being built for the Inverness & Aberdeen Junction Railway in 1857–58, English engineers fostered the foundation of two clubs in Forres.[68] At Dalbeattie, the game was promoted by southern workers in the granite quarries.[69] A few cricket matches are known to have been played in the area of Newton Stewart between 1853 and 1856, and the players included excise officers from the Bladnoch distillery and the engineer of the mines at Cairnsmore of Fleet, all Englishmen.[70]

Knowledge of how to play cricket was also spread by Englishmen who came to Scotland specifically for that purpose – professional cricketers. The first to travel north was John Sparkes (1777–c. 1853), a notable player in the south of England, who was brought to Edinburgh by the Grange Club in 1833 or 1834. Already in his late 50s when he arrived in Scotland, Sparkes is not known to have played in matches, but he coached and participated in practice. He also filled another important post – umpire – in setting standards. Like Thomas Lord, with whom he had played in London, Sparkes was a minor entrepreneur who ran his own eponymous cricket ground in Grove Street near Haymarket. The second professional in Scotland was Charles Lawrence (1828–1917), who was employed at Perth in 1846. Compared with Sparkes, he was at the other end of his career. After appearing in Ireland, he emigrated to Australia in 1861 and played a notable part in the early history of the game there. By 1870 there were about twenty professional cricketers in Scotland, almost all Englishmen.

The Scottish public schools, which modelled themselves on their much older English equivalents, were particularly aware of the popularity of cricket in England and, more generally, of the cult of athleticism which was fostered in England. The first school to form its own cricket club, in 1845, was Blair Lodge, near Polmont in West Lothian. Five other schools started clubs between 1850 and 1862.[71] In the early 1850s Merchiston took the innovative step of employing a professional to coach the boys, and to bowl to them.[72]

The final form of contact with cricket in England was through touring teams which spread enthusiasm for the game. From 1846 to 1879 a series of professional teams toured the British Isles, playing many games against local sides, taking advantage of the expanding railway network. In each match the strengths of the two teams were adjusted by allowing the local one to play up to 22 players, and by supplying one or two professionals to provide the skill of bowling – usually the greatest deficiency. The first and most famous touring team was the All England Eleven (AEE). They were managed by a shrewd and greedy Nottinghamshire player, William Clarke. A contemporary chronicler said, 'These encounters soon caused cricket to increase vastly all over England'.[73] The AEE first visited Scotland in 1849, when they played at Sparkes' ground in Edinburgh. By 1853 cricket was 'this exciting and now popular game' in Glasgow.[74]

The growth of cricket in Scotland was eased by patronage of

40.   Medal of Carron and Stenhouse Curling Club, Stirlingshire: members played
after dark by the light of the blast furnaces at Carron Iron Company. *National
Museums of Scotland.*

various kinds. A club might hope for some money or a ground, at
least. When the Duke of Buccleuch gave Hawick & Wilton C. C.
their field in 1860, he also paid for turf to be laid and a gateway
built.[75] In Galloway, H. Maxwell of Creebridge gave bats, balls and
wickets to Newton Stewart Maxwell C. C., and one of his family
similarly helped a club in Minnigaff, on the other side of the Cree.[76]
The Earl of Eglinton, who also presented trophies for horse-racing
and curling, gave the Eglinton Gold Cup in 1867 for competition
between teams in Ayrshire. Ayr, by beating Girvan Albion, won it
for the third time in 1874 and thus won it outright.[77]

Cricket acted as the springboard for the development of other
sports, particularly rugby and football. It provided grounds that were

already laid out and an administrative structure. The same pattern can be seen in England. Derby County and Birmingham football clubs evolved out of earlier cricket clubs. Kilmarnock CC, founded in 1856, took up rugby in 1869 and football in 1873 – the football team still play at Rugby Park. Glasgow Academicals, the first prominent rugby club in the west, were initially more interested in cricket. Members of Hawick & Wilton CC bought a rugby ball in 1872, to keep fit during winter: the rugby club soon devolved itself.[78] The first rugby match in Galashiels was played in November 1876 – on the cricket ground. Archibald Campbell, the founder of Clydesdale CC, was the first President of the Scottish Football Association, and two other Clydesdale cricketers, Ebeneezer Hendry and William Gibb, were on the first committee. Clydesdale were themselves an active football club: Hendry and Gibb were playing when they lost the first Scottish Cup Final to Queen's Park in 1874. Clydesdale's first ground at Titwood (Pollokshields) was used as a venue for major matches against English teams when Hampden Park was being rebuilt in 1883–84.[79] The West of Scotland's cricket ground at Partick was the scene of the first international football match in 1872, and of three subsequent ones.

CONCLUSIONS

The organisation of Highland Games in the Lowlands and Borders, even when they were called Lowland or Border Games, is an example of the way in which the Scots adopted Highland culture as part of their national identity. The hidden force behind them was, of course, Walter Scott. Games were present in significant numbers before the revolution in communication brought by the railway: the Glasgow & Edinburgh line did not open until 1842 and the bones of a national network came into being only in 1848. Railways made it possible for larger crowds to assemble, and for men to travel the 'circuit' and make a living from their prize money: this development had taken place by 1860. Donald Dinnie and William Tait were among the first Scottish sporting heroes. The railway thus occupies an ambiguous place in the shaping of the Scots' consciousness of being Scots. On one hand, it made English culture and English people much more accessible, but at the same time it allowed more people to see events which were Scottish in character.

This ambiguity also applies to local newspapers. One of their functions was to relay news from London and the Empire, and to encourage the Scots to think of themselves imperially. Sport in England was reported, particularly horse-racing. Yet at the same time newspapers gave prominence to curling and to a lesser extent golf, and the major Highland and Border Games were recorded in papers printed far from the location of the Games. William Donaldson has shown the vital role which the newspaper played in the development of popular literature in Victorian Scotland:[80] the local paper was also important in the growth of sport.

The publicity given by newspapers to sporting events and the printing of the names of winners was a means by which sport became more competitive. In all of society, competition was being given a more central place. For example, in the 1830s professors at Edinburgh University gave medals to their best pupils, but soon the medals were awarded not by individuals but by the institution, as a result of examinations scrutinised by a board of examiners. The bureaucratically appointed official had an increasing role in sports.

Travel, the music hall and the Volunteers were all British rather than Scottish developments. Yet, with limited exceptions, they did not involve the integration of Scots and English life until the end of the century: though some of the models came from the South, the events themselves were organised by Scots for Scots. At times they encouraged local identity, and this was certainly true of sport. Andrew Lang, who was brought up in Selkirk, wrote a memoir of Border cricket in the 1850s in which he revealed the sport as a means of expressing tenacious local rivalry between the towns. Visiting teams, if they won, were roughly handled by the local population, umpires were biased and fixtures were cancelled in anger and not re-established for years.[81]

The sports which were common in Lowland Scotland in the middle of the nineteenth century, with the exception of cricket, had long Scottish traditions. In the latter part of the nineteenth century the English influence is far clearer, as it was in other forms of popular culture,[82] affecting both the sports which were played (football, rugby) and also the social basis of sport, including the concepts of the gentleman amateur and the professional player. As with other types of cultural expression, sport was not driven by the dynamism of life in the cities – until the sudden growth of football after 1870. Change and expansion were taking place in leisure well before this date. The practice of going away for a holiday, even if only for a day, was promoted by Clyde, Forth and Tay steamers in the 1820s, and the 'free-and-easy' public house was developing into the music hall by the 1850s.

The re-establishing of the Volunteer Movement in 1859/60 gave men – particularly artisans and gentlemen, and particularly in the country – a new social structure for leisure in the guise of military service. Yet the Volunteer Regiments were organised by county, and led by local landowners: their platoons were identified with parishes. Local identity was emphasised along with their national role. Their shooting competitions were particularly important because they were highly organised and purely competitive: a man's score was an accurate reflection of his skill. Their importance in the history of sport has been hidden because shooting did not become a spectator sport. The way was clear for football.

REFERENCES

1. *AA*, 4 and 11 September 1834.
2. *EA*, 17 March, 4 and 11 August, and 16 October 1840, *MS*, 31 July 1840.
3. Tulloch (1907), 115–22.
4. *AJ*, 8 August 1855.
5. Quoted by Jarvie (1991), 31.
6. *GH*, 14 July 1826.
7. National Museums of Scotland H. 1958.1962.
8. *GH*, 11 January 1828.
9. Macfarlane (1906), 105.
10. Lamont (1830), 214–15.
11. Lamont (1830), 215; Burnett (1995/6).
12. Groves (1987), 2.
13. Sillery (1829), 122.
14. Dobson (1896), 74–6.
15. McNeill (1957–68), iv, 56–8, Banks (1937–41), ii, 64.
16. I am grateful to Alan Borthwick of the National Archives of Scotland for this.
17. *GH*, 30 August 1833.

18. *AJ*, 11 January 1860.
19. Personal communication from A. Fenton, 1997.
20. Now in the Musée de Cluny, Paris.
21. *MS*, 11 January 1850.
22. Mollyson (1893), 234–5.
23. *EEC*, 4 and 9 May 1850, *MS*, 3 and 10 May 1850.
24. *D&GS*, 2 October 1858.
25. *ibid.*
26. *A&SH*, 17 August 1867.
27. *A&SH*, 11 August 1866.
28. Melville (1935), 74; Simpkins (1914), 176.
29. *DT*, 31 August 1893.
30. *FH*, 2 October 1851.
31. *FH*, 12 August 1852; *GH*, 2 September 1833.
32. *DT*, 31 August 1842.
33. *KC*, 7 and 28 June 1844, *EEC*, 2 and 18 August, 5 July 1859.
34. *D&GS*, 13 August 1845, and *EEC* 26 July 1859.
35. *PC*, 24 July 1850.
36. *GH*, 27 July 1835.
37. With the exception of the chariot races, if the winning owner also owned the team who were second.
38. Adamson (1774), 21–2.
39. Adamson (1774), 22–3.
40. Wood (1977–91), ii, 63.
41. Quoted by Kerr (1890), 146.
42. Finlayson (1925), 195.
43. *AA*, 4 September 1862.
44. *AA*, 12 December 1844.
45. Thom (1813), 34–6.
46. Thom (1813), 36.
47. Hogg (1985), 43.
48. Strawhorn (1989), 138.
49. *AA*, 16 June 1870.
50. *AJ*, 5 September 1860.
51. *DA*, quoted by Clark (1876), 267–73.
52. Menzies (1894), 476–7.
53. National Museums of Scotland H. 1995.638.
54. *PerA*, 10 April 1856; the jug is National Museums of Scotland H. 1995.63.
55. *PCour*, 4 April 1905.
56. *KWP*, 30 April 1859.
57. *King*, 3 (1873), 6.
58. Bowen (1970), 83.
59. *EEC*, 11 July 1859.
60. *The Scottish Antiquary*, 11 (1897), 82.
61. *King's Annual*, 3 (1873), 25–7.

62. *Rules of the G. L. Cricket Club* [1819]. Handbill. Copy in Mitchell Library, Glasgow.
63. Peakodde (1835), iii.
64. *Ibid.*, iii.
65. *King's Annual*, 2 (1871), 62.
66. Robb (1985).
67. Bone (1898), 277.
68. Douglas (1934), 360.
69. Callan (1949).
70. *DGS*, 30 August 1856; *WFP*, 31 August 1854.
71. Carruthers (1950), 25.
72. *King's Annual*, 1 (1871), 71.
73. Quoted by Wynne-Thomas (1971), 72.
74. *GSP*, 20 August 1853.
75. *King' Annual*, 1 (1871), 62.
76. *WFP*, 12 May 1859.
77. *King's Annual*, 5 (1875), 18–21.
78. Scott (1981), 50.
79. Courtnay (1954), 28–30.
80. Donaldson (1986).
81. Lang (1890).
82. Harvie & Walker (1990), 343.

CHAPTER ELEVEN

The Scottishness of Sport
in Scotland

In the development of Scottish society and the lives of the Scots, a distinctive pattern of playing sport was created and enjoyed: this book has described it in the four centuries before 1860. Scotland's traditions have been shaped by her own history, but also by the social practices of other European peoples, most significantly the English.

It is difficult to make a comparison between the quantity of sport played in England and in Scotland between the Reformation and 1860, but there seems to have been significantly less north of the Border. The absence of lively church wakes meant that one of the most important contexts for sport was not present in Scotland. The nobility and the wealthiest gentry were the chief patrons of sport in England, and when their Scots equivalents indulged their sporting enthusiasms they did so primarily in England. The English sporting world focused on London and to a lesser extent Newmarket: there were no Scots parallels. Sunday sport, common in England in the first half of the nineteenth century,[1] did not exist in Scotland. The growth in the quantity of sport in Scotland, which has been identified between about 1790 and about 1840,[2] may have started from a low level.

The smaller quantity of sport in Scotland than in England explains the presence and character of some Scottish sports. Carters' plays were invented as a form of popular leisure to parallel parish ales and wakes in England. Élite horse-racing was probably as common in Lowland Scotland as in England, but it bulks larger in Scottish sporting history because of the comparative lack of other sports. Minor horse races are the more conspicuous because in the areas where they took place they were the only annual sporting events.

One of the most striking features of Scottish sporting history is the growth of curling between 1700 and 1900: the English equivalent was cricket. Curling could be played because it filled an enforced gap in the working year, and it was validated and controlled by the frequent presence of the minister, quite different from a rowdy wake. Curling obviously depends on Scotland's fairly frequent cold weather. Less obviously, it grew because men did not have an established place to go in winter – a Scots howff was not as respectable as an English inn – and so an outdoor venue was acceptable in the absence of an indoor one. Yet activity was needed to keep everyone warm: hence curling.

The different nature of inns and public houses in Scotland and England produced other sporting contrasts. In England, from the eighteenth century at least, they were the focus for local male society. England was a wealthier country than Scotland: there were far more large inns there, whose landlords were able to afford to build facilities such as skittle alleys and cockpits; and the traditional form of inn, with galleries round a courtyard, itself formed an amphitheatre. English public houses were of various kinds, but most were warm and companionable, and offered rooms for political and business meetings, coroners' inquests, consultations between doctor and patient or lawyer and client, and so on.[3] Drinking places in Scotland had a more limited role: leaving aside inns which served travellers, most were solely for drinking. With few exceptions change house keepers and landlords lacked the capital to develop sporting facilities or promote sport. Where innkeepers promoted wad shooting on one of the winter holidays they did so in the certainty of a quick profit from the entrance money and sale of drink: buying a bullock to slaughter to make up the prizes was a short term investment.

The special form which the Reformation took in Scotland gave the Scots Kirk great control over social behaviour. There is far more evidence from England for cruel animal sports.[4] Bull and bear-bating were common entertainments at festivals: thus the English bulldog and streets like the Bull Ring in Birmingham. Where bull-baiting appears in Scotland at any time after the Reformation, as at Maxwelltown in 1830, it sounds like a recent import from the south, and when reports of it in England appear in Scottish newspapers, it is with disapproval.[5] It was an insult to refer to the people of Newmilns as 'Newmills dog fechters'.[6] The 'famous' cock-fighting main in 1785 between Lanarkshire and East Lothian is the only recorded match between two Scottish counties, though in England they were common in the same period. Yet it was not merely animal sports which were missing in Scotland, for there was no hot hasty pudding eating, or grinning through a horse collar, or martial contests between men such as cudgelling, single stick and backsword play.

Whilst the near absence of cruel sports from Scotland may have been the result of the Kirk's general disapproval, there is a more specific explanation. In England the gentry were the patrons of cock-fighting and pugilism, breeding cocks, arranging mains and mills, and putting up purses.[7] The kirk deterred those who had a public position in society from carrying out these functions.

Smock racing, found all over England until moral pressure in the 1830s stopped it, was scarcely practised in Scotland. Smock races were foot races for women, sometimes accompanied by a hat race for men.[8] There is no pre-Reformation evidence for smock racing in Scotland; but neither are there clear English references before the seventeenth century, when its wide distribution indicates its antiquity. Because a smock race was normally accompanied by a race for men, it was one of the starting points for the development of athletics in Britain.

The Kirk forbade sport on Sundays. In England, sport on Sunday afternoon remained widespread in the first half of the nineteenth century. It was only stopped by evangelical insistence on the sanctity of the Sabbath, the same argument which had been won by Scots reformers two and a half centuries earlier. The Kirk was also intolerant of gambling, so often a stimulus to sport, though the comparative poverty of Scotland may also have limited betting.

In England and on the Continent, holidays and public entertainment still had a medieval flavour in the middle of the nineteenth century. They were held at times of the year which fitted into idle periods in the farming cycle, on saints' days or other religious holidays such as Easter Monday. They included many diversions, from eating, drinking, dancing, gawping at fat ladies and living skeletons, and theatrical performances, to bear-, bull- or badger-baiting, and as many as two dozen different sporting events. The character of Scottish holidays between 1700 and 1860 was different. Where there was sport, only one or two types were organised, typically horse races with perhaps a foot race afterwards. Although many examples can be found of Scots holidays which were held on saints' days, there were also many which were not. In the eighteenth century, the date of Leith races varied from year to year by several weeks, and the Dumfries and Kirkcudbright siller guns were held on the king's birthday.

In England, a 'substantial minority' of markets in England had sporting events associated with them, such as the wrestling and backsword play at the cattle market at Chesham in Berkshire.[9] Examples in Scotland are rare. Where one does arise, as at a fair at Milngavie in 1783 where a prize of two guineas was offered for a horse race by William Harvie, keeper of the change-house, it is clear that his aim was to increase his custom, and that Harvie himself had instigated the race.[10]

In Regency England popular entertainment was often meaty and violent: this kind of pleasure was far less common in Scotland. 'A major theme in the nineteenth century was to be the taming of English society.'[11] Scottish society did not need to be tamed to the same extent. The growth of sport in Scotland in this period involved the regularisation of two traditional sports, bowling and curling, the first by insisting on a completely flat green, the second by requiring circular curling stones. In both of these changes lawyers took a leading part, people in the middle ranks of society: they were the ones who wrote the rules. Lawyers and ministers had the power to affect sport in Scotland because mass culture scarcely existed in the way that it did in England. After the last running of Leith races in 1815 there was no annual event which drew enormous crowds until Paisley races began to attract Glasgow people twenty years later. Events such as the arrival of George IV at Leith in 1822 and the Eglinton Tournament in 1839 stand out because crowds rarely assembled in Scotland.

Association football appeared in Glasgow with the founding of Queen's Park in 1867: its rigorous amateurism in its earliest years links it to the English public school soccer-playing tradition. Within twenty years the game had become massively popular, dominating all other sports, particularly in Glasgow. It was an even more dramatic eruption than in England; it is probably the largest single change in the history of Scottish sport. Various causes of the sudden growth of football are clear: the Saturday half-holiday for working men, the vivid appeal of a short match (compared with cricket), and the emergence of entrepreneurs who organised and promoted the game.

In addition, Glasgow in 1870 was under-provided with competitive sport. Professional sportsmen had been working in England since the late eighteenth century, particularly in prize-fighting, cricket and pedestrianism.[12] We have seen that prize-fighting was always a marginal sport in Scotland, and though cricket was quite popular its standard was lower than in England. Neither did professional athletics develop in Scotland in the way that it did in London, the Midlands, Lancashire and Yorkshire. The sudden growth of games days in the second quarter of the century provided many annual events, but also created a demand for more frequent ones.

By the spring of 1871 the Scots still had sufficient sense of their identity as a distinct nation to make it seem reasonable to play an international match of rugby football against England, and nineteen months later to repeat the experience using the association code. Perhaps significantly, both games were played in Scotland and the first soccer international was played on St Andrew's Day: they can be seen as an unexpected consequence of the activities of the Earl of Eglinton and the National Association for the Vindication of the Rights of Scotland. The Scots thus participated in one of the defining moments in the shaping of modern sport, partly because of the enthusiasms of the Earl of Eglinton, who drew many of his ideas from Walter Scott and his vision of the Middle Ages. There is a link between medieval Scots archers practising for war against the English and commercial excesses of the World Cup at the millennium.

REFERENCES

1. Malcolmson (1973), 100–7.
2. Tranter (1987a).

3. Golby & Purdue (1984), 119–22.
4. For an overview of animal sports in England, see Malcolmson (1973), 45–51.
5. *Scotsman*, 14 August 1830.
6. Ramsay (1855), 34.
7. Malcolmson (1973), 56–71.
8. Goulstone (1982), 29–40.
9. Malcolmson (1973), 21–2.
10. *GM*, 23 October 1783.
11. Golby & Purdue (1984), 63.
12. Mason (1988), 36.

Bibliography

ABBREVIATIONS

DOST   Craigie, W. A. and others (eds), *A Dictionary of the Older Scottish Tongue* (Chicago and London, 1927-).

NSA   *The New Statistical Account of Scotland*, 15 vols (Edinburgh, 1845).

OSA   Sinclair, J. (ed.), *The Statistical Account of Scotland*, 21 vols (Edinburgh, 1791–99).

SND   Grant, W. & Murison, D. (eds), *The Scottish National Dictionary*, 10 vols (Edinburgh, 1931–76).

NEWSPAPERS

AA   *Ayr Advertiser*
AJ   *Aberdeen Journal*
A&SH   *Ardrossan & Saltcoats Herald*
D&GS   *Dumfries & Galloway Standard*
DA   *Dundee Advertiser*
DT   *Dumfries Times*
DWJ   *Dumfries Weekly Journal*
EA   *Edinburgh Advertiser*
EEC   *Edinburgh Evening Courant*
FH   *Falkirk Herald*
GA   *Glasgow Advertiser*
GC   *Glasgow Courant*
GH   *Glasgow Herald*
GM   *Glasgow Mercury*
GMJ   *Glasgow Morning Journal*
GSP   *Glasgow Saturday Post*
HA   *Hamilton Advertiser*
HC   *Haddingtonshire Courier*
KC   *Kelso Chronicle*
KWP   *Kilmarnock Weekly Post*
MC   *Mercurius Caledonius*
MS   *Montrose Standard*
NBDM   *North British Daily Mail*
PA   *Paisley Advertiser*
PerA   *Perthshire Advertiser*
PC   *[Perthshire] Constitutional*
PCour   *Perthshire Courier*

RI   *Renfrewshire Independent*
WFP   *Wigtownshire Free Press*

Adam, R. (ed.), *Edinburgh Records: the Burgh Accounts* (Edinburgh, 1899).

Adamson, H., *The Muses Threnodie*, 2 vols (Perth, 1774).

Aikman, J., *An Account of the Tournament at Eglinton* (Edinburgh, 1839).

Aiton, W., *General View of the Agriculture of the County of Ayr* (Glasgow, 1811).

Alexander, W. M., *The Place-names of Aberdeenshire* (Aberdeen, 1952). Third Spalding Club.

Anon. (1829), *Summary of the Rules and Regulations of the Six-Feet Club* (Edinburgh, 1829).

Anon. (1830), 'Border Games', *Edinburgh Weekly Chronicle*, 11 August 1830.

Anon. (1831), 'The St Ronan Games: a rhapsody', *Edinburgh Literary Journal*, 6 (1831), 73–8.

Anon. (1835), *Letters to King James the Sixth* (Edinburgh, 1835).

Anon. (1837), *Selections from the Minutes of the Synod of Fife* (Edinburgh, 1837).

Anon. (1839), *Selections from the Registers of the Presbytery of Lanark* (Edinburgh, 1839).

Anon. (1840), *The Topographical, Statistical and Historical Gazetteer of Scotland*, 2 vols (Glasgow, 1840).

Anon. (1842), *The Coltness Collection* (Edinburgh, 1842). Maitland Club.

Anon. (1871), *Extracts from the Records of the Royal Burgh of Edinburgh AD 1528–1557* (Edinburgh, 1871).

Anon. (1873), 'Will cricket soon die out?', *Percival King's Scottish Cricketers' Annual and Guide*, 3 (1873), 33–5.

Anon. (1876), *Extracts from the Records of the Burgh of Glasgow A.D. 1573–1642* (Glasgow, 1876).

Anon. (1882), *Extracts from the Records of the Burgh of Edinburgh A.D. 1573–1589* (Edinburgh, 1882).

Anon. (1887), *Extracts from the Records of the Royal Burgh of Stirling* (Glasgow, 1887).

Anon. (1890–91), *Muniments of the Royal Burgh of Irvine*, 2 vols (Edinburgh, 1890–91). Ayrshire and Galloway Archaeological Association, 17–18.

Anon. (1893), *Extracts from the Records of the Royal Burgh of Lanark* (Glasgow, 1893).

Anon. (1898), 'A New-Year's game' [yetlins], *The Scots Pictorial*, 2 (1898), 369.

Anon. (1927), *Extracts from the Records of the Burgh of Edinburgh A.D. 1589 to 1603* (Edinburgh, 1927).

Anon. (1939), *Ratis Raving*, ed. R. Girvan (Edinburgh, 1939). Scottish Text Society, 3rd series, 2.

Anstruther, I., *The Knight and the Umbrella* (London, 1963).

Archibald, J., *Alloa Sixty Years Ago* (Alloa, 1911).

Armet, H., 'The Society of Bowlers', *Book of the Old Edinburgh Club*, 29 (1956), 185–7.

Armet, H. (ed.), *Extracts from the Records of the Burgh of Edinburgh 1689 to 1701* (Edinburgh, 1962).

Ascham, R., *Toxophilus* (Wrexham, 1788).

Aubrey, J., *The Natural History of Wiltshire*, ed. J. Britton (London, 1847).

Balfour Paul, J., *The History of the Royal Company of Archers* (Edinburgh, 1875).

Banks, M. M., *British Calendar Customs – Scotland*, 3 vols (London, 1937–41).

Barbour, J., *Barbour's Bruce*, ed. M. P. McDiarmid and J. A. S. Stevenson, 3 vols (Edinburgh, 1980–85). Scottish Text Society, 4th series, 12–13, 15.

Barty, A. B., *The History of Dunblane* (Stirling, 1944).

Baxter, P., *Football in Perth* (Perth, 1898).

Birley, D., *Sport and the Making of Britain* (Manchester, 1993).

Blaine, D. P., *An Encyclopedia of Rural Sports* (London, 1840).

Blyth, H., *The Pocket Venus: a Victorian Scandal* (London, 1966).

Bone, D. D., *Fifty Years' Reminiscences of Scottish Cricket* (Glasgow, 1898).

Bowen, R., *Cricket: a History of its Growth and Development* (London, 1970).

Brailsford, D., *Sport, Time and Society: the British at Play* (London, 1991).

Brook, A. J. S., 'Notice of the Silver Bell of Lanark, a horse-racing trophy of the early seventeenth century, with some references to the early practice of horse-racing in Scotland', *Proceedings of the Society of Antiquaries of Scotland*, 25 (1890–91), 174–88.

Brooke, A. J. S., 'An account of the archery medals belonging to the University of St Andrews and the Grammar School of Aberdeen', *Proceedings of the Society of Antiquaries of Scotland*, 28 (1893–94), 343–469.

Buchanan, M., *Archery in Scotland: an Elegant and Manly Amusement* (Glasgow, 1979).

Buckroyd, J. M., 'Mercurius Caledonius and its immediate successors', *Scottish Historical review*, 54 (1975), 11–21.

A Burgess, *Brief Historical Reminiscences of the County and Town of Ayr ... and Directory* (Ayr, 1830).

Burke, P., *Popular Culture in Early Modern Europe* (Hounslow, 1978).

Burnett, J., *Sporting Scotland* (Edinburgh, 1995).

Burnett, J., 'The Kipper Fair and the cadgers' races at Newton-on-Ayr', *Review of Scottish Culture*, 9 (1995/6), 35–45.

Burnett, J. (1997), 'Shinty in nineteenth century Edinburgh, and a painting by Charles Altamont Doyle', *Book of the Old Edinburgh Club*, 4 (1998), 137–43.

Burnett, J. (1998a), 'The sites and landscapes of horse racing in Scotland', *The Sports Historian*, 18 (1998), 55–75.

Burnett, J. (1998b), 'A note on the Rattray ball game', *Proceedings of the Society of Antiquaries of Scotland* (1998).

Burnett, J. & G. R. Dalgleish, 'The Marchmont or St Ronan's Arrow', *Proceedings of the Society of Antiquaries of Scotland*, 125 (1995), 1175–86.

Burnett, J. & R. H. J. Urquhart, 'Early papingo shooting in Scotland', *Review of Scottish Culture*, 11 (1998), 4–12.

Burrell, W., *William Burrell's Northern Tour, 1758*, ed. J. Dunbar (Phantassie, 1997).

Burns, R., *The Complete Poetical Works*, ed. J. Mackay (Darvel, 1993).

Butler, L. St J. & P. J. Wordie, *The Royal Game* (Kippen, 1989).

Callan, I. A., 'Daniel: memories of Dalbeattie's famous old cricket ground', *The Gallovidian Annual*, 1949, 66–9.

Cameron, A. D., *The Man who Loved to Draw Horses* (Aberdeen, 1986).

Campbell, A., *The History of Leith* (Leith, 1827).

Campbell, G., 'The development of implements – clubs and balls', in Darwin (1952).

Carpentier-Bogaert, C., et al., *Les Bras de Fer: le Tir à l'Arc sur Perche Verticale* (Bethune, 1996). Documents d'Ethnographie Régionale du Nord-Pas-de-Calais, 7.

Carrick, J. C., *Around Dalkeith* (Dalkeith, 1904).

Carrick, J. C., *The Abbey of S. Mary of Newbattle* (Selkirk, 1907).

Carruthers, J. S., *The Story of Cricket in Scotland* (Dunlop, 1950).

Clark, R., *Golf: a Royal and Ancient Game* (Edinburgh, 1876).

Clark, R., 'The Whipman Play: a short history', in *The Whipman Play … 184th Celebrations* (West Linton, 1987), 14–15.

Clark, W. H., *The Six Incorporated Trades of Kircudbright: the, 'Silver Gun',*. (1961) Typescript in the Stewartry Museum, Kirkcudbright.

Comrie, J. D., *History of Scottish Medicine*, 2 vols, 2nd edn (Edinburgh, 1932).

Courtnay, S., *As Centuries Blend: One Hundred and Six Years of Clydesdale Cricket Club* (Glasgow, 1954).

Cowan, C., *Reminiscences* (Penicuik, 1878).

Craig-Brown, T., *The History of Selkirkshire*, 2 vols (Edinburgh, 1886).

Cramond, W., *The Records of Elgin 1234–1800*, 2 vols (Aberdeen, 1903–8).

Crawford, A., *The Crune of the Warlock of the Peil* (1838).

Crawford, T., D. Hewitt and A. Law (eds), *Longer Scottish Poems*, 2 vols (Edinburgh, 1987).

Cunningham, W., *The Diary and General Expenditure Book of William Cunningham of Craigends*, ed. J. Dodds (Edinburgh, 1887). Scottish History Society, 2.

Dalgleish, G. R., 'The "Silver Jack" trophy of the Edinburgh Society of Bowlers', *Proceedings of the Society of Antiquaries of Scotland*, 120 (1990), 189–200.

Dalyell, J. & J. Beveridge, 'Inventory of the plenishings of the House of the the Binns at the date of the death of General Thomas Dalyell, 21st August 1685', *Proceedings of the Society of Antiquaries of Scotland*, 58 (1923–24), 344–70.

Darnton, R., 'Workers revolt: the great cat massacre of the Rue St Severin', in his *The Great Cat Massacre and other Episodes in French Cultural History* (London, 1984).

Darwin, B. et al., *A History of Golf in Britain* (London, 1952).

Davies, P., *The Historical Dictionary of Golfing Terms* (London, 1993).

Dickson, J., *Cranstoun: a Parish History* (Anstruther, 1907).

Dickson, J., *Crichton: Past and Present* (Edinburgh, 1911).

Disraeli, B., *Sybil* (London, 1845).

Dixon, H. H., *Field and Fern … South* (London, 1865).

Dobson, T., *Reminiscences of Innerleithen and Traquair* (Innerleithen, 1896).

Dodds, A., 'The "Eglinton" hobby horse', *The Boneshaker*, 13 (1992) 13–18.

Donaldson, W., *Popular Literature in Victorian Scotland* (Aberdeen, 1986).

Douglas, G., *Vergil's Aeneid Translated into Scottish Verse*, 4 vols (Edinburgh, 1957–64). Scottish Text Society, 3rd series, 25, 27–8, 30.

Douglas, G., *The Shorter Poems of Gavin Douglas*, ed. P. J. Bawcutt (Edinburgh, 1967). Scottish Text Society, 4th series, 3.

Douglas, R., *Annals of the Royal Burgh of Forres* (Elgin, 1934).

Downie, W. F., *A History of Strathaven and Avondale* (Glasgow, 1929).

Dunkling, L. & G. Wright, *Pub Names of Britain*, 2nd edn (London, 1994).

Dunning, E. & K. Sheard, *Barbarians, Gentlemen and Players* (Oxford, 1979).

Durand, P., 'The game of bowls, and some Glasgow bowling clubs and trophies', *Old Glasgow Club Transactions*, 1936–37, 41–52.

Edington, C., *Court and Culture in Renaissance Scotland* (Phantassie, 1995).

Elder, J. S., *Some Memories of an Old Scottish Burgh, Maxwelltown* (Dumfries, 1897).

Encyclopedia Britannica, 11th edn, 29 vols (Cambridge, 1910–11).

Evans, R. D. C., *Bowling Greens: their History, Construction and Maintenance* (Birmingham, 1988).

Fairfax-Blakeborough, J., *History of Horse Racing in Scotland* (Whitby, 1973). Northern Turf History, 4.

Fenton, A., *The Northern Isles* (Edinburgh, 1978).

Fenton, A., 'Scottish ethnology: crossing the Rubicon', *Scottish Studies*, 31 (1992–93), 1–8.

Ferguson, J. P. S., *Directory of Scottish Newspapers*, 2nd edn (Edinburgh, 1984).

Fergusson, R., *Poems by Allan Ramsay and Robert Fergusson*, ed. A. M. Kinghorn and A. Law (Edinburgh, 1974).

Finlayson, M. J. (ed.), *An Anthology of Carrick* (Kilmarnock, 1925).

Finn, T., *The Pub Games of England* (London, 1975).

Fittis, R. S., *Sports and Pastimes of Scotland* (Paisley, 1891).

Fleming, D. H., 'The accounts of Dr Alexander Skene, Provost of St Salvator's College, St Andrews, relating to the extensive repairs of the College buildings ... 1683–1690', *Proceedings of the Society of Antiquaries of Scotland*, 54 (1919–20), 216–48.

Foulis, J., *The Account Book of Sir John Foulis of Ravelston 1671–1707*, ed. A. W. C. Hallen (Edinburgh, 1894). Scottish History Society, 16.

Fraser, G. M., *Historical Aberdeen* (Aberdeen, 1905).

Gardiner-Hill, H., 'The history of the rules of golf', in Darwin *et al.*, 17–41.

Geddes, A., 'Epistle to the President, Vice-Presidents, and Members of the Scottish Society of Antiquaries, on being chosen a correspondent member', *Archaeologia Scotica*, 1 (1792), 441–56.

Geddes, O., *A Swing Through Time: Golf in Scotland 1457–1743* (Edinburgh, 1992).

Geikie, W., *Etchings Illustrative of Scottish Character and Scenery* (Edinburgh, [1841]).

Gilles, R. P., 'Humours of the North. No. IX. Scotch lairds forty years ago', *Fraser's Magazine*, 22 (1840), 658–65.

Gillespie, J. H., *Dundonald: a Contribution to Parish History*, 2 vols (Glasgow, 1939).

Gillmeister, H., 'The origin of European ball games: a re-evaluation and linguistic analysis', *Stadion*, 7 (1981), 19–51.

Gillmeister, H., 'Wer erfand das Golfspiel? Der letzte Putt in einem langen Streit', *Schweizer Beiträge zur Sportgeschichte*, 2 (1990), 20–9.

Gillmeister, H. (1990a), *Kulturgeschichte des Tennis* (Munich, 1990).

Gillmeister, H. (1990b), 'The Language of English sports, medieval and modern', *Archiv*, 148 (1996), 268–85.

Girouard, M., *The Return to Camelot* (New Haven, 1981).

Golby, J. M. and A. W. Purdue, *The Civilisation of the Crowd* (London, 1984).

Gordon, E. C., *County Folk-Lore: Printed Extracts no. 2, Suffolk* (London, 1893).

Goulstone, J., *The Midsummer Games: Elements of Cult and Custom in Traditional English Sport* (Bexleyheath, 1982).

Grant, J., *History of the Burgh Schools of Scotland* (London, 1876).

Grant, J. (ed.), *Seafield Correspondence from 1685 to 1708* (Edinburgh, 1912). Scottish Text Society, 2nd series, 3.

Gray, W. F. and J. H. Jamieson, *A Short History of Haddington* (Edinburgh, 1944).

Grierson, H. J. C., *The Letters of Sir Walter Scott 1817–1819* (London, 1933).

Grierson, W., *Apostle to Burns: the Diaries of William Grierson*, ed. J. Davies (Edinburgh, 1981).

Groves, D., *James Hogg and the St Ronan's Border Club* (Dollar, 1987).

Guthrie, E. J., *Old Scottish Customs, Local and General* (London, 1885).

Hall, J., *Travels in Scotland by an Unusual Route*, 2 vols (London, 1805).

Hall, M. B., *John Cairnie and the Noddle Curling Club*,. Undated typescript in Largs Historical Society Museum.

Hamilton, D., *Early Aberdeen Golf* (Glasgow and Oxford, 1985).

Hamilton, D., 'The aristocratic myth: early Scottish golf', *Renfrewshire Local History Journal*, 8 (1997), 17–22.

Hamilton, D., *Golf – Scotland's Game* (Kilmacolm, 1999).

Hancock, D., *Citizens of the World: London Merchants and the Integration of the British Atlantic Community 1735–1785* (Cambridge, 1996).

Hardy, J., 'On bowling as an extinct Berwickshire game', *History of the Berwickshire Naturalists' Field Club*, 2 (1842–49), 51–68.

Harvie, C. and G. Walker, 'Community and culture' in W. H. Fraser and R. J. Morris (eds), *People and Soceity in Scotland II: 1830–1914* (Edinburgh, 1990), 336–57.

Harris, S., *The Place Names of Edinburgh* (Edinburgh, 1996).

Hay, D. (ed.), *The Letters of James V* (Edinburgh, 1954).

Hedderwick, J., *Backward Glances* (Edinburgh, 1891).

Henderson, E., *The Annals of Dunfermline and Vicinity* (Glasgow, 1879).

Henderson, I. T. and D. I. Stirk, *Golf in the Making*, 2nd edn (London, 1982).

Hogg, J., 'On the changes in the habits, amusements, and condition of the Scottish peasantry', *Quarterly Journal of Agriculture*, September 1832, 256–63, reprinted in J. Steel (ed.), *A Shepherd's Delight: a James Hogg Anthology* (Edinburgh, 1985), 40–9.

Hogg, J., *Highland Tours*, ed. W. F. Laughlan (Hawick, 1981).

Hole, C., *English Sports and Pastimes* (London, 1949).

Hole, C., *A Dictionary of British Folk Customs*, New ed. (Oxford, 1995).

Houston, A. M., *Auchterderran, Fife: a Parish History* (Paisley, 1924).

Houwen, L. A. J. R. (ed.), *The Dedis of Armorie: a Heraldic Treatise and Bestiary*, 2 vols (Edinburgh, 1994). Scottish Text Society, 4th series, 22–3.

Hudson, W., *Glimpses of Old Leith* (Leith, 1910).

Inglis, J., *Oor Ain Folk* (Edinburgh, 1894).

Irons, J. C., *Leith and its Antiquities*, 2 vols (Edinburgh, 1897).

James VI, *Minor Prose Works*, ed. J. Craigie (Edinburgh, 1982). Scottish Text Society, 4th series, 14.

Jarvie, G., *Highland Games: the Making of a Myth* (Edinburgh, 1991). Edinburgh Education and Society Series.

Johnson, E., *Walter Scott: the Great Unknown* (London, 1970).

Johnston, A. J. & J. F. Johnston, *The Chronicles of Golf 1457 to 1857* (Cleveland, Ohio, 1993).

Joyce, P. W., *A Social History of Ancient Ireland*, 2 vols (London, 1903).

Kay, J., *A Series of Original Portraits and Caricature Etchings with Biographical Sketches and Anecdotes*, 2 vols (Edinburgh, 1842).

Keith, G. S., *General View of the Agriculture of Aberdeenshire* (Aberdeen, 1811).

Kelsall, *Scottish Life 300 Years Ago* (Edinburgh, 1986).

Kennedy, W., *Annals of Aberdeen*, 2 vols (London, 1818).

Ker, W. L., 'The Papingo', *Transactions of the Glasgow Archaeological Society*, New Series 2 (1891–96), 325–39; reprinted in W. L. Ker, *Kilwinning* (Kilwinning, 1900).

Kerr, J., *The History of Curling and 50 Years of the Royal Caledonian Curling Club* (Edinburgh, 1890).

Kilmarnock Bowling Club, *Rules of the Club* (1867).

[Percival] King's Scottish Cricketers' Almanack (Edinburgh, 1871–87).

Lamb, H. H., *Climate: Past, Present and Future*, 2 vols (London, 1977).

Lamb, H. H., *Climate, History and the Modern World* (London, 1982).

Lamont, J., *The Diary of John Lamont of Newton* (Glasgow, 1830).

Lang, A., 'Border cricket' in A. G. Steel and R. H. Littleton, *Cricket* (London, 1890), 294–9. The Badminton Library.

Larwood, J. & J. C. Hotten, *The History of Signboards* (London, 1866).

Lauder, J., *Journals of Sir John Lauder, Lord Fountainhall* (Edinburgh, 1900). Scottish History Society, 36.

Lewis, P., 'The history of the golf ball in Britain', in A. Cochrane (ed.), *Golf – the Scientific Way* (Aston, 1995), 165–70.

Lindsay, D., *The Works*, ed. D. Hamer, 4 vols (Edinburgh, 1931–36).

Lockhart, J. G., *The Life of Sir Walter Scott*, 10 vols (Edinburgh, 1902–3).

MacDonald, J. N., *Shinty: a Short History of the Ancient Highland Game* (Inverness, 1932).

McDowall, W., *History of the Burgh of Dumfries*, 4th edn (Dumfries, 1986).

Macfarlane, W., *Geographical Collections Relating to Scotland*, 3 vols (Edinburgh, 1906). Scottish History Society, 33–4.

M'Kay, A., *History of Kilmarnock*, 4th edn (Kilmarnock, 1880).

Mackintosh, D. L., *Touchers, being the Story of Queen's Park Bowling and Tennis Club* (Glasgow, [c. 1946]).

Maclagan, R. C., *The Games and Diversions of Argyleshire* (London, 1901).

Maclennan, H. D., *Not an Orchid ...* (North Kessock, 1995).

Macleod, K. M., 'Auld Christmas customs', *Transactions of the Buchan Field Club*, 18 (2) (1964–89), 21–8.

McNeill, F. M., *The Silver Bough*, 4 vols (Glasgow, 1957–68).

MacNeill, M., *The Festival of Lughnasa* (London, 1962).

McNeill, P., *Tranent and its Surroundings* (Edinburgh, 1883).

MacQuoid, G. S. (ed.), *Jacobite Songs and Ballads* (London, 1887).

Magoun, F. P., 'Scottish popular football 1424–1815', *American Historical Review*, 37 (1931), 1–13.

Maidment, J., *A Book of Scottish Pasquils* (Edinburgh, 1868).

Malcolm, J., *The Parish of Monifieth* (Edinburgh, 1910).

Malcolmson, R. W., *Popular Recreations in English Society 1700–1850* (Cambridge, 1973).

Mandell, R. D., *Sport: a Cultural History* (New York, 1984).

Marshall, J. S., *Old Leith at Leisure* (Edinburgh, 1976).

Martine, J., *Reminiscences of the Royal Burgh of Haddington* (Edinburgh, 1883).

Martine, J., *Reminiscences and Notices of the Fourteen Parishes of the County of Haddington* (Edinburgh, 1890).

Marwick, J. D., *List of Markets and Fairs Now and Formerly Held in Scotland* ([London], 1890).

Mason, J., *The Border Tour*, 2nd edn (Edinburgh, 1826).

Matheson, D., *The Place Names of Elginshire* (Stirling, 1905).

Mason, T., *Sport in Britain* (London, 1988).

Maxwell, A., *Old Dundee* (Edinburgh, 1891).

Mayne, J., *The Siller Gun* (London, 1836).

Melville, J., *The Diary of James Melville 1556–1601* (Edinburgh, 1839).

Melville, L., *Errol: its Legends, Lands and People* (Perth, 1935).

Menzies, D. P., *The 'Red and White' Book of Menzies* (Glasgow, 1894).

Mitchell, J., 'Memories of Ayrshire about 1780', *Miscellany of the Scottish History Society: sixth volume* (Edinburgh, 1939), 245–334. Scottish History Society, 3rd series, 33.

Mitchell, W., *A Manual of Bowl-Playing* (Glasgow, 1864).

Moir, D. M., *The Life of Mansie Waugh, Tailor in Dalkeith* (Edinburgh, 1828).

Mollyson, C. A., *The Parish of Fordoun* (Aberdeen, 1893).

Morton, A., *Centenary of Newmilns Bowling Club* (Newmilns, 1962).

Murdoch, A., *Ochiltree* (Paisley, c. 1920).

Murray, D., 'The Rottenrow of Glasgow', *The Regality Club*, 3rd series (Glasgow, 1899), 35–85.

Murray, D., *Early Burgh Organization in Scotland*, 2 vols (Glasgow, 1924–32).

Murray, D., *Memories of the Old College of Glasgow* (Glasgow, 1927).

Murray, G., *Sarah Rae: and other Poems* (Greenock, 1882).

Murray, R., *The Armagh Bullet Thrower* (Armagh, 1976).

Nicholson, J., *Idylls o' Hame* (London, 1870).

Nimmo, W., *The History of Stirlingshire*, 2 vols (London, 1880).

Niven, T. E., *East Kilbride* (Glasgow, 1965).

Omand, R., 'Extracts from the Harveian address of 1874', *Edinburgh Medical Journal*, new series, 20 (1875), 97–104.

Ord, J., *Bothy Songs and Ballads* (Paisley, 1930).

Paton, H., 'The manuscripts of Robert Mordaunt Hay, Esq., of Duns Castle' in Historical Manuscripts Commission, *Report on Manuscripts in Various Collections*, vol. 5 (Hereford, 1909), 1–71.

Paton, H. M., *Supplementary Report upon the Manuscripts of the Earl of Mar and Kellie* (London, 1930).

Patterson, J., *History of the Regality of Musselburgh* (Musselburgh, 1857).

Patterson, T. G. F., 'Long Bullets in Co. Armagh', *Ulster Journal of Archaeology*, 9 (1946), 58–68, reprinted in E. E. Evans (ed), *Harvest Home – the Last Sheaf: a selection from the writings of T. G. F. Patterson relating to County Armagh* (Belfast, 1975), 90–103.

Patterson, W. H., *A Glossary of Words in Use in the Counties of Antrim and Down* (London, 1880).

Peakodde, Bailzie (pseud.), *The Pump* (Glasgow, 1835). Photocopy in the National Library of Scotland.

Pennant, T., *A Tour in Scotland*, 3 vols (London, 1790).

Penny, G., *Traditions of Perth* (Perth, 1836).

Pilley, P. (ed.), *The Story of Bowls: from Drake to Bryant* (London, 1987).

Pretsell, J., *The Game of Bowls: Past and Present* (Edinburgh, 1908).

Ramsay, A., *The Works of Allan Ramsay*, 6 vols (Edinburgh, 1944–74). Scottish Text Society, 3rd series, 19–20, 29, 4th series 6–8.

Ramsay, J., *Woodnotes of a Wanderer* (Edinburgh, 1855).

Ramsay, J., *Letters of John Ramsay of Ochtertyre 1799–1812* (Edinburgh, 1966). Scottish History Society, 4th series, 3.

Reeves, C., *Pleasures and Pastimes in Medieval England* (Stroud, 1995).

Reid, J. P., *The Skipper's Daughter: an East Lothian Tale of the Smuggling Days* (Haddington, [*c.* 1910]).

Robb, S., 'Selkirk in the twentieth century', in J. M. Gilbert (ed.), *Flower of the Forest: Selkirk, a New History* (Selkirk, 1985), 148–67.

Robertson, A. D., *Lanark: the burgh and its councils 1469–1880* (Lanark, 1974).

Robertson, D., *South Leith Records: second series* (Leith, 1925).

Robertson, D. & M. Wood, *Castle and Town: Chapters in the History of the Royal Burgh of Edinburgh* (Edinburgh, 1928).

Robertson, G., *A General View of the Agriculture of Midlothian* (Edinburgh, 1793).

Rodger, R. H., 'The Silver Ball of Rattray: a unique Scottish sporting trophy', *Proceedings of the Society of Antiquaries of Scotland*, 122 (1992), 403–11.

Rogers, C., *Social Life in Scotland*, 3 vols (London, 1884–86).

Salvio, D., *Irvine Marymass Festival: a Medieval Fair in Honour of the Assumption of Our Lady* (Irvine, 1970).

Scott, R. E., *Companion to Hawick and District*, rev. ed. (1981).

Scott, W., *St. Ronan's Well*, 2 vols (Edinburgh, 1832).

Scott, W., *The Poetical Works*, ed. J. L. Robertson (London, 1894).

Scott-Moncrieff, R. (ed.), *The Household Book of Lady Grisel Baillie* (Edinburgh, 1911). Scottish Text Society, 2nd series, 1.

Seton, G., *A History of the Family of Seton*, 2 vols (Edinburgh, 1896).

Shearer, J., *Antiquities of Strathearn* (Crieff, 1881).

Shirley, J., *The Dethe of the Kynge of Scotis* (Glasgow, 1837). Maitland Club.

Sillery, C. D., 'A trip to Innerleithen', *Edinburgh Literary Journal*, 1 (1829), 121–3.

Simpkins, J. E., *Examples of Printed Folk-Lore Concerning Fife* (London, 1914). County Folk-Lore, 7.

Sloan, G., *Stirling Races* (Stirling, 1986).

Smellie, T., *Sketches of Old Kilmarnock* (Kilmarnock, 1898).

Smith, A., *A Summer in Skye* (Edinburgh, 1865).

Smith, D. B., *Curling: an Illustrated History* (Edinburgh, 1981).

Smith, D. B., *The Roaring Game: Memories of Scottish Curling* (Glasgow, 1985).

Smout, T. C., 'Scottish-Dutch contact 1500–1800', in J. L. Williams (ed.), *Dutch Art and Scotland* (Edinburgh, 1992), 21–32.

Somerville, J., *Memorie of the Somervilles*, 2 vols (Edinburgh, 1815).

Stuart, W. J., *The History of the Aesculapian Club* (Edinburgh, 1949).

Strawhorn, J., *The History of Ayr* (Edinburgh, 1985).

Strawhorn, J., *The History of Irvine* (Edinburgh, 1989).

Strutt, J., *The Sports and Pastimes of the People of England*, new edn (London, 1841).

Strutt, J., *Queenhoo Hall*, 4 vols (Edinburgh, 1808).

Taylor, J., *Curling: the Ancient Scottish Game* (Edinburgh, 1884).

Thom, W., *Pedestrianism* (Aberdeen, 1813).

Tranter, N. L. (1987a), 'Popular sports and the industrial revolution in Scotland: the evidence of the Statistical Accounts', *International Journal of the History of Sport*, 4 (1987), 21–8.

Tranter, N. L. (1987b), 'The social and occupational structure of organized sport in central Scotland during the 19th century', *International Journal of the History of Sport*, 4 (1987), 301–14.

Tranter, N. L. (1989), 'Organised sport and the middle-class woman in nineteenth-century Scotland', *International Journal of the History of Sport*, 6 (1989), 31–48.

Tranter, N. L., 'Organized sport and the working classes in Central Scotland, 1820–1900: the neglected sport of quoiting', in Holt, R. (ed.), *Sport and the Working Classes in Modern Britain* (Manchester, 1990), 45–66.

Tranter, N. L., 'Quoiting in Central Scotland: the Demise of a Traditional Sport', *Forth Naturalist and Historian*, 15 (1992), 99–116.

Truckell, A. [Introduction] in McDowall (1986).

Tulloch, W. W., *The Life of Tom Morris* (London, 1907).

Vamplew, W., *The Turf: a Social and Economic History of Horse Racing* (London, 1976).

van Hengel, S. J. H., *Early Golf* (Vaduz, 1982).

Waring, T., *A Treatise on Archery* (London, 1832).

Warrick, J., *The History of Old Cumnock* (Paisley, 1899).

Watson, G., 'Annual Border ball games', *Transactions of the Hawick Archaeological Society*, 1922, 4–9.

Watson, T., *A Collection of Poems* (Edinburgh, 1835).

West, D., *The Elevens of England* (London, 1988).

Westwater, A., *Jenny Gray Pit – a Hundred Years Working* (Lochgelly, 1954).

Whamond, A., *James Tacket*, 7th edn (Motherwell, 1895).

Wilson, J. J., *The Annals of Penicuik* (Edinburgh, 1891).

Wingfield, M. A., *Sport and the Artist: Volume 1, Ball Games* (Woodbridge, 1988).

Wodrow, R., *Analecta*, 4 vols (Glasgow, 1842–43). Maitland Club.

Wood, H. H. (ed.), *James Watson's Choice Collection of Comic and Serious Scots Poems*, 2 vols (Edinburgh, 1977–91). Scottish Text Society, 4th series, 10 and 20.

Woodward, L., *The Age of Reform 1815–1870*, 2nd edn (Oxford, 1962). Oxford History of England, 13.

Wynne-Thomas, P., *Nottinghamshire Cricketers 1821–1914* (Nottingham, 1971).

Yorke, P. [T. Atkinson], *Three Nights in Perthshire* (Glasgow, 1821).

Index